本书获得：重庆市高等学校“十二五”市级重点学科"企业管理"专项经费支持
2015年中央财政支持地方高校发展专项资金项目“协同创新下的国际企业管理学科”经费支持
四川外国语大学旅游管理重点学科经费支持

国际旅游文化研究

主　编：罗文青　杨　红
副主编：黄　森　吴　昊

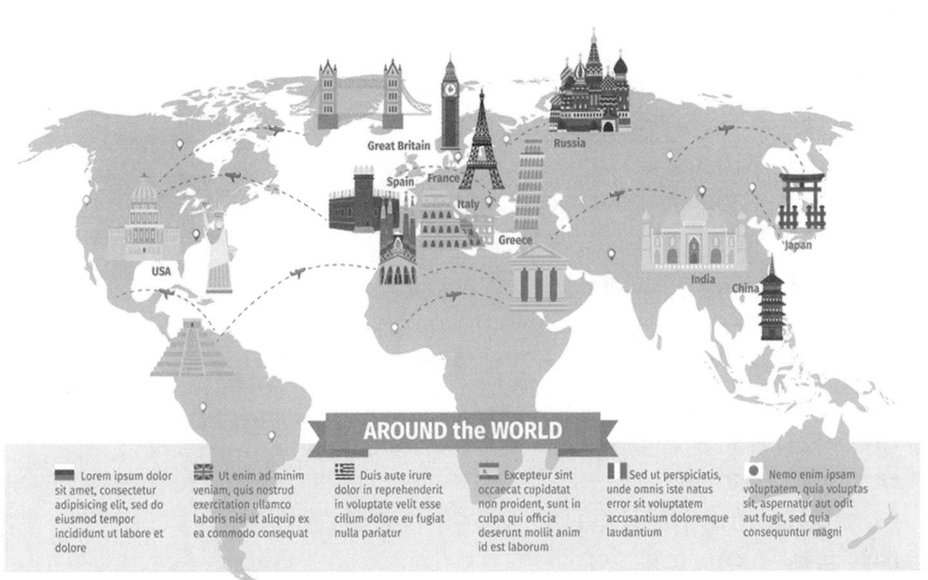

世界图书出版公司
广州·上海·西安·北京

图书在版编目（CIP）数据

国际旅游文化研究 / 罗文青，杨红主编．—广州：世界图书出版广东有限公司，2016.12
ISBN 978-7-5192-2263-5

Ⅰ．①国…　Ⅱ．①罗…　②杨…　Ⅲ．①旅游文化—世界—文集　Ⅳ．①F591-53

中国版本图书馆CIP数据核字（2016）第304016号

书　　名	国际旅游文化研究 Guoji Lüyou Wenhua Yanjiu
主　　编	罗文青　杨　红
责任编辑	张梦婕
装帧设计	吴伟边
出版发行	世界图书出版广东有限公司
地　　址	广州市新港西路大江冲25号
邮　　编	510300
电　　话	020-84451969　84453623　84184026　84459579
网　　址	http://www.gdst.com.cn
邮　　箱	pub@gdst.com.cn
经　　销	各地新华书店
印　　刷	广州市德佳彩色印刷有限公司
开　　本	787mm × 1092mm　1/16
印　　张	13.75
字　　数	250千
版　　次	2016年12月第1版　2016年12月第1次印刷
国际书号	ISBN 978-7-5192-2263-5
定　　价	38.00元

前　言

当今世界一体化背景下，国家提出实施对外开放战略，特别是“一带一路”战略，需要培养一批具有国际视野，通晓国际规则，能够参与国际事务与国际竞争的应用型、复合型非通用语种人才。重庆是西部大开发的重要战略支点，处在“一带一路”和长江经济带的联接点上，起着承东启西、连接南北的作用，而作为西南地区唯一的外国语大学，四川外国语大学肩负为西南地区培养具有国际视野、多元融合的高级涉外人才使命。凭借外语多语种的优势，四川外国语大学在发挥传统办学优势和学科优势的同时，正探索如何结合外语专业和社会需求联系起来，做好传统语言教学融入国别区域研究的结合，以融入重庆的经济发展，满足我国经济社会发展，特别是扩大对外开放新需要。

2014年12月，重庆市对外贸易经济委员会与四川外国语大学共同成立了重庆国际战略研究院，希冀搭建一个政届、学界、业届共同研究重庆市国际战略问题的平台，为重庆市全方位开放的战略格局提供政策制定参考。研究院的成立，为我们外语教学和国际事务的众多师生搭建了一个国际战略研究信息资料库、一个国际战略研究学术交流平台，以及国际战略研究人才交流与培育的平台。

正是在国家战略、重庆发展和学校发展的背景下，为开阔学术视野，围绕“国际旅游和文化”研究主题，四川外国语大学东方语学院和国际商学院的教师和研究生，根据自己专业对象国的信息资源，经过一年时间的辛勤努力，撰写了23篇论文，其中关于国际旅游、国别旅游方面的论文17 篇，关于国别文化研究的论文6 篇，涵盖了对阿尔及利亚、埃及、沙特阿拉伯、俄罗斯、韩国、日本、越南、泰国等国家的旅游文化方面的研究。

重庆国际战略研究院起步较晚，国别研究所也刚刚成立，基础不强，但我们希望通过这次尝试来推进传统语言教学与国别区域研究和社会发展想结合的思路，为以后更深入研究奠定基础。

感谢重庆国际战略研究院院长明国辉、副院长熊林、张艳，秘书长杨柏和高文等同志对本书的支持和关心，感谢世界图书出版公司对本书的大力支持，使本书得以顺利有效地出版。

由于时间仓促，加上编者学识有限，错误之处难免，恳请方家批评指正。

罗文青

2016年秋于重庆歌乐山下

目　录

再谈越南文化中的历史情结……罗文青　1

The Spatial Distribution of Agritourism in China: National Agritourism Demonstrations in China……杨　红　8

国际商品展示与交易中心发展的SWOT分析……黄　森　舒首凤　27

2016年埃及旅游业“寒冬期”及对策分析……吴　昊　37

关于日本近年来发展观光立国的政策，措施及实效……毛卫兵　45

关于重庆地区中韩旅游合作发展的思考……金日权　56

“一带一路”背景下重庆低碳旅游发展研究……呙小明　67

阿尔及利亚罗马遗址旅游资源研究……潘雷　闵　敏　74

“一带一路”背景下提升我国邮轮旅游竞争力初探……邹思晓　85

阿尔及利亚撒哈拉沙漠旅游资源研究……闵　敏潘　雷　92

“一带一路”战略下开展国际旅游合作的策略选择……姬妍婷　102

谈俄罗斯文化的双重性……包淑萍　109

中国与“一带一路”沿线国家进行旅游目的地营销合作的分析……黄雅婷　116

泰国旅游资源概况与2015年旅游业发展形势分析……赵银川　125

中国旅游国际传播中的问题及对策研究……黄　俊　李　超　134

沙特旅游业的现状和前景……黄婷婷　141

中国大陆泰国文学研究综述——以公开发表论著和CNKI网论文为中心分析……蒙昭晓　148

中国出境游市场的发展趋势及其原因……金福实　157

国内智慧旅游研究的回顾和展望——基于CNKI相关文献的统计分析……王文健　164

关于中越经济外交的一些思考——从电商角度……任丹丹　178

略论越南“船文化”……刘艳芬　189

论中韩文化之争——以“端午节”为例……徐绿枝　195

浅析越南佛教中的女性崇拜……张　睿　207

再谈越南文化中的历史情结

罗文青

摘要：越南文化以儒释道为主，以历史人物和典故命名街道地名表现出越南对历史过往“感恩戴德”的浓厚情结，越南的习俗节庆、语言文字割不断华夏文化对其深远的影响和传承，可见越南文化仍是以东方文化为主体，越南文化的根与中国文化紧紧相连，对此我们应有既认同又宽容的豁达态度。

关键词：越南；文化；历史情结

一、引言

越南是东南亚地区的一个国家，也是中国的邻邦，全称是越南社会主义共和国。历史上对现今越南国境，称呼屡经更替：古代称“交趾”“象郡”“安南”，968年从中国独立出去，称为“大瞿越”，1803年开始出现“越南”这个称呼；1945年，越南八月革命胜利，建立越南民主共和国；1976年南北统一，称为越南社会主义共和国。过去人们指称的“安南人”也就是“越南人”。

说到越南文化，到过越南的中国人，很多都有似曾相识的感觉，因为在很多方面，越南和中国特别相似。虽然，越南很强调其文化具有民族特色，但我们还是感受到：越南有着很浓重的源自华夏文化的历史情结。之前笔者发表过一篇题为“越南文化中的历史情结”小文章，时隔十年，经历了在越南留学以及一直从事越南语教学科研工作的体验，对越南文化有了更多了解，今天再撰此文与大家探讨。

二、越南文化以儒释道为主

人们一般把儒学、佛教、道教简称为儒释道。从文化角度来看，在东南亚各国中，越南和新加坡都是属于儒释道为主的文化[①]，所以和中国很相似。

越南是一个多民族国家，主体民族京族是当地旧苗裔与华夏南迁族群融合而成的，因此在族群起源上，越南民族与中华民族有着密切的历史渊源关系。从公元前2世纪至公元3世纪以来，随着华夏族群的南迁，中国的传统文化也开始传入安南，其中祖先崇拜、祭祖习俗和孝道尊严等华夏文化一直在越南得到沿用，这份历史情结一直保持至今。

首先，越南全国上下都有祭祖习俗，分为家祭、族祭和国祭三种。在越南，无论是城市还是农村，无论是大公司还是小商店，无论是富人还是穷人，家家户户都在家里最庄重的地方设置供台，安放祖先牌位，摆放香烛、灯烛、花瓶、果盘和酒器等，供桌上方常常用汉字书写。家祭的时间一般是祖先的忌日，每月农历初一、十五，以及重大传统节日，如春节、清明、端午、中元、重阳、中秋等，家里有重大事件如婚礼、葬礼、生育、考试、病痛、打官司等，也要祭拜祖先，以求庇护和恩泽。与中国族祭相似，越南民间也非常盛行族祭，祭祀地点一般在宗族祠堂，供桌上放置宗族始祖牌位，族祭时家族各支系的子孙都要到场，仪式相当隆重。越南的国祭是在每年农历三月初十，这天会在越南北方富寿省雄王庙举行祭拜雄王的祭祀活动，也称为“祭祖日”。祭雄王日也是雄王庙会，这是祭祀活动中最庄严隆重的活动。

其次，越南尊崇儒学，把儒家传统思想称为儒教。二千年来儒家对越南的社会和家庭产生了巨大影响，潜移默化地影响着人们的思想文化和生活习惯。“忠孝节义”“三纲五常”等观念成为家喻户晓的伦理规范，《四书五经》等儒学经典成为普及的通俗读物，忠、孝、勤、俭、廉、正成为传统的道德因素，表现在家庭生活中就是男尊女卑、长幼有序和重男轻女。在越南人的观念中，男主外女主内，妇女照顾老人、小孩和丈夫，承担所有家务是天经地义的职责。越南人在称呼上也是长幼有序，如果不按辈分，会被认为是极没教养。饭桌上小辈要先邀请长辈，对长辈说话要带敬语，离家出门要向长辈辞别。越南的家庭伦理观念和中国很相似，中国不少影视作品深受越南民众喜欢，就是由于越南人对中华儒家道德的高度认同。在尊崇儒学的社会风气熏陶下，越南每个家庭，尤其是儒士家庭十分重视教育，形成了全民尊师重教和讲究文明礼节的社会风尚。

再次，越南崇奉佛教和道教，宗教信仰具有较强包容性。佛教已传入越南近两千年，并得到广泛传播，越南各地寺庙处处可见，几乎每个村庄都有拜佛的

① 《东南亚文化》(古小松主编)，中国社会科学出版社，2015年，第189页。

庙或者庵，并且寺庙悬挂的牌匾、楹联几乎都是用汉字书写。道教也对越南影响深刻，广泛流传对真武帝君的信仰，北部和中部有许多奉祀真武大帝的宫观和神祠。河内西湖边的真武观和还剑湖边的玉山寺道观，所奉祀的真武大帝、文昌帝君、关帝和吕祖等都是中国广泛流传的道教神祇。越南的寺庙，常常是既供奉佛教人物，又摆放道教神案。此外，越南信奉的母道教和高台教也是以道教为主，母道教的庙观与道教宫观相似，而高台教则吸收了中国儒家和佛家的伦理观念，神仙基本搬用道教的神仙体系。虽然，越南的中南部也信仰天主教、基督教和伊斯兰教，但从教人数远无法和儒释道相比。

三、越南以历史名人和故事命名街道地名

这类地名可以分为两小类，一类是以名人命名，这些名人包括神话传说人物、历代封建皇朝的皇帝、将士、文人以及近现代的革命烈士、爱国人士、领导领袖等。人物地名在河内街巷地名中最为常见，且大部分是以名人命名，可以说名人地名是是河内街巷地名的一大特色。有人曾对河内旧市区内717条街道进行统计，以人名命名的街道占291条，占街道总数的40.59%[①]。

这些名人包括神话传说人物、古代人物或是当今名人，其中以神话传说人物命名的有安阳王路、瓯姬路、雄王路、雒龙君路等。以古代名人命名的有100多条街巷，这些人物主要为历代皇帝、文人名将，如丁先皇路、李太祖路、李常杰路、陈仁宗路、黎太祖路等。以近现代名人命名的也有100多条，主要是作家、诗人、学者、领袖及革命爱国人士等，如南高街、陶维英街、阮攸路、黎笋路、范文同路、潘佩珠路等。

越南历史上也出现不少杰出的女性，因此在河内地名中也出现一些以女性人名命名，如武氏熟街、裴氏春街、段氏点街。由于越南女性有跟随夫姓的习俗，所以有时还会出现以丈夫姓氏命名的，如赵夫人街、清官县夫人街等。

另一类是记载民间传说或史实的地名。民间传说源自神话或者衍生于历史故事，这类故事反映了越南社会底层老百姓朴素的世界观，对神仙鬼怪的敬畏。河内还剑郡有一座寺庙叫白马寺，相传李太祖在建升龙城时屡建屡塌，于是派人到龙杜寺祈求保护，祈神仪式完毕后突然出现一匹白马，李太祖跟随马的脚印建筑升龙城并最终成功，因此修建这座寺庙供奉神灵白马，取名为白马寺。河内市中

① 闫京育,《河内街道命名文化探究》, 2011年广西民族大学外国语学院本科毕业论文，第5页。

心有名的还剑湖，得名的由来也是源于越南李朝李太祖向神龟借剑打败外敌后将剑物归原主的神话传说，还有二征夫人郡内的白藤路也是因越南历史上有名的白藤江战役而得名。

越南行政省市地名通名上，我们也能看到中国地名文化对越南地名的影响。由于中越历史上的特殊关系，越南的行政区划通名受中国政区地名通名的影响很多，河内作为历代皇朝的京都，其政区地名通名的历史沿革充分体现了中国地名文化对越南地名的影响。中国古代的行政区划单位屡有变化，曾出现有郡、道、路、府、县、州等，这些行政通名都曾出现在越南的行政通名中。时至今日，越南仍实行省制，国家划分为省、中央直辖市，省划分为省辖市和县，中央直辖市划分为郡、县和县级市，县划分为乡、镇，省辖市划分为坊、乡，郡划分为坊。

再次，河内地名有以历代皇帝的年号及庙号命名，以皇帝年号及庙号命名起源于中国。且在河内地名中也有因为与当时皇帝及其帝王的宗族同名或同字而被更改的现象，这种现象叫做避讳，这是封建社会一种特殊的制度。这些地名命名方式与中国地名的命名方式相同。从这些地名现象，我们可以看到华夏文化在河内甚至是整个越南的影响。

越南以历史名人来命名城市街道，体现了越南对历史人物的纪念和崇拜，证明越南对饮水思源、学会感恩的“德”，以实际事例诠释了儒家思想，越南在行政地名上也无法割断其与华夏政治历史文化上的渊源关系，表现了越南具有浓厚的历史情结。

四、越南民俗节庆酷似华夏

越南的历法与中国几乎一样，既用公历，也用农历，并且越南完全使用农历来推算传统节日，如春节、中秋、端午、中元等。越南同中国一样使用天干地支来纪年，也与中国一样有二十四个节气。十二生肖是中国传统文化的重要部分，而越南的十二生肖与中国也大同小异，除了一个为“猫”年（中国为“兔年”）不同，其他十一个都一样。而越南这些民俗的形成和流传至今，都是源自与中国有着密切的渊源关系，割舍不了的历史情结。

越南与中国的节庆习俗也几乎一模一样，发展趋势也是惊人相似。比如春节，和中国一样，也是越南一年中最重要的节日，并且也同样视为辞旧迎新的日子，也是最重要的家庭团聚的节日，同样习惯在腊月开始置办年货，年二十三送灶王爷上天，贴春联，买年画，包粽子，做年糕，放鞭炮，吃年夜饭，年初一拜年，发红包，讲吉利话，家里张贴“福”字以及“福禄寿”，和中国完全一样。越南的春节也有花市，家家户户都要买几株桃花或者一盆金橘摆放在家里，这点和中国南方很相像。难怪有些到过越南的中国人感叹说：越南简直就是一个缩小的中国，世界上找不出比越南更像中国的国家了。

清明节也是越南的一个重要节日，一般在农历三月或四月初。同中国一样，越南也借清明节扫墓和踏青，祭祀先人。同中国的时间一样，越南的端午节在农历五月初五，也有吃粽子和驱虫的习俗，越南人认为，吃粽子可以求得风调雨顺和五谷丰登。虽然用于驱虫的方法因地而异，但都是通过采摘草药来驱邪避冲。

越南也是在农历八月十五过中秋节，这天晚上，越南人有点彩灯和吃月饼的习俗，并举行各种文化体育娱乐活动，孩子们提着各种灯笼在月光下玩耍，边吃月饼和水果，边听大人讲故事，就像是过儿童节。越南的中秋月饼，或是在春节、端午节时吃的粽子，在做法和形状上和中国不尽相同，但也都是很类似。

越南的婚礼也和中国一样，有纳彩、问名、纳吉、纳征、请期、亲迎等六礼，随着社会发展，婚礼形式有了很大改变，但有一样始终不曾改变，那就是婚礼上一定必须张贴中国的“红双喜”字。

要说出越南本土习俗与中国有什么明显不同的地方，那就是越南春节不像中国北方那样要包饺子，还有一点就是，在越南结婚时一定要有一长串新鲜槟榔，这点在中国并不常见。

总的看来，越南的这些习俗节庆都有一个共同特点，都是用阴历来推算，都是和华夏文化有很明显的传承关系。

五、受汉字影响的越南语言文字

越南人最早使用的文字是汉字，被称为“儒字”。两千多年来，越南留下大量的古籍文物都是使用汉字书写记载的，甚至连家谱都是用汉字记录的。越南历史上曾一度创造和使用“喃字”，产生过一些民族风格浓郁的文学作品，但总的来说还是使用汉字时间长并且更广泛。由于历史的原因，越南语与汉语关系密切，除发音和中国广东话相像外，词汇上也借用了大量的汉根词，据统计有70%左右的词汇是借汉词，特别是现代越南语还保存了一套“汉越音”，用这套汉越音系统可以读出所有的汉字。这类汉根词大量保留了古汉语词的痕迹，如“铜壶—钟表”“进士—博士”“书院—图书馆”“甘结—承诺”，前者是汉越音的越南语，能对应于古汉语，后者是现代汉语的词汇语义。可见，从语言文字上，我们也不难看出古代汉语对越南语言文字的影响和继承。

今天大多数越南人使用的是现代越南语，已看不懂也读不懂汉字了，他们已不一定知道汉语对其的影响，但汉语情结仍然难以消除，如前面提到的婚礼上的红双喜必须是汉字，祭祖、宗教活动也要使用汉字，庙宇和古建筑的牌匾、楹联也都是保留着汉字，甚至家里墙上的挂饰也使用汉字。随着中越关系正常化，学习汉语在越南成为热门，近期越南教育部培训部还提出小学和初中要增加汉语和俄语两门外语课程，可见，越南方面已清楚地意识到，掌握汉语对越南来说是何等重要，懂汉语不仅能促进中越两国人民之间的交流和沟通，还有利于中越经贸合作和共谋发展，有助于提升民族的文化素养。

六、余论

当然，越南文化也不仅仅只是受中国文化的影响，它还吸收了印度和西方文化，处在中西文化和中印文化交汇的前沿。越南从19世纪法国人到来之后开始接受西方文化影响，20世纪50年代法国人离开越南后，一直到20世纪70年代中期，越南南部还接受了来自美国等西方国家文化的影响。西方文化的影响至今仍明显地体现在越南的语言、饮食、建筑等方面，如越南人把使用了两千多年的汉字改成了拼音文字，日常生活也会食用面包，喝啤酒和咖啡，南北建造了不少哥特式的西洋建筑等等。越南当代文化中保留下来的具有鲜明土著文化特色的印记是很少的。

不过，相比较而言，无论是印度文化还是西方文化，对越南文化的影响都只是表层，而华夏文化对于越南来说，由于是通过族群承传的，所以它已深入越南人的血液和基因之中，已不可能分清哪些是汉文化，哪些是越南文化。就拿儒学来说，它已经在越南两千多年，潜移默化地影响人们的思想、文化、教育和习惯行为，即使后来西方思想文化冲击越南传统文化，儒教影响削弱，但儒教毕竟已方方面面影响并深深扎根于越南社会与生活之中。所以越南文化仍然是以东方文化为主体，越南文化的根与中国文化紧紧相连。

既然越南文化与华夏文化有着根深蒂固的渊源关系，“打断骨头连着筋”，“剪不断，理还乱”，因此对越南来说，应正视华夏文化对越南深远影响的客观事实，不应刻意回避或是试图消除汉文化影响而割断中越纽带。所以对于文化中的历史情结，越南既要承认，也要豁然对待。另一方面，从文化角度看，顽强且独立自主是越南民族的重要精神，也是越南文化的重要特色，越南是一个具有强烈民族独立意识的国家，胡志明曾说“没有什么比独立自由更可贵的”，因此对中国来说，不应总把“汉文化影响”挂在嘴边，过分强调自己文化对对方的影响，要充分尊重对方自身的意见，特别是在当今世界文化多元化背景下，要给对方留存一些思考和选择的时间和空间。

参考文献：

[1]古小松.东南亚文化.中国社会科学出版社，2015年1月.

[2]孙衍锋等.越南文化概论.世界图书出版公司，2014年12月.

[3]范宏贵.越南历史与社会主义革新.广西民族学院外国语学院教材，2001年7月.

[4]罗文青.越南文化中的历史情结.东南亚纵横，2005年第10期.

[5]古小松.越南-历史，国情，前瞻.中国社会科学出版社，2016年3月.

[6]闫京育.河内街道命名文化探究.本科毕业论文，广西民族大学外国语学院，2011年.

[7]黄秋莲.越南河内地名研究.广西民族大学亚非语言文学硕士论文，2013年.

（作者简介：罗文青，女，四川外国语大学东方语学院，教授，博士，研究方向：越南语言文化）

The Spatial Distribution of Agritourism in China: National Agritourism Demonstrations in China

Hong Yang, Bai Yang, Wei Chen

Abstract: Although agritourism has been an important element in the growth of China's tourism and has developed dramatically in recent years, its spatial distribution pattern has not been known in detail. After tracking the historical development of agritourism in China, this paper presents the spatial distribution pattern of NADs (National Agritourism Demonstrations) in China and their spatial relationship to tourist origin based on the statistical analysis of 359 NADs in China designated by CNTA (China National Tourism Administration). It confirms that agritourism in China is mainly concentrated in eastern coastal provinces. The geographic association coefficient is applied to identify four agritourism clusters which exhibit tourist market orientation.

Key words: agritourism; spatial distribution; NADs; China

1. Introduction

Tourism has long been considered as a complementary tool and an effective catalyst of rural socio-economic development and regeneration (Opperman, 1996; Fleischer & Felsenstein, 2000; Sharpley, 2002; Briedenhann & Wickens, 2004). In many countries, such as America, Canada, Australia, New Zealand, tourism is employed as an engine of economic growth and diversification in rural areas (Hall & Jenkins, 1998). Agritourism is regarded as a valuable and growing sector of the overall tourism market (Hummelbrunner & Miglbauer, 1994). In China, agritourism is usually defined as tourism products which are connected with the agrarian environment, agrarian products or agrarian stays (Yang & Zhao, 2001; Cheng & Mei, 2004). The development of agritourism offers potential solutions to many of the problems facing rural areas (Gannon, 1994). Therefore, according to Fleischer & Pizam (1997), agritourism in many countries has enjoyed substantial encouragement, support and, in some cases, even direct financial assistance from both the public and private sectors.

China is a large country abundant in agritourism resources. Numerous scenic spots and attractions, long agricultural traditions, rich agrodiversity and colorful folk customs provide great potential for developing agritourism (He, 2004; Xie, 2007). However, unlike countries in Europe and North America with agritourism development history of approximately 100 years, China did not start agritourism until the early 1980s. Since 1998 when the Chinese central government identified tourism as a "pillar industry" (State Council of PR China, 1998), supportive government steps were taken one after another. Agritourism, as a means to spur the country's rural economy and social development, has been given great priority by tourism authorities at both national and provincial levels (Shao, 2007a). The promotion of agritourism, as a derivative of political will, is considered an urgent need to enhance the New Socialist Rural Construction which serves as a campaign to effectively deal with "Three Nong" issues: the issues of agriculture, farmer and rural areas (their initials all pronounce "Nong" in Chinese), develop modern agriculture, achieve a level of integration between urban and rural areas, change the urban-rural dual structure, and reduce disparities between urban and rural areas. In addition, agritourism is also put into the broad government agenda of income and employment generation and the diversification of tourism products. Adherence to the policy of reform and opening up has brought China a steadier, sustainable and healthier political and economic environment for development (Zhang, 1997). Combined with a favorable policy of stimulating domestic tourism, the fast growing national economy and the marked improvement in living standards give rise to a level of growth of agritourism at an unprecedented speed.

The fast development of agritourism in China has caught the interest of many Chinese scholars. Their studies have investigated the characteristics and current state of China's agritourism (Wang, 2007), definitions of agritourism (Han, 2000; Yang et al., 2001; Cheng & Mei, 2004), agritourism classifications (Ding &Sun, 2000; Lu, 2002), the origin of agritourism (Guo et al., 2000), and agritourism development issues (Mei, 2005; Zhang, 2011, Zhang, 2012). However, the spatial distribution of China's agritourism still remains a void in terms of any detailed analysis of China's spatial distribution pattern. This paper, therefore, aims to analyze the regional and provincial distribution state of agritourism in China.

Tourism in China is a "government-led" industry. The former Chinese president of CNTA (China National Tourism Administration), He indicated that Chinese governments at various levels do their best to promote the growth of tourism, including providing guide lines, allocating funds, training personnel, initiating projects, overseeing service quality, stipulating regulations and marketing. One concrete evidence is made clear with the designation of NADs (National Agritourism Demonstration) conducted by CNTA who aims to promote the sustainable development of agritourism in China. Through spatial analysis of the 359 NADs, this paper intends to present the spatial distribution state of Chinese agritourism. First, Table 1 illustrates the standards for NADs to identify the agritourism definition, significance and functions of NADs in China. Second, statistical analysis provides a picture of the current spatial distribution features of China's agritourism from the provincial perspective. Then, spatial density and the Geographic Association Coefficient are also calculated to examine the relationship between the tourist market and agritourism destinations, NADs.

2. China's Agritourism Development—an overview

Although China is a country with a long tradition of agricultural culture, her agritourism origin dates back less than three decades (He, 2004; Xie, 2007). Between 1979 and 1984, systemic and effective reforms were instituted in China's agricultural system. In the rural areas, these reforms decollectivized agriculture by a contract responsibility system based on individual households, which successfully increased productivity, the amount of available arable land, and peasant per capita income. Simultaneously, peasants in China were given more freedom for their agricultural production and other economic activities. This success stimulated substantial support in the countryside for the emergence of agritourism. The original activities, probably without any government intention, were derived by rural residents' spontaneous business behaviours to improve their living conditions (Gao et al., 2009). The business types and services provided include family-run hostels, restaurants, shortdistance transportation, retailing, photographing, horse renting and rickshaw services (Gao, 1997). This period of time is called the embryonic stage of China's agritourism. During this stage, neither local nor central authorities were involved in these spontaneous business activities in rural areas (Shu, 1997). In 1988, the Lychee Tourist Festival was first launched in Shenzhen, a prefecture-level city. Since then, China's agritourism market has seen a boom in popularity.

In the 1990s, more and more citizens spent their holidays in inexpensive accommodation in villages close to their cities, particularly from neighboring large cities such as Guangzhou, Shanghai, and Beijing (Shu, 1997). In 1996, the CNTA and The State Council Leading Group of Poverty Alleviation and Development jointly held the national conference on poverty alleviation through tourism in Zhangjiajie of Hunan Province, which was a hallmark event in the agritourism development in China (Gao, 2008). The concrete evidence of the growing interest in agritourism manifested when, according to estimated statistics, more than 7 projects were conducted that reached 100m RMB for investment in sightseeing agritourism from 1996 to 1997 (Lv & Liu, 2006). In 1998, the CNTA related the theme of Huaxia Urban-rural Tourism to the year and put forward the slogan "taste rural dishes, accommodate in rural houses, participate in formworks, view rural scenery, and enjoy rural lifestyles" in an effort to give China's agritourism a great boost (Tian, 2007). In 1999, the first forum on Chinese ecotourism was held in Xishuang Banna in Yunnan Province. The event induced the establishment of the Chinese Ecotourism Association and the Declaration on Chinese Ecotourism. At the same time, 1999 was declared officially as the Year of Chinese Ecotourism. Given that agritourism was seen as an effective means of achieving not only the regeneration of rural areas but also a variety of ecotourism-policy objectives, it has become and remains an established priority of the ecotourism and sustainable development agendas in China.

In the 2001 National Tourism Work conference, Vice Premier Qian Qichen noted that in the new century, tourism's function in leading the development of other industries should be stressed; tourism development should help facilitate the improvement of the structure of the national economy; as implementation measures, some projects of agritourism, ecotourism and mountain tourism around suburban and rural areas could be planned and constructed (Sun, 2006; Gao, 2009). Besides the intention to promote the economies of Chinese rural areas, to maintain the continuous and healthy development of agritourism and regulate the market was another essential purpose of establishing the National Standards on the Evaluation of Industrial and Agricultural Tourism Demonstrations (Trial Version) promulgated by CNTA in 2002 (CNTA, 2002). The Standards is an important policy instrument for China's agritourism development (Gao, 2009). Based on the Standards, almost all provincial tourism authorities took positive actions to organize and stimulate applications for the national title. They first undertook a self-evaluation and then made improvements following the specified criteria. Two years later, CNTA conducted a final assessment and entitled 306 applicants throughout the country as the first batch of National Industrial and Agricultural Tourism Demonstrations, specifically 203 NADs (National Agriourism Demonstrations) and 103 NITDs (National Industrial Tourism Demonstrations) (CNTA, 2004). By 2005, a total of 359 NADs were listed on the CNTA's official website (CNTA, 2005).

In 2006, the government's vigorous efforts to develop agritourism in China were enhanced by the official announcement that 2006 to be the Year of Chinese Agritourism. The magnitude of agritourism in China was made clear when CNTA issued the Guidelines for Agritourism Development. In 2007, CNTA designated the promotion theme as China's Harmonious Urban-rural Tourism, and initiated the agritourism projects named " Baiqianwan Projects" (Bai in Chinese means hundred; Qian means thousand; Wan means 10 thousand) with an aim to present 100 distinctive counties, 1000 distinctive towns and 10000 distinctive villages (Shao, 2007). Since 2010 to 2015, CNTA cooperating with China Agriculture Ministry (CAM) has cultivated 100 national leisure agriculture and rural tourism demonstration counties and 300 national leisure agriculture demonstrations (CAM, 2015).

To summarize, it can be seen that over the last two decades, the development of agritourism in China has been characterized by the rapid growth. Great efforts were made to encourage the revitalization and promotion of traditional Chinese agricultural practices as an integral element of the agritourism product. It is also evident that the central government agency, the CNTA, has provided significant financial and technical support to develop agritourism in China.

3. National Agritourism Demonstrations in China

3.1 National standards for NADs

In the framework of National Standards on the Evaluation of Industrial and Agricultural Tourism Demonstrations (Trial Version), NADs are defined as agritourism attractions that appeal to visitors by integrating agricultural production processes, rustic scenery, peasantry's working and living scenarios into tourism. The Standards (see Table 1) adopts an evaluation score for every type. The total score for all the ten types is 1000. In addition, a bonus item granted up to 50 scores comprises the appendix in the Standards. Every applicant scoring 700 or above can be entitled as a National Agritourism Demonstration, while given the preferential policies for China Western Development, those from western areas can be qualified to obtain the title with a score of 650 or above. It provides a synoptic list suitable for appraising China's agritourism entities and allows different provincial tourism authorities to assess current levels of agritourism development in the area under evaluation. It is a valuable instrument for the assessment of the positive potential of that area. The Standards describes the applicants' main problems from economic, environmental and social perspectives and guide them to conduct improvements which can induce the standardization of the market. More importantly, it allows areas to integrate these indicators in such a way that decision-makers and the government can analyze the degree of sustainability of China's agritourism, and then find the causes and propose countermeasures where required.

Table 1 An indicator system for NADs evaluation

No.	Indicator type	Indicator	Score
1	Number of visitor arrivals and economic returns (200)	1.1 Number of annual visitor arrivals 1.2 Tourist annual income	100 100
2	Social benefits (150)	2.1 Number of direct employees 2.2 Number of indirect employees 2.3 Added-value (i.e. sale of self-made products, souvenir, etc.) 2.4 Tourism tax	70 30 30 20
3	Ecological and environmental benefits (50)	3.1 Environmental evaluation by Environmental Protection Department	50
4	Tourism products (100)	4.1 Number of tourism spots 4.2 Evaluation of the appeal of tourism spots made by inspectors 4.3 Number of tourism lines & tourism arrangement 4.4 Length of stay	30 30 20 20
5	Tourism infrastructure (140)	5.1 Reception facilities 5.2 Tourism transportation 5.3 Dinning facilities 5.4 Shopping facilities 5.5 Catering facilities 5.6 Direction board both in Chinese and English 5.7 Tourism board both in Chinese and English 5.8 Toilet	30 30 10 10 10 10 10 30
6	Tourism management (60)	6.1 Line management 6.2 Marketing management 6.3 Tourism quality & complaints management	20 20 20
7	Tourism operation (130)	7.1 Tourism independent accounting entity 7.2 Tourism promotion 7.3 Potential visitors 7.4 Reception services 7.5 Visitor satisfaction	20 20 30 30 30
8	Tourism security (80)	8.1 Tourism security rules and regulations 8.2 Tourist accident 8.3 Medical facilities 8.4 Potential safety hazard	20 20 20 20

continued

No.	Indicator type	Indicator	Score
9	Neighboring environment and accessibility (60)	9.1 Neighboring environment 9.2 Accessibility	20 40
10	Development potential (30)	10.1 Tourism resources & programs needed to develop 10.2 Sustainable development 10.3 Medium and long term plan for tourism development	10 10 10

3.2 Spatial distribution of 359 NADs

China is considered as one of the most agri-diverse countries in the world, and with its ancient civilization and a history of several millennia has a wide variety of agriculture systems. In addition, China is dominated by numerous topographies, climatic variability and biological diversity, and is populated by diverse cultural minority groups. Therefore, China has a huge potential for developing agritourism. On the basis of data published by NTA, the proportion within 31 provinces/municipalities/autonomous regions of China by is calculated and listed in Table 2 where 359 NADs in the first two batches entitled by NTA are shown. Table 2 and figure 1 suggests that the 359 NADs were located widely across the whole county, but its spatial distribution is uneven, with significant clustering occurring, notably in the eastern areas accounting for more than half of the total. There is a dense cluster of NADs found in eastern provinces/municipalities, such as Shandong, Jiangsu, Liaoning, Hebei, Zhejiang, Guangdong, Beijing, Shanghai and Tianjin, respectively, 55, 43, 34, 15, 14, 14, 7, 5 and 4, but other provinces, such as Ningxia, Qinghai and Tibet, all have a few NADs, the lowest in Tibet with one. Agritourism in China is a relatively new approach in the broad government agenda of the diversification of tourism products and its development does not only depend on the regional resources but is also influenced by such external factors as the regional economy, transportation, operation modes, human resources and tourist origins. Even if inland China is endowed with resource advantages for agritouism compared with the eastern coastal areas, inconvenient transportation, communication and insufficient infrastructure, combined with unsatisfactory tourism facilities, handicaps agritourism in the interior. Therefore, the agritourism development in China exhibits a disparity between eastern coastal areas and interior China.

Table 2 Provincial distribution of NADs in China

No.	Province	NAD(s)	Proportion(%)	No.	Province	NAD(s)	Proportion(%)
1	Shangdong	55	15.32	17	Beijing	7	1.95
2	Jiangsu	43	11.98	18	Gansu	7	1.95
3	Liaoning	34	9.47	19	Hubei	6	1.67
4	Guizhou	18	5.01	20	Yunnan	6	1.67
5	Sichuan	17	4.74	21	Shanghai	5	1.39
6	Anhui	17	4.74	22	Jiangxi	5	1.39
7	Hebei	15	4.18	23	Tianjin	4	1.11
8	Zhejiang	14	3.90	24	Jilin	3	0.84
9	Guangdong	14	3.90	25	Shaanxi	3	0.84
10	Shanxi	13	3.62	26	Hunan	3	0.84
11	Henan	12	3.34	27	Hainan	2	0.56
12	Guangxi	11	3.06	28	Fujian	2	0.56
13	Inner Mongolia	10	2.79	29	Ningxia	2	0.56
14	Xinjiang	10	2.79	30	Qinghai	2	0.56
15	Heilongjiang	9	2.51	31	Tibet	1	0.28
16	Chongqing	9	2.51				

From a provincial perspective, Shandong province ranks first in the number of NADs with a proportion of 15.32%, followed by Jiangsu, Liaoning, Guizhou, Sichuan, Anhui, Hebei, Zhejiang, Guangdong, and Shanxi (see Table 2). Shandong Province is situated along the eastern coastal lines and in the lower reaches of the Yellow River. Shandong, the cradle of ancient Chinese civilization, enjoys the advantages of geographical location, a long history and rich culture, and abounds with rich tourism resources. Shandong is recognized to be a most important grain and cotton producing region and the largest peanut-producing base of the state. Meanwhile, it is also affluent in fruits and vegetables, enjoying the fame of being the largest

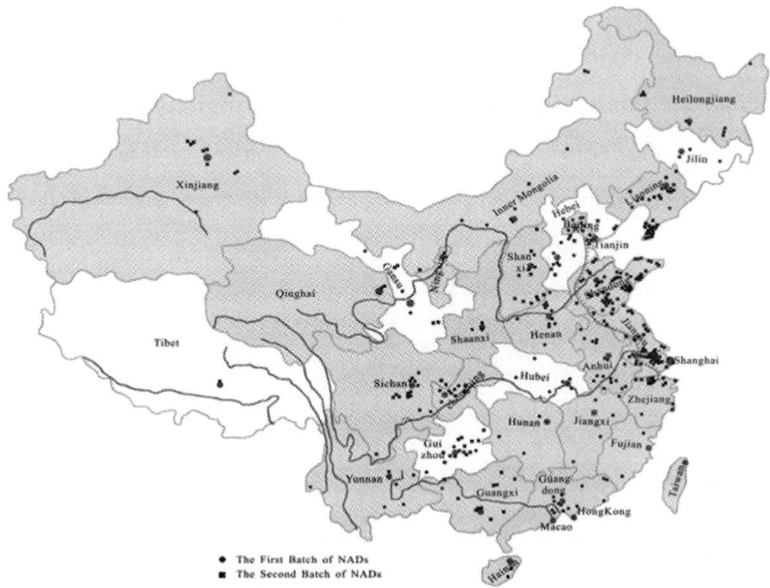

Fig. 1 Spatial distribution of 359 NADs in China

"Vegetable Basket" in China. Its infrastructures prove to be complete and convenient. Due to the rapid, healthy and sustainable development of its economy and the all-the-more reasonable industrial mechanism, its agritourism development plays a leading role in the nation. It has established some well-known agritourism destinations with Qingdao as the "Dragon Head", and Weifang, Rizhao as the forelands, generating quite impressive economic benefits and social impacts.

In table 3, the spatial density of NADs in China is indicated. Spatial density is an important indicator of the spatial nature of tourism destinations. It can serve as an indicator of the relative clustering degree of NADs for a region. Spatial intensity here is calculated by comparing the number of NADs in a province with its areas and can be considered as a guide for conducting a reasonable spatial organization in a region. On the basis of the number of NADs in the 31 provinces/municipalities/autonomous regions, the average spatial density in China as a whole was 0.376. Shanghai held the highest spatial density with a ratio of 8.065, followed by Jiangsu, Beijing, Shandong, and Tianjin, with a ratio of 4.191, 4.167, 3.595, and 3.540, respectively. According to the statistical data, as reflected in Table 3, the 31 provinces can be divided into three groups: the first group is the top ten provinces/ municipalities/

regions with relatively high spatial density ratio of over 1.00, which is far higher than the average ratio, characterized by leading agritourism development in China; the second group includes the following six provinces/regions with the spatial density ratio higher than the national average level but much lower than the first group; the third group is the remaining 15 provinces/regions with the lower ratio than the national average.

Table 3 Spatial density of NADs in China (by 2014)

No.	Province	NAD (s)	Area (10,000 km^2)	Density (per 10,000 km^2)	No.	Province	NAD (s)	Area (10,000 km^2)	Density (per 10,000 km^2)
1	Shanghai	5	0.62	8.065	17	Sichuan	17	48.8	0.348
2	Jiangsu	43	10.26	4.191	18	Hubei	6	18.7	0.321
3	Beijing	7	1.68	4.167	19	Ningxia	2	6.64	0.301
4	Shandong	55	15.3	3.595	20	Jiangxi	5	16.6	0.301
5	Tianjin	4	1.13	3.540	21	Heilongjiang	9	46.9	0.192
6	Liaoning	34	14.57	2.334	22	Fujian	2	12	0.167
7	Zhejiang	14	10.18	1.375	23	Jilin	3	18.7	0.160
8	Anhui	17	13.9	1.223	24	Gansu	7	45	0.156
9	Chongqing	9	8.2	1.098	25	Yunnan	6	39.4	0.152
10	Guizhou	18	17	1.059	26	Shaanxi	3	20.5	0.146
11	Shanxi	13	15.6	0.833	27	Hunan	3	21	0.143
12	Hebei	15	19	0.789	28	Inner Mongolia	10	118	0.085
13	Guangdong	14	18.6	0.753	29	Xinjiang	10	160	0.063
14	Henan	12	16.7	0.719	30	Qinghai	2	72	0.028
15	Hainan	2	3.4	0.588	31	Tibet	1	122	0.008
16	Guangxi	11	23.63	0.466					

What becomes obvious is that many NADs are distributed around the big cities (see Figure 1 where red dots represent capital cities of every provinces), such as Shanghai, Beijing, Tianjin and Chonqing, four Chinese municipalities listed in the first group.

Urban areas play a critical role in tourism development, not only as tourist origins or destinations, but also as hubs that provide transportation, hospitality, infrastructure, and facilities to support tourism in peripheral areas (Li et al., 2009). According to the study of Wu, Tan, Zhao, Qiu, and Fang (1997), 80% of urban residents in China prefer to visit destinations within 500 km (310.5 miles) of where they live (Wu et al., 1997). In addition to this accessibility, which is an important pull factor (Boniface and Cooper, 1994), the relatively complete tourism support system, the steady and fast economic growth and social development, the holiday systems, namely the two-day weekend and the Golden week, combined with the authority led promotion projects, facilitate urban dwellers' pursuit of physical, outdoor activities and enjoyment of an aesthetically pleasing, tranquil countryside and contribute to the dense cluster of NADs around these big cities. Shanghai, a spectacularly modern city, is one of the best examples, ranking first in spatial density of NADs (Figure 1 and Table 3). Shanghai is situated on the bank of the Yangtze River Delta, and has absolute advantages over other domestic cities to develop agritourism.

From a geographical perspective, tourism consists of three major components: the origin of tourists, tourist destinations, and routes traveled between these two locations (Leiper, 1979). The Coefficient of Geographic Association (G-coefficient) can be employed to evaluate the degree of geographical coincidence of two comparable variables, namely tourist attractions (as tourist destinations) and population (as the origin of tourists) (Wu and Tang, 2003). The analysis of geographic association between NADs and the tourist market can incorporate data on the government's planning and decisions pertaining to agritourism development. A sufficient tourist source is necessary for developing agritourism in China. Usually, the number of urban residents is considered equivalent to the number of tourists generated from a city, because urban residents contribute significantly to the growth of China's domestic tourism (Cai et al., 2001; Wu and Cai, 2006; Li et al., 2008). Therefore, within the context of China's agritourism development, urban dwellers are considered as the major origin of tourists.

In this paper, the G-coefficient between NADs and the origin of tourists is calculated considering 359 NADs in the 31 administrative regions. The G-coefficient can be expressed by the following formula: where represents a percentage of NADs in *i*th province over 31 provinces, represents a percentage of urban population over all the country, *n* is equal to 31 and represents the number of provinces in China. The G-coefficient can assume values from 1 to 100. The bigger the value of G-coefficient — within the above range — the greater the geographical or spatial association of NADs and tourist market, and vice versa. The G-coefficient for the whole of China as well as the G-coefficients for four major agritourism clusters are indicated in Table 4. The national G-coefficient is 99.69 which shows that the degree of geographical coincidence of NADs and urban population in every province is very high, and from this it can be apparent that NADs are characterized by the tourist market orientation.

Table 4 Spatial density and G-coefficient of NADs in China (by 2014)

Agritourism cluster	Province/ municipality in agritourism cluster	NADs	Proportion (%)	Spatial Density (per 10,000 km^2)	Urban population (10,000 persons)	G-coefficient
Eastern Coastal Area	Shanghai, Zhejing, Jiangsu	62	17%	2.94	8068	99.76
Circum-Bohai-Sea Area	Beijing, Tianjin, Hebei, Liaoning, Shandong	115	32%	2.23	11282	99.81
Middle Area	Hubei, Anhui, Henan, Shanxi	48	13%	0.74	8918	99.78
Southwest Area	Chongqing, Sichuan, Guizhou, Guangxi	55	15%	0.56	6539	99.83
China	31 provinces	359	100%	0.38	56157	99.69

China's agritourim can be described as exhibiting a cluster distribution. Considering the spatial density and the G-coefficient illustrated in Table 4, NADs in China are concentrated in four clusters, namely Eastern Coastal Area, Circum-

Bohai-Sea Area, Middle Area, and Southwest Area. 32% of NADs in China are concentrated in Circum-Bohai-Sea Area, a region which has rich agricultural resources, superior position, convenient transportation network, fully equipped infrastructure, high aggregation of talents, combined with a huge consumer market, reinforces the agritourism development. The area exhibits a dense agritourism cluster with several large cities as centers, namely Beijing, Tianjin, Dalian, Shenyang, Qingdao and Rizhao. Eastern Coastal Area is another dense agritourism cluster with a high NAD spatial density of 2.94, which is far higher than the national average level. The region is characterized by the most developed economic zone, with Shanghai as a center, which is renowned as the Land of Fish and Rice and enjoys great advantages of developing agritourism, such as a huge tourist market, developed agricultural and tourism systems. The Middle Area, with Zhengzhou as a centre, owns good position and very convenient transportation network, which means high accessibility for tourism. But its relatively underdeveloped economy, insufficient infrastructure, unsatisfactory tourism facilities handicapped the development of agritourism in this area. The Southwest Area covers Chongqing, Sichuan, Guizhou and Guangxi with 55 NADs. Considering the large area, its NADs spatial density of 0.56 is lower than that in the first three areas. But the area is endowed with a high percentage of China's natural resources, populated by diverse cultural minority groups. In addition, abundant ecotourism resources distributed in the south west China and increasing tourist demand in rural places reinforce the prospects of agritourim growth in the future.

4. Conclusion

Tourism is employed as an engine of economic growth and diversification in rural areas (Hall & Jenkins, 1998). In China, agritourism has enjoyed substantial encouragement, support and direct assistance from both the public and private sectors. Many government-endorsed agritourism policies were launched as one element of China's agritourism development strategy. The official announcement of NADs is one of actual implementation of these policies.

This paper has sought to explore the spatial pattern of agritourism in China. Owing to the limitation of available statistics, the paper analyses only the first two batches of NADs in China. Generally speaking, NADs in China reveal a spatial concentration in eastern regions and are less concentrated in middle and west China. Coastal regions obtain the majority share of NADs in China. From a provincial perspective, NADs are mainly distributed in coastal provinces such as Shandong, Jiangsu and Liaoning. Based on the statistical figures of NAD spatial density in Table 3, 31 administrative regions can be categorized into three groups. It appears that the first group exhibits a greater density of agritourism. The G-coefficient has been calculated to explore the degree of geographical coincidence between the tourist market specifically urban residents and NAD distribution within four major agritourism clusters. The results suggest that the spatial distribution of NADs is demand-oriented, i.e. characterized by tourist market orientation. The analysis also hints at the presence of four major agritourism clusters in China, namely Eastern Coastal Area, Circum-Bohai-Sea Area, Middle Area, and Southwest Area. In addition, the spatial analysis also suggests that the scale of agritourism in China is very impressive and agritourism has become a new growth pole of economic development in rural areas.

The framework of geographical areas proposed by the present analysis could form the basis for research seeking to understand how the development of agritourism in China is affected by external constraints, such as the origin of tourist. This study represents an attempt to increase awareness of the spatial linkage between agritourism destinations and tourist generating areas in China. It is evident that such research would provide suggestions for regional policy planning and decisions pertaining to local agritourism development and can be used for future benchmarking.

The analysis presented in this paper is of an exploratory nature, seeking to provide a basis for further research concerning developing China's agritourism. A better understanding of the spatial distribution patterns of agritourism will be helpful in estimating the volume of agritourism demand and enhance policy making for agritourism spatial planning in China.

References:

[1] Barbieri C., Mshenga P.M., 2008, The role of the firm and owner characteristics on the performance of agritourism farms, *Sociologia Ruralis*, 48, 166-183.

[2] Boniface B., Cooper C.P., 1994, *Geography of Travel and Tourism* (2nd ed), Oxford: Butterwoth Heinemann.

[3] Briedenhann, Wickens, 2004, Tourism routes as a tool for the economic development of rural areas—vibrant hope or impossible dream?, *Tourism Mangement*, 25(1), 71-79.

[4] Cai L., Hu B., Feng R., 2001, Domestic tourism demand in China's urban centers: Empirical analysis and marketing implications, *Journal of Vacation Marketing*, 8(1), 64-74.

[5] Cheng D.P., Mei H., 2004, Literature review on Chinese agritourism development, *Reformation and Strategy*, 10: 28-31.

[6] China Agriculture Ministry (CAM), 2015, National leisure agriculture and rural tourism demonstration counties and national leisure agriculture demonstrations, Available at http://www.moa.gov.cn/zwllm/tzgg/tz/201512/t20151222_4959527.htm.

[7] China National Tourism Administration (CNTA). 2002, Circulation on the issuance of evaluation standards of national industrial and agricultural tourism demonstrations (Trial Version), Available at http://www.cnta.gov.cn/gb2/gonggaoview.asp?id=6628 (accessed 18 December 2009).

[8] China National Tourism Administration (CNTA), 2004, First batch of national industrial and agricultural demonstrations list. Available at http://www.cnta.gov.cn:8000/Forms/ExcellentDes/ExcellentDesList.aspx?newsID=606542338669&classID=807811952743&imgOn=5&menuType=ExcellentDes (accessed 18 December 2009).

[9] China National Tourism Administration (CNTA), 2005, National industrial and agricultural demonstrations list, Available at http://www.cnta.gov.cn

[10] (accessed 18 December 2009).

[11] Ding Z.M., Sun, J.S., 2000, Research on the development of sightseeing agriculture in China, *China Agricultural Economy*, 12: 27-31.

[12] Fleischer A., Pizam A. 1997, Rural tourism in Israel. *Tourism Management*, 18 (6), 367-372.

[13] Fleischer A., Pizam A. 2000, Support for rural tourism: Does it make a difference?, *Annals of Tourism Research*, 27, 1007-1024.

[14] Gannon A. 1994, Rural tourism as a factor in rural community economic development for economies in transition, *Journal of Sustainable Tourism*, 2 (1+2), 51-60.

[15] Gao S. 1997, The experiences, problems and solutions of poverty alleviation through tourism, *Tourism Tribune* 12(4), 4.

[16] Gao S. 2008, The current state and new development ideas of China's rural tourism, In *Analysis and Forecast of China's Tourism Development 2008*, Zhang G., Liu D. (eds), Social Science and Literature Press: Beijing: 221–232.

[17] Gao S., Huang S., Huang Y., 2009, Rural tourism development in China. *International Journal of Tourism Reserch*, 11: 439-450.

[18] Guo H.C., Liu J.P., Wang Y.C., 2000, Sightseeing agriculture development, *Economic Geography*, 2, 119-124.

[19] Hall C.M., Jenkins J., 1998, The policy dimensions of rural tourism and recreation, In Butler R., Hall C.M., Jenkins J. (Eds.), *Tourism and recreation in rural areas* (pp. 19-42), Chichester: Wiley.

[20] Han L., 2000, The study on the sustainable development of China's sightseeing agriculture, *Agricultural Economy*, 10: 9-10.

[21] He J.M., 2004, Research on Chinese rural tourism, *Tourism Tribune*, 9(1): 92-96.

[22] He G.W., 1998, Address at the 1998 National Conference on Tourism. China Tourism News in *Chinese Tourism Newspaper*, Mar. 26.

[23] Hummelbrunner R., Miglbauer E., 1994, Tourism promotion and potential in peripheral areas: The Austrian case, *Journal of Sustainable Tourism*, 2(1+2), 41-50.

[24] Leiper N., 1979, The framework of tourism, *Annals of Tourism Research*, 6(4), 390-407.

[25] Li M., Wu B., Cai L., 2008, Tourism development of world heritage sites in

China: a geographic perspective, *Tourism Management*, 29, 308-319.

[26] Lu H.K., 2002, Sightseeing agriculture and its development, *Tribune of Study*, 7, 31-33.

[27] Lv H.J., Liu B., 2006, The current status and countermeasures of China's agritourism development, *Shanxi Agricultural Science*, 5, 95-97.

[28] Mei H., 2005, The study on quantitative evaluation of agritourism resources, *Science and Technology Progress and Policy*, 12: 65-68.

[29] McGehee N.G., 2007, An agritourism systems model: a Weberian perspective, *Journal of Sustainable tourism*, 15, 111-124.

[30] National Bureau of Statistics of China (NBSC), 2005, http://www.stats.gov.cn/tjsj/ndsj/ (accessed 18 December 2009).

[31] Opperman M., 1996, Rural tourism in southern Germany, *Annals of Tourism Research*, 23 (1), 86-102.

[32] Phillip S., Hunter C., Blackstock K., 2009, A typology for defining agritourism, *Tourism Management*, DOI:10.1016/j.tourman.2009.08.001.

[33] Qian W., 1999, Tourism in China and professionalism: an insider's perspective, *Asia Pacific Journal of Tourism Research*, 4 (1), 22-29.

[34] Shao Q.W., 2007, The speech on 2007 national tourism conference, Available at http://www.gov.cn (accessed 18 December 2009).

[35] Sharpley R., 2002, Rual tourism and the challenge of tourism diversification: the case of Cyprus, *Tourism Management*, 23, 233-244.

[36] Shu B.Y., 1997, The current status and future prospects of China's sightseeing agritourism, *Tourism Tribune*, 5: 41-43.

[37] Tian F.J. 2007, Sightseeing agritourism literature review, *Areal Research and Development*, 26 (1), 107-112.

[38] Wang X.L., Zhang Z.Y., Wang Z.B., 2007, Rural tourism and agritourism, *Inquiry into Economic Issues*, 2: 155-158.

[39] Wu B., Cai L., 2006, Spatial modeling: Suburban leisure in Shanghai, *Annals of Tourism Research*, 33 (1), 179-198.

[40] Wu B., Tang J., Zhao R., Qiu F., Yang Y., 1997, A study on destination choice behavior of Chinese urban residents, *Acta Geographica Sinica*, 52 (2), 97-103.

[41] Wu B.H., Tang Z.Y., 2003, A Study on Spatial Structure of National 4a Grade Tourism Attractions in China, *Human Geography*, 18(1), 1-5, 28.

[42] Xie Y.P., 2007, On the progress of the research on eco-agricultural tourism in China, *Journal of Shaoyang University* (*Natural Science Edition*), 4(2), 105-109.

[43] Yang Y.M., Zhao M.M., Lei X., 2001, Thinking of developing ecological agriculture tourism of Yunnan, *Inquiry into Economic Problems*, 1, 119-121.

[44] Zhang W., 1997, China's domestic tourism: impetus, development and trends, *Tourism Management*, 18(8), 565-571.

[45] Zhang W.J., 2011, Agritourism: industrial integration and urban-rural interaction, *Tourism Tribune*, 26(10), 11-12.

[46] Zhang Y.C., 2012, Study on the industrial convergence and agritourism development in balancing urban-rural development, *Tourism*, 154(7), 154-157.

（作者简介：杨红，女，四川外国语大学国别经济与国际商务研究中心，教授，博士，研究方向：国际旅游管理）

国际商品展示与交易中心发展的SWOT分析

黄 森 舒首凤

摘要：自2013年自贸区的设立开始，一种新的商业模式——国际商品展示与交易中心，如雨后春笋般出现，然而国际商品展示与交易中心的发展现状、面临问题以及未来发展方向尚不明确。本文在通过对全国各个省份的国际商品展示与交易中心进行资料搜集以及部分实地调研的基础上，运用SWOT分析法，分析国际商品展示与交易中心的发展现状、存在模式、面临问题，得出国际商品展示与交易中心应当利用依托保税区的优势、成立协会并交流合作，在优化自身的物流与信息化管理的基础上，加大营销力度、平衡发展进出口商品贸易。

关键词：国际商品展示与交易中心；保税商品；进口商品；SWOT分析

国际商品展示与交易中心，是依托保税物流中心、保税港区、综合保税区、自贸区（以下简称“保税区”）的商品展示功能，进行商品展示与销售的场所。中国现行商品展示与交易中心，除具备传统的进口商品展示与销售功能外，还配备跨境电商的线下体验、进口商品的直销分销、进口商品与服务体验以及休闲娱乐等功能。国际商品展示与交易中心的出现，一方面是因为国内消费者对于国外产品的需求增加:从最初的代购到后来海淘的迅速发展，都反映出人们对海外商品的青睐；另一方面也跟国家积极推进跨境电商的试点（李文一，2014）有关，跨境电子商务试点退出后，跨境电商迅速发展，但是发展中遇到了瓶颈：由于线上销售产品，人们看不到摸不着，无法直观地判断商品的好坏，因此销量受限，为了满足消费者体验式购物的强烈要求从而突破销量瓶颈，许多跨境电商跟保税区完美结合，国际商品展示与交易中心应运而生。

国际商品展示与交易中心，作为一种新兴的商业模式，在发挥保税商品展示功能的同时也产生了一系列影响。首先国际商品展示与交易中心，满足了人们对海外商品日益增加的需求，让人们更加直观地感知海外商品，避免盲目消费。其次，国际商品展示与交易中心的出现，无疑会给国内产品带来更大压力，让国内的企业能够在外界压力下，提升自身创新能力，争取能够生产出更高质量的产品，来满足国内消费者的需求。最后，进口商品的销售不仅仅是商品的交易，在一定程度上也是国家间的贸易合作与文化交流，这对加强国家间的友好合作关系、增进国家间的了解，也有一定的促进作用。

一、国际商品展示与交易中心的发展现状

国际商品展示与交易中心是一种新的商业模式，所以在进行SWOT分析前，需要明晰国际商品展示与交易中心的发展现状和存在模式，以便为其发展提出可靠的建议。

（一）国际商品展示与交易中心的概况

国际商品展示与交易中心在数量和分布上的发展状况。国际商品展示与交易中心的发展，跟国家自贸区的建立有一定的关系，中国为了更好地融入世界的发展，完善开放型经济体制，于2013年建立上海自贸区。随后广东、天津、福建自贸区于2015年4月21日挂牌，各地综合保税区、保税物流中心、保税区也陆续批复。保税区具有商品展示的功能，落地成型即为我们所见的保税商品展示中心。2013年国际商品展示与交易中心，大多处在规划或者项目谈判签约阶段，真正成型的商品展示与交易中心寥寥可数；2014年作为中国跨境电商元年，一定程度上刺激了国际保税展示中心的发展，截至2014年年底国际商品展示与交易中心共有12家；直至2015年，国际商品展示与交易中心得到了井喷式的发展，据不完全统计，2015年全年，新开业的国际商品展示与交易中心共有61家；2016年，大多数国际商品展示与交易中心基本成型，统计截至2016年5月底，新开业的国际商品展示与交易中心有11家。观察图1，国际商品展示与交易中心的区域分布，国际商品展示与交易中心多分布在华北、华南、华东三个区域，原因是之一是这三个区域都是有自贸区试点，投资人在进行项目投资时，有可以模仿的对象；另一方面这些区域人们整体消费水平高，进口商品大多属于中高端消费水平，这样商品才有销路，商家才有利可盈。

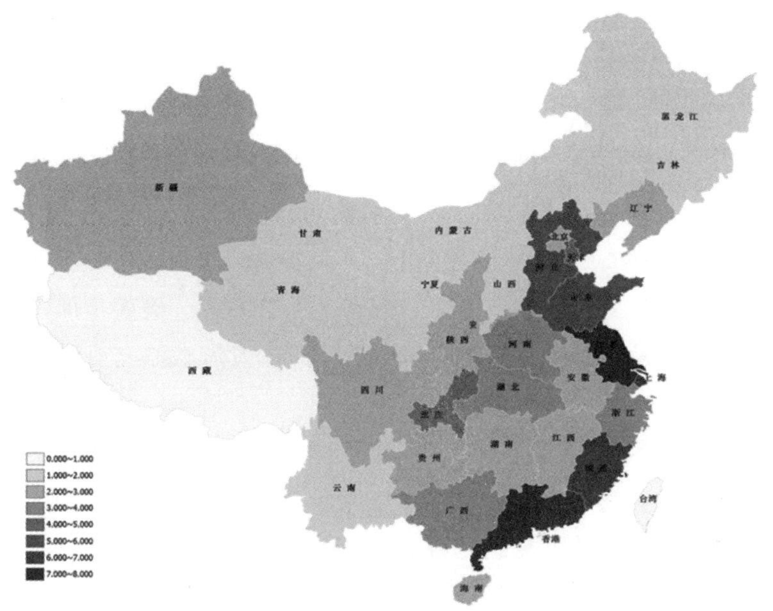

图1　中国国际商品展示与交易中心分布图

（二）国际商品展示与交易中心的模式

截止到2016年5月，全国共有进口国际商品展示与交易中心84家，按业态划分，可以分为进口商品直销、跨境电商、保税展示交易三种模式，三种模式对比见表1。与传统模式相比，国际商品展示与交易中心的运营模式有四大特色：一是进口商品以保税状态进入平台展示、陈列，销售时完税；二是海关对平台商品实施电子监管和状态管理，采用“分批出区、集中报关”，商检对平台商品进行预商检；三是保税商品在交易平台实现销售，消费者支付货款时，货款与税款实现即时分离，保证税款及时入库；四是如商品销售不佳或三个月内没有售出，可灵活返回区内继续进行保税仓储并重新进行全球分拨，平台具有自贸功能（钱继光，2014）。

进口商品直销模式，一般以“国际超市”的形式存在，主要经营人们日常所需的必需品，涵盖食品、日用品、化妆品、酒类、钟表等国外进口商品，以进口海鲜与水果为特色。这种销售模式，人们可以直接购买商品，现场付款提货，跟平常逛超市没有区别。现存直销中心，有两种发展战略，一种是与市中心繁华地段联动战略，将“国际超市”开到人们家门口，方便人们购买；另一种战略是，布置在国际国际商品展示与交易中心内部，作为进口商品销售必不可少的一部分存在，即进口商品直销、跨境电商落地、保税展示交易三者结合。例如，上海DIG外高桥进口商品直销中心、河北的I.B.D.进口保税商品直营中心，广东的IGOSHOP全球商品跨境直购体验中心等。

跨境电商模式，顾名思义，是一些跨境电商为了满足人们现场体验的需要，而存在于线下的实体店铺，即人们熟知的跨境电商“线下展示交易中心+线上购买平台”O2O体验中心，人们在线下实体店可体验商品，购买却必须在网上下单，再通过物流快递寄送到顾客手中。商品类型涵盖日用品、生鲜食品、奶粉、母婴用品、箱包服饰、化妆品、电器、数码产品、酒等。例如“保税国际、万国优品、京东母婴、爱购保税”等。跨境电商模式的发展战略与直销中心模式是相同的。

保税展示交易是指经海关注册登记的海关特殊监管区域内企业在区内或者区外开展保税展示交易的经营活动（中华人民共和国黄埔海关，2015）。“保税展示交易”是上海自贸区“可复制、可推广”的十四项创新制度之一（朱伟良和黄少宏，2015）。简单地说，是指进口货物存放在保税区内，可以进行商品展示与销售，这种形式下，商品在未销售出去之前不用缴纳税费，只有在商品销售出去以后，才进行报税工作。这种模式极大地减少了企业的资金占用与报税成本。商品种类从生活用品、中高端奢侈品到进口汽车应有尽有，满足了人们日常生活所需。由于保税商品出区展示需要全额缴纳货物的税款担保金，所以保税展示交易一般都存在与海关监管下的保税区内，现在很多地方综合保税区或者保税物流中心，都建有比较大型的国际商品展示与交易中心，能够满足人们各种购物需求。由于一般保税区都处于常住人口比较少的区域，为了吸引人气，国际商品展示与交易中心通常会打造一个集休闲娱乐、旅游度假、购物、商务、餐饮于一体的商业中心。例如，天津欧贸中心、福建利嘉商贸中心等。

二、国际商品展示与交易中心发展的SWOT分析

表1 国际商品展示与交易中心发展的SWOT分析

	优势	劣势
	1.商品原装进口 2.商品成本相对低廉 3.通关便利	1.位置偏僻 2.部分商品送达不及时 3.知名度较低 4.中心发展状况良莠不齐
机会	SO战略	WO战略

续表

	优势	劣势
1. “一带一路”战略 2. 国内产品质量遭质疑 3. 保税区政策支持 4. 鼓励跨境电商的发展	1. 加大营销宣传 2. 引导消费 3. 加强客户体验	1. 与人流量大的地方联动 2. 整合跨境物流
威胁	ST战略	WT战略
1. 竞争激烈 2. 尾货处理 3. 进出口失衡	1. 平衡进出口贸易 2. 信息化商品管理	1. 丰富国际商品展示与交易中心的业态 2. 成立行业协会，资源共享

（一）优势分析

第一，国际商品展示中心的商品是原装进口。展示交易中心销售的货物均在国外原产地采购，经过正规渠道报关进口、商品检验，可保障货品来源。

第二，国际商品展示与交易中心商品通关便捷。对于保税区进口的商品，海关实行“集中报备、税收健全、清单出库、汇总纳税”的政策，利用信息化技术和信用考核机制，将以前的出区报税改为对信用度好的企业实行商品登记出区，固定时间集中批量报税，大大提高了通关效率。

第三，在前两项的基础上，商品具有了成本优势。首先，大力压缩流通成本。国际商品展示与交易中心，在进行商品采购时，加大原产地自采力度，同时很多进口代理商，很多都是一级代理商，直接和一级代理合作，能大大压缩商品的流通成本。事实上，市场上进口商品贵的原因，主要不是因为关税，而是流通成本。比如进口巧克力的关税税率是8%，增值税率17%，计算下来进口综合税率约26%。但国内出售的进口巧克力价格往往比原产地贵100%以上，大头被经销商赚走了。其次，优惠的税收政策。2016年4月8日之前，国家的跨境电商实行“保税进口，行邮出区”的政策，即商品进口存放在保税区中，可以先不用缴纳税费，待商品销售出区，以征收“行邮税”的方式出口，比一般贸易优惠很多。而税改之后，国家针对跨境电商的税收政策，虽然有调整，但是相对一般贸易，还是有很大的优惠。再次，灵活使用保税优势。比如率先在自贸区开张的“保税展示交易平台”，商品在展示过程中是保税的，卖出去才交进口关税，供货商不用事先垫付税款，卖不完的货还可以全球调拨，由此降低的资金成本，可以用来向消费者让利。

（二）弱势分析

第一，存在商品日期不新鲜、款式落后，商品送达不及时的问题。由于保税进口商品，从国外进口的过程中，采购、运输、报关本身都需要一定时间，再加上由于人们对进口保税商品中心的熟知度不够，或者还未养成在保税进口商品展示中心购买物品的习惯，因此进口商品大都存在日期不够新鲜、款式不够新颖的弱势。另一方面，一部分商品通过跨境电商在海外集中购买，邮寄到客户手中，电商一方面为了节约物流成本，会等待货物集中完毕，一起寄回国内，需要花费一定时间，货物到达保税区，还要办理清关手续，而海关在非工作日停止清关，通常商品要15天以上才能达到客户手中，交易周期过长，客户“交钱提货”的消费习惯没有改变的话，会不适应这种购物方式。

第二，国际商品展示与交易中心位置偏僻，缺乏人气。国际商品展示与交易中心通常与保税物流中心、保税港区共同存在，这些地方通常设在位置偏僻的郊区，街区不够繁华、常驻人口较少、人流量不够大，因此新建的国际商品展示与交易中心，在营销与广告做得不够好时，会面临人气不旺、无人知晓的局面。

第三，国际商品展示与交易中心知名度低。一方面，国际商品展示与交易中心，作为一种新的商业模式，刚刚进入人们的生活，很多人需要购买国外商品，但是却不知道有这样的商场存在，造成信息不对称；另一方面，人们对国外商品的知晓度也不够。虽然人们对国外商品趋之若鹜，但是仅仅局限于一些爆款和热销产品，国际商品展示与交易中心的商品，都是原装进口，能够满足生活的各种商品百货，人们对于某些商品本身的属性以及在原产国甚至是国际上处于何种消费档次都不太了解，造成产品信息传递的不对称。

第四，国际商品展示与交易中心，发展现状良莠不齐。由于全国各地的发展水平、消费水平的差异，国际商品展示与交易中心为了适应不同的消费水平，整体的商业规模以及售卖的商品种类大小多少不一，有的地方建立一条龙的消费体验商业中心，有的地方却只是存在一个国际超市。

（三）机会分析

第一，国家“一带一路”战略的提出，给国际贸易带来契机。一方面，“一带一路”战略下，中国与沿线国家的联系越来越密切，贸易往来有所增加；另一方面，“一带一路”战略下，中国国内开始发展物流业，中国境内通往欧洲各地的中欧班列物流专线，带动了中国以及相关国家的物流连通，使货物贸易更加方便快捷。

第二，国内产品质量不高，给进口商品的进入提供契机。近年来，随着人们消费水平的提升，人们更加追求高质量的产品，加上国内外商品价差较大以及国内商品质量频出丑闻，国内消费者更加倾向于购买进口产品。

第三，国际商品展示与交易中心可以依靠保税区的政策优势。目前，全国海关监管区域主要有六种类型。从政策功能上看，由低到高依次是：保税区、出口加工区、保税物流园、跨境工业园区、保税港区和综合保税区。其中，根据《保税区海关监管办法》《中华人民共和国海关保税港区管理暂行办法》《中华人民共和国海关对保税物流园区的管理办法》规定，保税物流园、保税区、综合保税区、保税港区、贸易试验区具有保税仓储、商品展示、转口贸易的功能，即商品在保税区内储存、展示，可以不用缴纳税费，商品没有内销，还可以再出口到其他国家，无需办理手续以及缴纳税费。

第四，国家鼓励跨境电商的发展。国家批复了10个城市的保税区（分别为上海、重庆、杭州、宁波、广州、郑州、深圳、福州、平潭、天津），拥有跨境电商试点资格，试点城市可以开展跨境备货业务，即电商平台或第三方商家直接备货到保税区，然后从杭州、宁波、郑州等国内保税区仓库直接发货，购物速度和国内网购几乎没有区别。而跨境电商的另外一种直邮模式，即消费者先下订单后，国内跨境电商平台聚集足够的货（主要目的是分摊物流成本），然后从已经备好货或者临时采买货的美国仓、韩国仓等地邮寄到国内，极大地降低了物流与采购成本。

（四）威胁分析

第一，同类产品购买渠道多，竞争激烈。国际商品展示与交易中心，交易的对象是进口商品，而国内现有的奥特莱斯、进口超市也进行国外商品的销售，同时人们也可以通过海外直邮、代购、出国自己购买的方式，获得海外商品，因此同质产品的替代性比较大，竞争激烈，国际商品展示与交易中心，如何利用自身优势、吸引消费者尤其重要。

第二，尾货处理不当，造成资源浪费（盛柯文等，2012）。由于需求不足等原因导致的商品销路不好，商品将如何处理的问题，现行模式没有做好尾货处理的计划，造成商品浪费、资金周转困难的后果。

第三，商品出口较少，造成发展失衡。国际商品展示与交易中心，目前侧重点在于进口商品的销售，而忽视了商品的出口。2015年，中国跨境电商交易规模为5.4万亿，同比增长28.6%，其中出口占比达到83.2%，进口比例16.8%；因此商品出口是大趋势，如果单纯是进口商品展示与交易，中心人流量受限，业态发展不完整，造成部分物流等资源的浪费。

综合分析，国际商品展示中心，依托保税区、跨境电商的政策优势，经历2015年井喷式增加之后，当下面临着商品销路不畅、中心人气不旺等问题。在现今激烈竞争情况下，更好地利用自身优势，进行积极营销，在做好进口商品展示与交易中心的基础上，推进国内商品的展示与出口。

三、国际商品展示与交易中心的发展对策建议

（一）SO战略：加大营销，引导消费，增强体验

国际商品展示与交易中心，诞生与发展的环境与政策都很有利，进口的商品也具有质量优、价格低的特点，所以国际商品展示与交易中心自身具有内部优势。但是由于国际商品展示与交易中心是一种新兴的商业模式，最初通常存在于相对偏僻的保税区内，所以普通人群很难了解到这样一种商业模式的存在，更不会前去购物，而语言、地域等的差异导致大部分人对国外商品了解不多、关注与消费不足。因此国际商品展示与交易中心在开业之初，需要加大对营销的投入力度。首先通过媒体、实体广告投入等宣传方式，扩大国际商品展示与交易中心的知名度，特别是针对目标群体，即中高端消费者的推广，可以在机场、高铁等地，通过实体广告的投入进行宣传；接下来，当国际商品展示与交易中心聚集到一定人流量的时候，应该通过现场的一系列互动体验活动，让客户更深入地了解商品，引导人们对进口商品的消费。

（二）WO战略：与人流量较大的地方联动，同时整合跨境物流

国际商品展示与交易中心，可以与中心繁华城市、旅游景区、汽车展示中心等人口相对比较集中的地方合作，让国际商品展示与交易中心融入到人们的生活中，扩大其影响力，让更多的人去接触和了解国际商品展示与交易中心；同时也可以借鉴“重庆模式”，即重庆市在主城繁华地段以及著名旅游景点解放碑，搭建了“区外保税商品展示交易中心延展平台”，将保税商品延展至区外主城商业中心进行保税展示，实现真正意义上的“前店后仓”。

跨境物流网络系统缺乏协同（冀芳和张夏恒，2015），具体表现在仓储、运输、海关、配送等物流功能缺乏协同，国内物流、国际物流与目的国物流衔接缺乏协同，跨境物流与语言、习俗、技术、政策等物流环境缺乏协同。目前跨境物流的主要模式包括国际邮政小包、国际快递、海外仓、国际物流专线、边境仓、

保税区与自贸区物流、集货物流、第三方物流与第四方物流等。未来跨境电子商务物流发展，需要推动跨境电子商务与跨境物流的协同发展和跨境物流网络协同；采用多种跨境物流模式共用的方式，推动以第四方物流为代表的物流外包模式升级，实现跨境物流本地化运作，加强与本土物流公司合作等。

（三）ST战略：平衡进出口，信息化管理商品

国际商品展示与交易中心现在的发展重心是进口商品的销售，出口产品业务量不大。但是商品在进口时候，会建立一些合作伙伴关系以及物流方面的基础设施，这些资源都可以为国际贸易中的出口所用，同时发展出口还可以增加国际商品展示与交易中心的人流量，增加人们对此的关注度。

同时国际商品展示与交易中心依托保税区存在，有着通关便利以及转口贸易的天生优势，所以将国际商品展示与交易中心的商品进行信息化的管理，以便及时地检测到商品的余量、保质期、销量等情况，以此来方便快捷地进行商品货物的调拨与转口。

（四）WT战略：丰富业态，成立协会，资源共享

商业发展至今，呈现出新的贸易模式。单纯的商品展示与交易，已经不能满足人们日常的需求，必须抓住消费者的“体验”环节，满足他们的社交、休闲需求，当然也不仅仅局限在吃饭、看电影等体验上，要挖掘更多的消费者情感需求。因此集购物、休闲、旅游、餐饮、娱乐等于一体的项目，是商业发展的必然趋势，完善的配套设施不仅能满足周边居民假日购物休闲需求，同时也吸引了消费者前来购物。

此外，国内国际商品展示与交易中心虽然数量逐渐增多，但是发展的质量良莠不齐，各地的国际商品展示与交易中心，应该充分利用自己的地方优势，促进国际商品展示与交易中心的发展。一方面可以成立行业协会，让发展较好的国际商品展示与交易中心的管理经验传播出去，让各地借鉴学习，以提高整体行业知名度。另一方面，成立行业协会，各地的国际商品展示与交易中心成为会员后，会员间可以相互进行货源的调拨，加强会员之间的合作，以应对外部竞争。

参考文献：

[1]李文一.郑州市跨境贸易电子商务发展战略研究[D].北京交通大学，2014.11-12.

[2]钱继光.加快推动宁波保税商品展示交易中心建设——以上海自贸区森兰商

都建设模式为鉴[J]. 宁波经济(三江论坛), 2014, 11:45-47.

[3]中华人民共和国黄埔海关.黄埔海关积极复制推广上海自贸区制度，推动保税展示交易在广州开展[EB/OL].http://www.customs.gov.cn/publish/portal114/tab61064/info767093.htm, 2015-01-25.

[4]策划 谭亦芳 南方日报记者 朱伟良 黄少宏 实习生 魏申. 跨境电商体验店不会被叫停[N]. 南方日报, 2015-01-26001.

[5]盛柯文，洪涛，高原雪. 我国尾货市场战略选择与发展的SWOT分析[J]. 管理现代化, 2012, 04:31-33+47.

[6]冀芳，张夏恒. 跨境电子商务物流模式创新与发展趋势[J]. 中国流通经济, 2015, 06:14-20.

（作者简介：黄森，男，四川外国语大学国别经济与国际商务研究中心，副教授，博士，研究方向：国际经济管理；舒首凤，女，四川外国语大学国别经济与国际商务研究中心，硕士研究生）

2016年埃及旅游业“寒冬期”及对策分析

吴　昊

摘要：埃及旅游资源丰富，文化古迹众多。埃及旅游业是国家经济的支柱产业之一，是外汇收入的重要来源，也是第一大创造新就业机会的部门。阿拉伯之春埃及革命爆发后，受到政治动荡和恐怖主义威胁的影响，埃及旅游业面临发展困境，2015年末俄罗斯客机遭炸弹袭击事件的联动效应，使得2016年埃及旅游业举步维艰，步入“寒冬期”，导致埃及美元短缺继续恶化，相关产业均受到负面影响，失业率持续增加。面对埃及旅游业颓势，埃及政府应稳定政局，加大反恐力度，确保游客安全，采取倾斜性政策，切实采取措施恢复埃及旅游业的生机。

关键词：埃及；旅游业；寒冬期；对策；2016

埃及地跨亚、非两洲，北濒地中海，东临红海，是亚、非之间的陆地交通要冲，也是大西洋与印度洋之间海上航线的捷径，战略位置十分重要。埃及是世界上历史最悠久的文明古国之一，旅游资源丰富，文化古迹众多，金字塔、狮身人面像、尼罗河、红海、卢克索神庙、阿斯旺大坝、开罗、亚历山大、西奈、黑白沙漠等等，都是埃及的标签，悠久神秘的文化背景，迷人旖旎的自然风光，星罗棋布的名胜古迹，四通八达的交通网络，为埃及旅游业带来了得天独厚的优势。埃及旅游业十分发达，在国家经济中占有重要地位。

一、旅游业是埃及经济支柱产业之一

旅游业作为一个综合性产业，涉及国民经济的多个行业和部门，包括交通、建筑、通讯、贸易、餐饮、文化娱乐等，具有产业关联度高、综合带动能力效应明显等特点。发展国际旅游业能够增加外汇收入，降低换汇成本。旅游业作为劳动密集型产业，就业门槛低，就业范围广，就业层次多，能为社会提供大量的就业机会。

埃及有着丰富的旅游资源、完善的娱乐设施，让世界各地的游客心驰神往，埃及在世界旅游的版图上一直占据着重要地位。旅游业是埃及国家经济的支柱产业之一，是埃及外汇收入的重要来源，同时也是埃及第一大创造新就业机会的部门。

2011年阿拉伯之春埃及革命之前，埃及旅游业保持了良性发展。1993—2000年间，埃及旅游业占国内生产总值的平均数是12.5%。进入21世纪后，埃及旅游业发展迅猛，旅游人数从2001年的464.85万人增加到2009年的1253.6万人，年平均增长率为13.2%，旅游收入从2001年的43亿美元增加到2010年的115.91亿美元，年平均增长率达到了11.6%。以2006—2008年为例，2006年埃及接待外国游客870多万人次，旅游外汇收入达68亿美元；2007年，接待外国游客980万人次，旅游收入为76亿美元，比上年增长11.76%；2008年，接待外国游客1230万人次，旅游收入为108亿美元，比上年增长42.1%，占所有非贸易收入的40%。

2011年1月25日埃及革命之后，埃及旅游业虽然面临诸多困难，发展有所衰退，但依然不能撼动旅游业在埃及经济中的重要地位。2012—2013财政年度，旅游业占埃及国内生产总值的7%，如果加上旅游业的相关产业，这一数据将达到11.3%，占外汇收入的19.3%，排在侨汇之后是外汇收入的第二大来源，解决了整个埃及12.6%的就业。根据世界旅游业理事会的统计，每9个埃及人中就有1个人的收入来自旅游业。所以，旅游业在埃及经济中扮演着十分重要的角色，是埃及经济发展的推动力，是国民收入的重要来源。

二、2016年埃及旅游业步入“寒冬期”

2012—2013年穆尔西执政期间，埃及旅游业得到了很好的发展，旅游人数为1220万人，比同期增长11.5%，旅游业收入达到98亿美金，但之后旅游业的发展急转直下，2014年埃及旅游业产值几乎缩水一半，旅游收入仅为51亿美金，塞西领导下的第一个财政年度的旅游收入只是74亿美金。

从2011年1月25日埃及革命开始，埃及旅游业就经历着倒退，负面事件接踵而至，政治上的动荡，安全局势的不稳定，是影响埃及吸引游客的最主要因素。埃及领导人努力想让外国游客认为埃及的旅游环境是安全的，但2015年末俄罗斯客机遭炸弹袭击的事件让所有努力都成为泡影。

俄罗斯一直是埃及旅游业最大的市场，2014年共有310万俄罗斯游客抵达埃及，英国和德国的游客人数仅次于俄罗斯。2015年末俄罗斯客机遭炸弹袭击以后，基于安全考虑，包括俄罗斯、英国、德国等多个国家宣布暂停来往埃及的航班并撤离游客，这直接导致到埃及旅游人数的锐减。埃及旅游部长表示，2016年第一季度埃及游客人数仅为120万人，而2015年的同期数据是220万人，意味着同比下降了近一半。以2月为例，埃及吸引了近35万游客，而去年同期数据是64万。外界预测，2016年很有可能成为数十年来，埃及旅游业最不景气的一年。世界旅游业理事会预计，2016年埃及旅游业收入续跌4%。

据英国《每日邮报》报道，埃及著名景点金字塔甚至出现了一个游客都没有的冷清场面。除金字塔外，埃及另一个人气景点海边度假胜地沙姆沙伊赫的游客也寥寥无几，许多知名大酒店开出的房价低得简直让人不敢相信，仅为先前房价的十分之一。沙姆沙伊赫的旅游行业萎缩了90%，50多家潜水中心关闭，旅游投资者遭受着巨大压力，无力承受现在的状况。

埃及旅游业举步维艰，正在经历历史上最黑暗的灾难，毫无疑问，2016年是埃及旅游业的"寒冬期"。

三、埃及旅游业遭遇"寒冬期"的原因

（一）持续政治动荡的消极影响

自2011年埃及陷入政治动荡以来，埃及的旅游业就不断遭受打击。数据显示，2011年的政治骚动吓跑了数百万游客，当年游客数量骤降37%，从2010年的1470万跌至2011年末的900万人。阿拉伯之春、阿拉伯世界的动荡、恐怖主义事件的频发，这一切不仅对埃及旅游业产生了不利的影响，还使整个阿拉伯世界的旅游业都受到了波及。

2015年对于阿拉伯国家的旅游业来说都是艰难的一年，埃及、突尼斯等国的旅游业收入减少了近半数。埃及的游客人数从2010年的1470万下降到600万；突尼斯的旅游业收入减少了35%；摩洛哥旅游人数同比下降1%，旅游业收入下降1.3%；约旦旅游人数同比下降9%，旅游业收入下降5%，从2014年的43.84亿美元下降到40亿美元。

（二）恐怖主义袭击威胁和民航事故

持续的恐怖主义袭击威胁以及一系列的民航事故，让埃及旅游业雪上加霜，6个月里埃及民航发生了三次事故，让埃及旅游业彻底陷入"寒冬"。

2015年10月31日，一架从埃及海滨城市沙姆沙伊赫起飞前往俄罗斯圣彼得

堡的A321型俄航客机在西奈半岛中部坠毁，机上217名乘客和7名机组人员全部遇难，俄方在残骸中找到的黑匣子显示，该客机是被炸弹炸毁的，伊斯兰国称是他们在客机中设置的炸弹爆炸引发的。2016年3月29日，埃及一架载有88人的客机起飞后不久遭到劫持，在塞浦路斯机场紧急降落，不过最后证实这只是一起个人上演的“闹剧”，与恐怖主义无关。2016年5月19日，一架5月18日从巴黎戴高乐至埃及开罗的埃及客机在进入埃及领空的地中海上失联。随后，埃及外交部确认在希腊喀帕苏斯岛水域发现属于航班的残骸，确定客机已经坠毁。

2015年以来，埃及发生的一系列恐怖主义事件在很大程度上加大了埃及国内机场的风险，造成旅客大量流失。俄航客机事件对埃及旅游业来说是一个毁灭性的打击，许多航空公司拒绝飞往沙姆沙伊赫。在埃及航空引入新的安全防护措施来保护乘客安全之后，易捷航空和汤森航空仍然表示不会飞往埃及沙姆沙伊赫。

2014年，从世界各地到埃及的游客人数达到990万，东欧的游客人数占45.1%，其中，俄罗斯在东欧游客中占了70.45%，西欧的游客人数占31.6%，英国是西欧国家中所占比例最高的，为29%，紧随其后的是德国。换言之，俄罗斯是埃及旅游业最大的市场，英国和德国是仅次于俄罗斯的第二大旅客来源，来自俄罗斯、英国、德国的游客人数约占50%。2014年俄罗斯到埃及旅游的人数达到了310万，其中200万游客的旅游目的地是沙姆沙伊赫，俄罗斯游客为埃及带来了25亿美元的收入。

俄航坠机事件后，来自欧洲的旅客下降了18%，并且这个数据有增无减。埃及政府虽然想方设法地吸引俄罗斯和英国的游客，但俄航坠机事件发生后，普京命令俄罗斯航空公司暂停运行俄罗斯飞往埃及的航班，旅游公司和旅行社暂停销售前往埃及的旅游产品，并采取措施帮助5万俄罗斯游客从埃及返回。除俄罗斯外，英国、德国等也采取了类似措施，英国有2万游客从埃及返回，欧洲多家航空公司都拒绝在沙姆沙伊赫降落。这对于埃及旅游业来说，无疑是一个沉重的打击。

根据埃及中央银行估计，俄航客机坠机事件将给埃及旅游业带来毁灭性灾难，埃及总统塞西曾表示摧毁俄罗斯客机的人旨在摧毁埃及旅游业，摧毁埃及和俄罗斯的关系。从俄罗斯航班在西奈坠机以来，埃及至少损失了12到13亿美元的收入。在损失了俄罗斯和英国游客之后，沙姆沙伊赫和霍尔格达有40多家酒店歇业，整个住宿业每月损失20亿埃镑，合2550万美金。而在此之前，来自俄罗斯和英国的游客数量每周可以达到3.5万。

四、旅游业“寒冬期”对埃及经济的影响

（一）美元短缺进一步恶化

2011年初埃及发生动荡以来，外汇储备从最高点360亿美元不断下滑，并持续在低位徘徊。埃及的三大外汇来源为侨汇、旅游和苏伊士运河通行费。2011年1月25日革命之前，埃及旅游业的收益接近130亿美金，之后就一路下滑，2015年埃及的旅游收入仅为61亿美元，比2014年下降15%。受到安全局势不稳定和保险费用不断上涨的影响，很多海运公司不再通过苏伊士运河，而是绕道非洲的好望角，造成2015年苏伊士运河的通行费不升反降，为51.75亿美元，比2014年减少2.9亿美元。此外，由于海湾国家经济形势低迷，埃及侨汇收入也有所下降。2016年2月埃及外汇储备为165.3亿美元，仅能满足3个月的进口，而2016年埃及还需要26亿美金来填补世界货币基金组织和卡塔尔的债务。

美元短缺成为困扰埃及经济发展的最大问题，国内经济陷入恶性循环：外汇短缺导致进口困难，进而影响出口，出口不振又加剧外汇短缺。世界经济复苏乏力，美国加息、新兴经济体增长放缓、货币贬值，更加大了埃镑贬值压力。匮乏的外汇储备无法继续支撑稳定汇率，2016年3月中旬，埃及央行宣布将埃镑兑美元汇率一次性贬值13%，银行间拍卖价从原来的7.73降为8.85，此举旨在非官方市场的美元进入官方市场，增加了美元流动性，同时央行宣布将采取更加弹性的汇率政策，暗示埃镑未来有可能继续贬值。

（二）相关产业受到负面影响

埃及旅游业遭遇的一连串恶性事件，重挫了埃及旅游业复兴的希望。俄罗斯客机在西奈坠机事件使得埃及的旅游业在外国游客数量、运营酒店数量、旅游收入等各项指标上都濒临崩溃。俄航坠机事件发生后，埃及股票市场应声下跌，交易所指数下跌到6801点，是2015年9月以来的最低水平。

很多行业和旅游业息息相关，首当其冲的就是运输行业，埃及所有运输业都受到了负面影响，航空运输每个月的损失是两亿八千万美金。此外还有旅游商店收入，餐饮业收入，住宿业收入，游轮收入等等，都在遭受损失。这就意味着很多与旅游业相关的公司会产生坏账，无法还贷，又会对埃及银行造成负面影响。

埃及对于外资的依赖度是很高的，特别是服务业和生产业。俄罗斯客机坠机事件对于埃及吸引外资投资有着极大的负面影响，伊斯兰国宣称对该事件负责，这就给投资者提供了埃及并不安全的明确信号，投资环境的不安全无法吸引外国

投资者下定决心在埃及投资。

（三）失业率持续增加

每增加100万名游客，就可以为埃及带来20万个新的就业机会，对于埃及这个拥有近亿人口，且面临人口增长率偏高、劳动力过剩等问题的国家来说意义重大。埃及现在的失业率已经达到12.8%，旅游业的衰退进一步导致失业率的增长。在旅游业“寒冬期”的影响下，仅仅是住宿业，就有70%的酒店关门，新增大量失业人口。

如果埃及政府不能及时对原有和因旅游业萧条新增的失业人口给予相应的社会保障，提供职业技能培训，帮扶再就业，那么相应的社会问题又会随之而来。

五、对策分析

面对埃及旅游业的“寒冬期”，埃及观光部部长拉希德指出，近年来埃及政治、经济动荡不安，再加上接连发生的民航事件，未来埃及将需付出高于过往10倍的努力重振旅游业。目前，埃及政府正致力于重振旅游业，希望将其恢复到在国民经济中应有的地位，到2020年使旅游收入达到260亿美元。

如前文分析，埃及旅游业遭遇“寒冬期”是由于政局动荡，恐怖主义袭击威胁的影响，所以要重振旅游业，重中之重是稳定政局，加大反恐力度，确保游客安全。恐怖事件的发生，会使游客产生畏惧心理，改变先前的旅游决策。加大对恐怖主义的打击力度，增派警力，提高安检级别，确保旅游者的安全是埃及旅游业复兴的必要条件。同时，应该加强宣传力度，让全世界游客了解到埃及是安全的旅游目的地，埃航是安全的航空。

旅游业的发展离不开政府的宏观调控和支持，在面临困境的时候，应该采取一些倾斜性政策，重视中国这个巨大市场。埃及作为“一带一路”起点的国家，自古以来就与中国保持着良好的双边关系，而且与中国达成了全面战略伙伴关系。埃及总统塞西自2014年上任后，先后三次访问中国，还作为嘉宾国领导人出席了G20杭州峰会。

2015年赴埃及旅游的中国游客人数达12万人次，创下历史新高；2016年是“中埃文化年”，7个月赴埃及的中国游客已达10万人次，保持了良好的发展势头，全年预计将达到20万人次。但如果把这些数据和中国出境游人数相比较，会发现赴埃游客所占比例太小。2015年中国出境游总人数超过1.2亿人次，规模连续三年排名世界第一，出境旅游消费总额连续5年居全球第一，带动了全球旅游行业的发展，中国市场应该成为埃及的重点关注对象。

为吸引中国游客，埃及政府做出了一些努力，首先是出台了简化签证的政策。2016年7月19日，埃及驻上海总领事馆微博公布，中国护照持有者在符合以下条件情况下，可在埃及取得个人落地签证：1.随身携带至少2000美金现金（或其他等值货币）；2.持有酒店（4星级或以上）确认的预订信息；3.持有已出票的离境（埃及）机票。埃及想借此举进一步争取中国客源，只是三个附加条件显得力度不大，诚意不足。此外，埃及旅游业界组团参展2016广东国际旅游产业博览会，一场持续3个月的埃及旅游线上媒体和户外媒体推广活动，正在北京、上海、广州、成都等地全面开展。为了便利游客出游，目前埃及航空公司从广州飞往开罗的航班，已经由原来的每周5班增加到每周7班；北京、上海、成都等地已经开通飞往埃及的包机业务。

小结

埃及旅游业是国家的经济支柱和推动力，是埃及外汇的重要来源，也是埃及第一大创造新就业机会的部门。阿拉伯之春埃及革命爆发后，受到政治动荡和恐怖主义威胁的影响，埃及旅游业面临发展困境，2015年末俄罗斯客机遭炸弹袭击事件的联动效应，使得2016年埃及旅游业举步维艰，步入"寒冬期"，导致埃及美元短缺进一步恶化，相关产业均受到负面影响，失业率进一步增加。面对埃及旅游业颓势，埃及政府应稳定政局，加强反恐，确保游客安全，加大宣传力度，开发好中国市场，相信埃及旅游业会再次迎来属于自己的春天。

参考文献：

[1]埃及旅游业陷入"寒冬", http://news.ifeng.com/a/20160526/48846687_0. shtml
[2]http://www.aljazeera.net/programs/economyandpeople/2016/5/28/
تحديات-السياحة-العربية-وأسباب-تراجعها
[3]刘晖.埃及旅游业，飘摇中的"热气球"[J].世界知识，2013(7).
[4]刘晖.阿拉伯国家旅游业发展一瞥[J].阿拉伯世界研究，2006(2).
[5]刘晶.恐怖主义对埃及旅游业的影响及政府的应对措施[J].内蒙古民族大学学报(社会科学版)，2011(3).
[6]丁隆.埃及货币断崖式贬值，哪些经验教训值得借鉴?
http://money.163.com/16/0331/11/BJG0PFP400253B0H.html

[7]重新平衡外汇市场之举(经济透视)
http://finance.ifeng.com/a/20160323/14284291_0.shtml

（作者简介：吴昊，女，四川外国语大学东方语学院，副教授，博士，研究方向：阿拉伯语语言学，阿拉伯社会文化）

关于日本近年来发展观光立国的政策，措施及实效

毛卫兵

摘要：自2003年以来，日本确立并实施了观光立国战略。该战略是基于日本国家发展的需要，把旅游观光产业作为日本国家战略体系的重要组成部分之一。日本政府在观光立国战略体系的框架下制定颁布并实施了一系列的政策措施，共同构筑了一个支撑国家旅游发展战略得以顺利实施的系统。即主要通过1）调整旅游行政组织管理体系，2）建立旅游法律体系，3）以地方自治体为中心，地方与政府的协调合作，4）旅游人才培养体系等紧密合作，有计划地推动旅游业的建设以达到战略目标，且取得了令人注目的实效。2016年日本政府策划制定出建立『旅游观光先进国家』的新目标，这标志着日本“观光立国”战略进入了一个新的阶段。日本观光旅游战略发展历程和政策措施的制定的经验对我国旅游产业的发展具有借鉴意义。

关键词：入境游客；观光立国；观光立国行动计划；新成长战略

一、日本观光立国战略的发展历程

近年来，日本的入境旅游市场快速发展。2015年访日的外国游客达到史上最高1,973万7000人，比上年增长47.1%[①]。而在2002年，日本接待的外国游客为524万人次，仅占当年全世界各国各地区接待旅游者的 0.7%。可以说当时日本入境旅游业的发展与其他旅游大国相比还有较大的差距，而这也正好让日本入境旅游业具有了更大的后劲优势及发展空间。

日本入境旅游市场的快速发展是内因与外因共同作用的结果。其中，内因为

① 『2016年版观光白书』日本国土交通省观光厅

日本国内的各种因素。这些内在因素成为推动日本入境旅游市场发展的主导力量，这股力量源自于日本政府相关政策的策动和引导。从思想上使日本的全体国民都能够理解推进观光立国不是简单地劝导大家游山玩水，而是从工业立国、贸易立国一边倒的状态中脱离出来，从立国的高度去理解振兴旅游业的意义。日本政府肯定了推进观光立国战略对于提高国家“软权力”的促进作用，赋予了观光立国战略以很高的政治意义。从国家战略高度来重新理解旅游业的意义，把观光立国作为其发展为政治、经济大国必要途径。外因是随着近年来世界游客的不断增长和亚洲各国经济急速增长，带来了访日旅游旺盛的需求。在这样良好的外部环境下，使日本政府的访日旅游促进战略得以奏效。

众所周知，日本近现代发展走的是技术立国和贸易立国之路，产业政策的重点一直放在制造业上，从而实现了战后日本经济腾飞的奇迹。20 世纪 90 年代以后日本经济持续萧条，以往以制造业为中心的产业政策已经不能带来经济的新增长。为了拉动经济回升，日本政府推出“观光立国”的发展战略。

2003年是具有转折意义的一年，这一年日本首相小泉纯一郎在国会施政演说中提出“观光立国”的战略，其主旨在于振兴日本的旅游产业，使旅游业成长为日本的支柱产业之一，成为新的经济增长点，并力争到 2010 年实现来日外国游客人数倍增的目标，即从当时的每年约500万人次增加到每年1000万人次。2003年7月31日，观光立国关系阁僚会议制定并发布了《观光立国行动计划》。其主要由观光立国宣传普及计划、发掘日本国家和地区社会魅力的计划、日本品牌海外宣传计划、观光立国环境治理计划、推进观光立国体制改革计划5部分内容组成，明确指出推进观光立国的243项政策措施。内容涵盖了旅游业发展的六大领域（餐饮、住宿、交通、游览、娱乐、购物），并且对每个领域都提出了具体要求，政策涵盖范围十分广泛[①]。这一战略性计划的提出大大促进了日本入境旅游的发展。

2009年9月，民主党战胜自民党上台执政之后，鸠山内阁在其施政纲领《新成长战略基本方针》中，对观光立国战略提出了2010年—2020年新发展战略目标：2020年前争取访日外国游客达到2500万人次，由此产生的经济波及效益10万亿日元，增加就业人数56万人。鸠山内阁倒台后，2010年6月18日，菅直人内阁正式制定并公布了《新成长战略：复兴“充满生机的日本”的方案》施政纲领，基本延续了鸠山内阁实施的旅游产业政策。

① 『为了实现观光立国的行动计划-「一面向访日外国游客2000万人时代一」』观光立国推进阁僚会议，2003年7月 参考

《新成长战略：复兴“充满生机的日本”的方案》最大特点是目标明确而且细致（参照图1）。方案首先就2016年的中期目标进行量化，即2016年要实现访日外国游客达2000万人次，然后根据实际情况再调整2020年的战略目标为2500万人次。在此基础上，要力争将来访日外国游客达到3000万人次。并把2010年、2013年、2016年的入境游客人数目标细分到具体客源国家。把中国、韩国、中国台湾地区、中国香港地区作为重点客源市场来看待。由此看来政策目标不仅非常明确而且还十分具体。在日本旅游业政策的发展过程中，该国始终把旅游业的功能与地位上升到国家层面予以研究，每一个时期的旅游发展战略都将旅游业的综合性及关联性的经济特征进行全面分析。

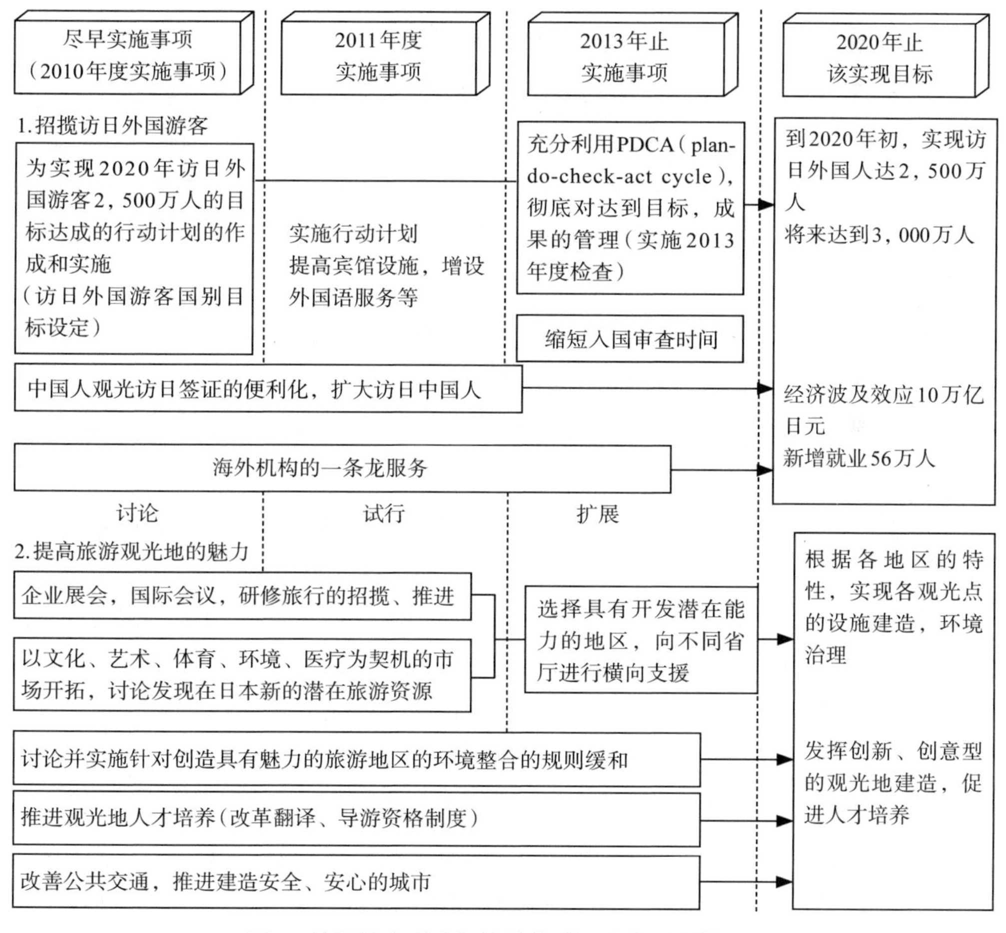

图1　搞活地方观光经济的战略～观光立国推进～

资料来源：『新成长战略计划-Ⅳ 搞活地方观光经济的战略战略～观光立国推进～』日本政府2010年6月18日阁僚决定书，参考制作

二、观光立国战略的政策和措施

振兴旅游业需要全社会各个方面的联动与协作，因此，如何有效地推动观光立国行动计划本身的实施，也需要方方面面的意见建议，以及有关的政府机构、民间企业或是地方的公共团体的紧密协作，才能全力推动各项政策的实施。为实现观光立国战略目标，日本政府主要采取构建完备的战略推进体制和政策措施来推进观光立国的发展。具体通过：1）调整旅游行政组织管理体系，2）建立旅游法律体系，3）以地方自治体为中心，有计划地推动地方旅游业建设，4）旅游人才培养体系等的紧密结合，共同构筑成一个支撑国家旅游发展战略的顺利实施的系统。

（一）国家旅游行政组织管理体系的调整

目前，日本政府关于旅游宏观管理组织结构是在观光立国大臣的领导下，由日本观光厅（JTA：Japan Tourism Agency）负责实施观光旅游的战略政策；日本政府观光局（JNTO：Japan National Tourism Organization）负责入境旅游的营销以及申办国际会议等工作，各级地方政府根据本地区的具体情况配合观光厅实施国家旅游政策。

为了提高旅游管理机构的行政级别，政府在2003年10月1日通过颁布《国际观光振兴机构法》，全面改革了原来作为协调旅游相关部门的最高行政机构的国际观光振兴协会，成立了“独立特殊行政法人国际观光振兴机构”，又称日本政府观光局（JNTO：Japan National Tourism Organization）。其主要任务是在主要旅游市场国家设立办事处，针对竞争激烈的海外旅游市场，展开对日旅游的招揽及宣传活动。

同时，政府也加强了国土交通省观光部的力量，新设置观光厅，在观光立国担当大臣的直接领导下具体负责推进观光立国战略。改变了过去单纯依靠日本国际观光振兴会吸引外国游客的局面，形成了政府引导、官民一体的旅游观光宣传组织机构，并在美国、韩国、中国等重要的客源国展开了声势浩大的宣传攻势。

具体来说，2003年9月，政府增设了观光立国担当大臣职位（由国土交通大臣兼任），并于2008年10月在国土交通省内设置观光厅，专门负责观光立国的具体工作。民主党执政以后，在旅游行政管理机构上进行了较大改革。2009年12月，为进一步推进观光立国，日本政府在国土交通省内成立了跨省厅的观光立国推进本部，本部长由国土交通大臣担任，成员由其他省厅的副大臣组成。负责推进观光立国战略方面的具体工作。国土交通省下属的各地方运输局和当地政府紧密合作，与中央政府保持一致，积极贯彻实施中央政府的观光立国政策措施，共同推进观光立国的发展。以国土交通部部长（观光立国担当部长）为总部部长及所有属的副部长等人组成。总部下设工作组分管各自的任务。例如：法务部（完善出入境审核体制），外交部（通过驻外使领馆，促进公告和签证发放手续的快捷、顺利），文部科学部（促进文物保护单位的保护和使用、文化振兴、留学生交流、教育旅游等），厚生劳动部（促进上班族休假，实施旅馆设施环境卫生管理等），农林水产部（促进城市与农村共存、和谐等），经济产业部（促进服务产业的繁荣，受欢迎产业的培育，工业旅游等），环境部（促进国立公园和世界自然遗产的保护，环保旅游等）。由此，观光立国战略在行政组织层面上获得了支撑。旅游厅推进与其他部、厅进行合作，履行旅游行政职责。这也是当前日本政府推进观光立国战略的最高行政机构。

（二）利用法律的方式明确产业地位

加强旅游法律体系建设，增强法律对旅游经济发展的配套与保护。利用法律的方式明确产业地位、产业功能、长期发展目标及其实施战略的机构设置和机制的保证。

在现代旅游业发展过程中，日本制定了许多相应的法律法规，建立了较为完备的法律体系，为旅游业的顺利发展起到了保驾护航的作用。其旅游法律具有完整的体系涉及面广。由基本法、专门法及相关法构成。其中基本法是旅游业的根本大法，规定了日本旅游业发展的基本方针等重大原则。专门法针对旅游相关领域的行业范围、经营活动、行为准则等做出了严格的规定。相关法是从不同的角度对旅游业发展的相关领域做出规定。从整体到部分，从概念到具体，各项法律法规面面俱到。据不完全统计，到目前为止，日本的旅游法规及相关法共有 76 项之多。

2006年12月13日，日本参议院通过并公布了《观光立国推进基本法》，该法于2007年1月1日起正式实施。这部法律实际上是完全修正了日本于1963年制定的旧的《观光基本法》，将自2003年以来日本国内对旅游业的整体认识和全新观点以法律的形式确定下来，明确地把旅游业确定为21世纪日本的重要政策支柱。该法律规定，政府应当以综合地计划地推进与促进观光立国有关的政策措施为目的，制定观光立国推进基本计划。此基本法以法律的形式规定了政府今后围绕观光立国的主要工作任务[①]。根据《观光立国推进法》第10条规定，国土交通大臣（观光担当大臣）必须认真听取交通政策审议会的意见，及时制定《观光推进基本计划》。《观光立国推进基本计划》制定后还要通过内阁会议批准，再提交国会审议批准后才能正式实施。因此，与之前的《观光立国行动计划》相比，《观光立国推进计划（2007—2011）》的最大特点是法律地位明确，是具有法律效力的国家旅游发展战略规划。此外，依据《观光立国推进基本法》还制定了《生态旅游推进法》、《观光圈整备法》，适时实施了《景观法》。由此，观光立国战略就在法律层面上获得了稳固的支撑。

（三）以地方自治体为中心，地方和政府有计划地推动地方旅游业建设

日本的基层地方自治体叫市、町、村及东京都的特别区，地方政府分为都道府县。现有786个市、757个町和184个村合计1727个市町村，加上23个特别区，共有1750个市町村，此外还有47个县级单位即1都（东京都）、1道（北海道）、2府（京都府和大阪府），以及43个县。日本旅游业的投资主要是依靠地方和民间的财力。在政府推行旅游经济的带动下，各级地方政府充分认识到发展文化观光产业对振兴地方经济的重要作用，纷纷根据当地实际情况制定中长期规划，加大宣传力度，推出各种具有地方特色的文化遗产、民间艺术、传统工艺和祭祀活动，举办各种规模的文化节等。例如2015年11月21日，印度尼西亚首都雅加达的高级购物中心“中央公园商城”举办了“日本旅游博览会”，旨在促进当地市民来日旅行。此次活动上，日本旅游业者和日本各自治体观光局用展台大力宣传“我们的城市”的魅力。其中最具吸引力的是甲府市的展台，甲府市是山梨县下的自治体，使了浑身解数来吸引外国旅客。山梨县既有富士山，又有与之相连的自然风光和特产。该PR活动已成为官民共同的一大事业。

熊本县地方政府为了提高当地的被认知度，一改以往一贯严肃的政府形象，通过“打破盘子”的创新精神，设计师的奇思妙想和营销工作人员的正确营销策略，成功地设计创作了作为熊本市吉祥物“熊本熊”，大大提高了熊本县的知名度。2013年4月，日本地方经济综合研究所的调查显示，九州、关西和首都圈地区的居民对熊本县的印象分别从 2011年的第6位，第6位和第7位，上升至第2位，第3位和第5位。此外，民众前往熊本县观光旅游的意愿也有大幅提升。申请授权的商品从 2011 年的 3600 件，升至如今的 20000 件。根据日本银行的计算，吉祥物“熊本熊”出道的头两年（2011年至2013 年），它就为熊本县带来了

① 『关于观光立国推进法』日本国土交通省观光厅 参考

1244亿日元的收益。另外，九州早已成为受中国台湾、中国香港游客青睐的观光地。现在，九州也在向中国大陆游客招手，他们同广州的饭店开展合作项目进行人才交流，希望通过交流了解中国游客的爱好，以便更好地为中国游客服务。像京都、冲绳这样具有文化优势和旅游资源优势的地方自治体，更是提出了文化立市、旅游立县的战略口号。

（四）推行旅游专业人才的培养

日本旅游业目前直接吸纳就业210万人，间接吸纳就业450万人，是日本近年来吸纳劳动力持续增长的产业之一。而高素质的从业人员队伍是保持高质量产业发展态势的保证。为提高旅游人才素质、加强国际竞争力、振兴旅游业，日本加大了旅游从业人员的建设力度，积极培养观光旅游业人才，在大学中增加旅游观光相关联的系·学科的入学定员人数（图3）。例如：2006年，高崎经济大学设置了与旅游观光相关联的学科，入学定员合计为3,000人（包括5系28学科），并计划在5年内增加1,095人（11学科）。2007年和歌山大学也准备设立观光相关联的学科，北海道大学作为国立大学也初次准备设立观光专业学科。目前，日本已有50多所大学设有旅游及相关专业。但是在观光旅游专业人才的培养方面还存在着不足之处。目前旅游相关性大学中以人文·社会科学为中心的学科相对较多，经营性的学科比较少（图4）。随着观光旅游业务，旅游消费的急速扩大，为了能提供高品质的旅游观光服务，还需要在人才培养方面进行改革。另外，日本旅行业协会、全国旅行业协会、全国农协观光等社团机构也加大导游队伍建设，推出实行导游资格认定制。

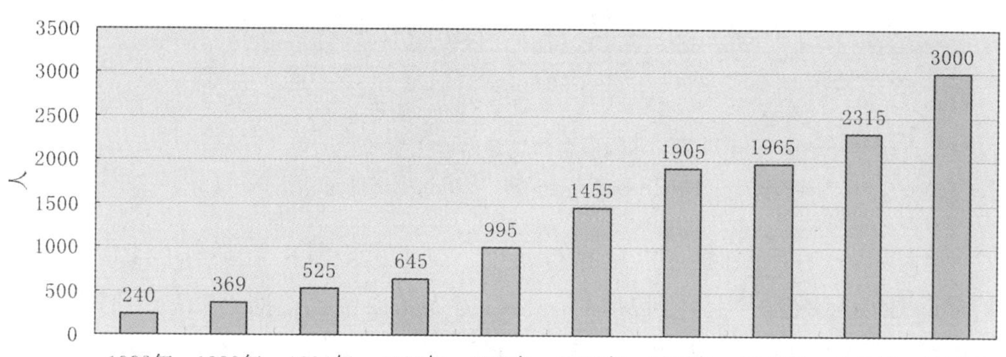

图2　大学中开设旅游观光相关联的系·学科入学定员合计人数

纵轴：2006年观光旅游的相关联的系·学科入学合计人数（研究生除外）

横轴：旅游观光关联的系·学科设立年份

资料来源："观光立国政策实施现状，资料2"日本观光厅2007年1月

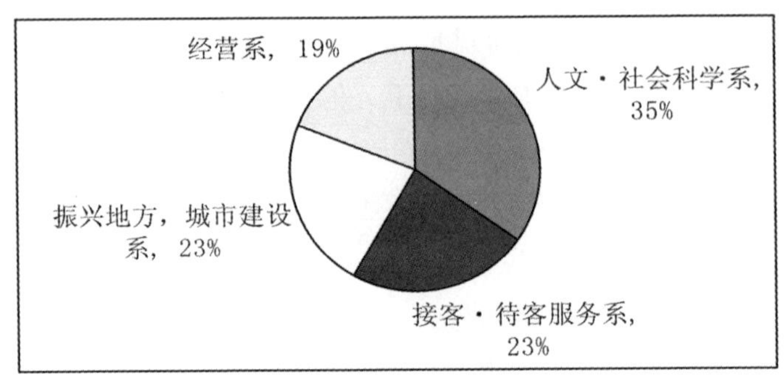

图3 旅游性大学学科中按教育内容分类的比例

资料来源："观光立国政策实施现状，资料2"日本观光厅2007年1月

三、政策措施的实效

在政府的观光立国的战略政策引导下，日本的入境游客得到了迅速的发展（图4）。由2003年的521.2万人次增加到2008年的835.8万人，而在2014年日本入境游客的人数突破了1000万，增长到了1341.3万人次，出境人数为1690.3万人次，入境人数占出境人数的77.8%，可以说是日本发展国际旅游业的重大突破。

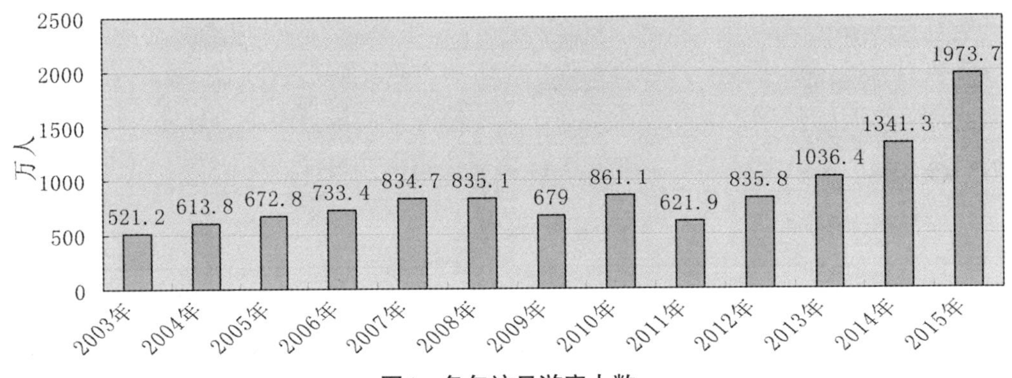

图4 各年访日游客人数

资料来源："2016年观光白皮书"日本政府观光局（JNTO）

全世界各国接受外国游客的排行榜中，日本也由原来2013年的1,036万人（27位，亚洲第8位），上升到2014年1,341万人（22位，亚洲第7位），不论人数和排位都得到上升。其次随着入境游客的急速增多，在旅游过程中所消费的各类旅游产品及相关消费资料，包括基础消费（如住宿，餐饮，交通，游览等方面的消费）和非基础消费（购物和娱乐方面消费）也随着增加。访日外国游客的消费也给日本带来了旅游消费的巨大需求市场。2014年的访日游客的消费额达到2万

278万亿日元，比去年增长了43%，占日本个人消息总额的1%，2015年达到3万4,77亿日元，比2014年比增长率71.5%(图5)。由此可见，旅游业对国民经济的作用不可忽视。

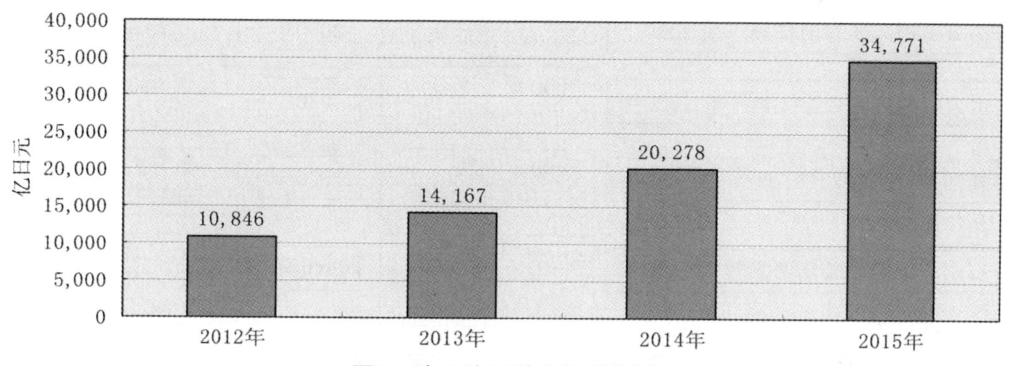

图5 访日外国游客年消费额

资料来源："访日外国旅游客消费倾向—访日外国人消费者动向调查与分析—"2015年报告书，日本政府观光局（JNTO）

四、未来日本支柱产业"旅观光游业"的展望（VISION）

根据联合国世界观光机构亚太中心（UNWTO）发布的世界观光动向，2015年的国际观光游客比去年增加5,100万人，达到11亿8,400万人。预测到2030年将达到18亿人。特别亚洲国家的国际游客将成为主要的增长力量。日本政府已经认识到这股强大的力量将成为日本经济增长的新动力。随着外国旅游客达到2000万人的目标已基本实现，日本"观光立国"战略进入了新的阶段。日本政府已开始着手下一步新的目标和对应策略。在此背景下，2016年3月30日的观光立国阁僚会议会议中，策定发表了"未来成为日本支柱产业'观光旅游业的'展望(VISION)"(图6)。日本将朝着新的目标，地方与政府，官民一起着手把日本建设成为"旅游观光先进国家"。

挑战新目标!

访日的外国人旅客人数	2020年	4,000万人数（约2015年的两倍）	2030年	6,000万人数（约2015年的两倍）
访日外国人游客消费额	2020年	8万亿日元（约2015年的两倍）	2030年	15万亿日元（约2015年的两倍）
地方的外国人住宿天数	2020年	7,000万人住宿（约2015年的3倍）	2030年	1亿3,000万人住宿（约2015年的3倍）
外国人回头客人数	2020年	2,400万人数（约2015年的两倍）	2030年	3,600万人数（约2015年的两倍）
日本人国内旅游消费额数	2020年	21万亿日元（最近5年平均值增加5%）	2030年	22万亿日元（最近5年平均值增加5%）

图5　未来日本的支柱产业观光旅游业的新目标

资料来源:《2016未来日本支柱产业“观光旅游业”的构想》观光立国阁僚会议2016年3月30日。

参考文献:

[1]古屹.浅析日本旅游经济的发展及对我国的启示.《经济纵横》, 2015.

[2]金春梅，凌强.日本观光立国战略模式及启示.《日本问题研究》, 第162期, 2012.

[3]汤伊心.试论日本日本发展国际旅游业的经验及借鉴.《前沿》, NO9, 2015.

[4]纐纈光元.10年目を迎える観光立国日本.《Report Vol.148共立総合研究所》, 2013.

[5]Kagawa Makot.Thinking of the Meaning of the ‘Tourism-based Japan’: Review on the History of the Japan Tourism Policy. Special Issue in Celebration of 20th anniversary of the Faculty of Sociology, Ryutsu Keizai University. 2010.(in Japanese).

参考网页:

[1]http://www.mlit.go.jp/kankocho/(日本国土省观光厅(JTA))

[2]http://www.jnto.go.jp/jpn/(日本政府观光局(JNTO))

[3]http://www.cao.go.jp/index.html　(日本内阁府)

[4]http://www.kantei.go.jp/jp/sinseichousenryaku/sinseichou01.pdf(“Ⅳ 搞活地方观

光经济的战略—观光立国推进—”日本政府2010年6月18日阁僚决定书）
[4]http://unwto-ap.org/（联合国世界观光机构亚太中心）

（作者简介：毛卫兵，男，四川外国语大学国别经济与国际商务研究中心，副教授，博士，研究方向：国际旅游经济）

关于重庆地区中韩旅游合作发展的思考

金日权

摘要：1997年3月，八届全国人大五次会议批准成立，6月18日正式挂牌，重庆作为中国最年轻的直辖市，是中国内陆西南部、长江上游的经济、政治、文化中心，拥有丰富的文化旅游资源。随着国家对第三产业的高度重视，国内第三产业的蓬勃发展，越来越多的地区政府在定位旅游产业作为经济增长的支柱产业，随着国内旅游业的不断快速发展，重庆的旅游业也逐步有秩序地发展。中韩两国作为一衣带水、隔海相望的邻国，发展两国间的经济、政治、文化合作是必然趋势。本文通过对重庆市旅游产业现状分析，针对重庆开发相关旅游商品、与韩国旅游合作发展等问题，提出相应对策，以推动重庆市中韩旅游产业的快速合作发展。

关键词：重庆、韩国、旅游产业、多元化、合作发展

中国改革开放30多年来，随着世界旅游业的蓬勃发展，中国旅游业也保持了健康、持续、快速的发展态势，特别是国内旅游和出境旅游两大市场，这与中国政府重视旅游业的发展和改革开放以来打下的坚实经济基础是分不开的。旅游业的持续发展有力地推动了我国服务业总体规模的扩大和整体质量的提升，成为我国服务业发展的主要因素之一。改革开放也给我国入境旅游业带来了新的契机，为入境旅游市场的发展提供了有利因素。近年来，随着旅游宣传扩大、各地方政府更加重视旅游产业发展、交通基础设施不断改善以及体育赛事和各种盛大展会在中国的成功举办，进一步促进了入境旅游的发展。

重庆作为我国最年轻的直辖市，也是非常重要的历史文化名城，旅游资源十分丰富。自然旅游资源方面：拥有两处世界自然遗产、国家重点风景名胜区、国家级森林公园等。人文旅游资源方面：拥有一处世界文化遗产、集多种文化于一体，全国重点文物保护单位等高品位的旅游资源。重庆市政府已决定将旅游业作

为重庆市的支柱产业之一。旅游业在重庆地区经济发展中作用日益凸显，对整个城市的经济拉动性，文化产业飞速发展作用日益增强。

一、重庆市旅游产业发展现状

（一）旅游产业规模和相关产业现状

旅游景区：2014年末，国家A级旅游景区共有178个，增加25个。其中：5A级旅游景区6个，与上年持平；4A级旅游景区63个，增加14个；3A级旅游景区69个，增加7个；2A级旅游景区38个，增加4个；1A级旅游景区2个。

旅行社：2014年末，全市共有559家。其中：出境游旅行社62家，比上年增加12家；赴台游旅行社8家，与上年持平；一般旅行社497家，增加33家。

旅游星级饭店：2014年末，旅游星级饭店共249家，新增星级饭店17家，撤消星级饭店称号25家，总数比上年减少8家。其中：五星级27家，新增4家；四星级54家，新增2家；三星级131家，新增10家；二星级37家，新增1家。

旅游船：2014年末，五星级及五星级标准游轮共31艘，其中已挂牌五星级游轮23艘，比上年增加8艘。经营重庆“两江游”企业3家，共有“两江游”游船7艘。

温泉旅游项目：2014年末，全市已建成并正常营业的温泉旅游项目33个，成为“中国温泉之都”、“世界温泉之都”有力支撑。

（二）旅游产业的社会经济发展现状

据统计，2014年重庆市共接待海内外游客3.49亿人次，比上年增长13.2%；旅游总收入达2003.37亿元，增长13.1%。其中：全年接待入境旅游人数263.76万人次，旅游外汇收入13.54亿美元，分别增长8.9%和6.8%。受全球经济影响，2014年全国入境旅游呈下滑趋势。但重庆市通过加快推进旅游重点项目建设，加强旅游品牌创建，加大旅游宣传和营销力度，又一次实现了入境旅游逆势增长。入境游客前三位的地区为：港澳台、亚洲、欧洲。入境旅游人数前五位的国家为：韩国、日本、美国、泰国、新加坡。

2014年，重庆经济持续向好，城乡居民收入水平和生活质量不断提高，出境旅游市场持续发展壮大。全年新增出境游旅行社12家。通过出境旅行社组织的出境旅游者120.84万人次，比上年增长31.4%。其中出国游增长强劲，出国游人数达96.96万人次，增长41.9%；出境游目的地前5位国家为：泰国、韩国、新加坡、马来西亚、日本。从数据中可以看出：目前，韩国是重庆入境旅游市场的第一大客源国。

二、中韩国际旅游发展现状及成果

加强中韩双方在旅游领域的交流与合作，不仅可以促进两国旅游业的发展，增进两国人民之间的了解和友谊，进而促进两国以及亚太地区的经济发展，维护整个地区的和平与稳定（张广瑞，1998，（冬季号）：52）。中韩两国，隔海相望，地缘相近，人文相亲，文缘相通。特别是中国改革开放以来，经济高速发展令世界瞩目，两国关系不仅在政治、经济、文化相融相通。随着经济发展的带动，旅游业得到了迅速的发展，特别是两国的出入境旅游方面，出现了相互依存，相互发展的共赢局面。

自1989年1月韩国政府解除国民出境旅游限制以来，韩国出境旅游市场增长迅速。中韩两国在1992年8月正式建交，1994年4月韩国解除旅华限制，刺激了访华韩国游客的快速增长，短短20年的时间，韩国已成为中国最重要的旅游客源国之一。1998 年5 月韩国被正式指定为中国公民出境旅游目的地国家，2000 年6 月中国解除公民赴韩旅游的地区限制，中国公民赴韩国出境旅游市场发展迅速。

根据国家旅游局和国家统计局的统计，至2010年开始，韩国就位居我国入境旅游最主要的客源国第一位。韩国访华游客，主要是观光休闲，因距离较近、旅程短、航班次数多，再加上中国旅游商品相对价格便宜、旅游费用较低等优势。据统计，2015年全年韩国游客访华达444.44万人次，超过日本游客访华249.77万人次，稳拿中国入境旅游第一大客源国。

中韩两国在旅游领域的交流与合作，不仅可以促进两国旅游业的发展，还可以扩大两国间的民众往来，增进相互友谊，促进地区经济的繁荣与社会的发展。中韩两国自1992年建交，一直在经济和贸易、旅游等方面扩大开展交流和合作。自2006年以来，中韩日每年都会举办三国旅游部长会议，该会议以“旅游、合作、和谐、共赢”为主题，以旅游为桥梁，加强了三国的旅游交流，深化了三国间的旅游合作。为促进中韩两国旅游产业共同发展，2011年5月30日，中国国家旅游局局长邵琪伟与韩国文化体育观光部长官郑炳国在韩国江原道共同签署《中韩旅游交流合作协议》。双方将在推进“中韩互访年”、提高游客便利化水平、扩大两国青少年教育旅游往来、扩大人力资源交往、提高旅游商品质量、加强信息和旅游统计资料交换等六大领域加强交流合作。根据《协议》中韩双方将根据各自国家的法律和法规，鼓励两国政府旅游部门及其有关机构之间开展合作与交流，鼓励、支持民间交流合作以促进旅游业和旅游产业的发展，扩充相关配套设施，开发多种多样的旅游景点。双方同意每年举行一次“中韩旅游部长会晤”，坚持召开“中韩旅游交流与合作事物级协商会议”(邱菲，2016，13(1))。

韩国作为半岛国家，面积只有9.9万平方千米，却可以说旅游业已达到比较高的发展水平，成为亚洲旅游业发达国家之一，原因何在？而中国也一直把大力发展入境旅游作为旅游业发展的工作重点来抓，中国的旅游业发展前景十分光明。政府主导型发展战略以及正确的政策导向、完善的旅游法规、健全的旅游机构，韩国政府通过实施旅游资源开发计划、加强旅游基础设施建设和加强国际旅游产品营销等措施，提升了文化旅游大国形象，实现了旅游业的可持续发展（王继庆2005，14(5))。总言之，韩国旅游产业的成功经验对促进中国旅游业的健康、稳步发展有着可以借鉴的启示。

三、重庆地区中韩旅游合作发展优势

（一）开发设计“追寻抗日复国足迹之旅”

重庆历史悠久，重庆与韩国的关系久远密切，1910年朝鲜半岛沦为日本殖民地。日本废除“大韩帝国”政府，设立“朝鲜总督府”。1919年，朝鲜境内爆发了声势浩大的“3·1”反日起义运动。并于1919年在上海法租界成立“大韩民国临时政府”，成为韩国抗日独立运动的领导核心力量。后来中国抗战全面爆发，韩国临时政府在南京国民政府的支援下，从上海、杭州、长沙等一路西迁，于1939年搬迁至重庆，由国民政府全面出资安置于今天的重庆市渝中区七星岗莲花池38号，被称为“韩国民族独立运动的圣殿”。

重庆大韩民国临时政府在独立运动领袖——金九的带领下与中国军民一起积极坚持抗日奋战，为韩国的民族复兴做出了极大的贡献，创造了辉煌的抗日独立业绩。1945年8月日本战败投降，二战结束，韩国也迎来了自己祖国的光复，在重庆的韩国临时政府完成了自己的使命，于1945年8月开始分批陆续归国（甘露，2013，30(6))。从1919年到1945年，韩国临时政府在中国流亡了近27年，在重庆工作和生活的这六年时光，是韩国临时政府在中国开展独立运动最重要、最活跃的六年，也是韩国独立运动史上最引以为自豪和辉煌的时期。

图1 重庆大韩民国临时政府旧址

图2 修复后大韩民国临时政府旧址

韩国临时政府回国之后，于1995年8月被正式修复成为重庆大韩民国临时政府旧址陈列馆并向对外开放。该陈列馆每年接待大量韩国游客，其中包括不少韩国政要领导、知名人士和企业家等前来参观。它已成为中韩两国友谊历史的见证，也成为了重庆和韩国经济、文化、旅游等产业交流的桥梁。

图3 重庆韩人村旧址

图4 重庆韩人村幼儿园开学纪念照

重庆时期大韩民国临时政府的流亡爱国志士以重庆为根据地，开展抗日复国运动，所以这里被韩国人视为“革命圣地”。与重庆其他自然文化旅游市场不同，深化开发设计“大韩民国重庆临时政府旅游商品”能够使韩国人感受到民族精神的升华。还可以把几处重庆时期的“韩人村旧址”等加进来联合宣传，或加以“历史+观光”Storytelling，肯定对提高重庆大韩民国临时政府旧址的口碑和知名度带来一定扩大宣传效果，也将促进重庆韩国客源旅游市场的持续发展。

（二）“韩流”到“汉风”，拓展多元化旅游产品

作为同属儒家文化圈的中韩两国，都以儒家思想为根基，自古以来在文化、历史、地理、人文，甚至种族上就有很深的渊源，甚至也可以说有着较为相近的文化结构和文化心理。因此，两国在“文化”上具有独特的亲和力及共享之处。中韩两国通过几千年的文化交流和融合，韩国将传承了大量儒家文化所留下的“有形”和“无形”的传统文化遗产，并用于“旅游观光”产业。

重庆与韩国的友好关系也不断加强，双方在经贸、艺术、文化、科技、教育等领域的合作交流日益深化，2005年朴槿惠、2007年全斗焕、2011年郑云灿、2012年孙鹤奎等韩国政要领导人相继来渝访问，重庆多任重要领导也相继赴韩访问。2007年6月重庆率先与韩国仁川广域市缔结友好城市；2008年重庆与韩国全罗南道建立友好关系；2009年武隆县与韩国全罗北道缔结友好交流区县；2010年12月，重庆与釜山广域市结为友好城市。双方的交流互访，为重庆和韩国搭起友谊的桥梁，也结出累累硕果。

近几年，韩流的热度在中国一直只增不减，尤其在西南地区的重庆，每年都会开展一系列经贸、文化交流活动。2005年起，轮流频繁开展“重庆·韩国友好周”庆典；2008年重庆友好代表团赴韩国参加“第7届韩国仁川—中国庆典”大型活动；2010年重庆举办“2010 重庆—韩国美食展”；2013年举办“2013K-FOOD FAIR”；2014年“重庆农食品博览会”；2015年“重庆·京畿道文化产业交流会”；“2015年重庆—韩国时尚文化节”；2016年重庆举办“大邱—庆尚北道旅游年展会”，“2016重庆韩流商品博览会”等各种大型会展。

图5 2016重庆·韩流商品博览会

图6 2015重庆·京畿道文化产业交流大会

会展旅游是一种新型、高品质、高附加值的专项旅游产品，重庆作为一个最年轻、最活力的直辖市，具有明显的区位优势。未来“一带一路”发展战略中充分发挥西部地区经济中心城市集聚辐射功能，金融、货运、贸易中心功能会取得更大的提升。目前，重庆市已建成7个展览场馆，其中包括2个规模较大的场馆，即重庆国际会展中心和重庆展览中心。据市商委统计，2014年全年，重庆举办展会662个，举办节庆活动520个，举办各种会议活动5038个，会展业直接收入85.3亿元，由会展业拉动的消费更是高达682.4亿元，重庆也连续六年被评为“中国十大影响力会展城市”。

重庆会展产业真正要做大做强，做出影响力，还需要提升自身品质。重庆急需打造的是真正有影响力的“国际范”会展，而这种“国际范”还需要很多外界支撑，这几年韩国政府、企业、商家频来重庆举办并参加会展，加大开设与韩国的直飞航线，对建设会展旅游业是非常重要的。目前，重庆与韩国正规直飞航线只有重庆至仁川往返航线一条，还有两条国际客运旅游专线航班往返济州岛和大邱广域市。以后需要更加拓展“国际会展+旅游观光”多元化旅游模式。

不仅这些大型会展，每年还有很多韩国知名歌星、演员来重庆开演唱会及粉丝见面会，足以看出重庆市场的受欢迎度。演艺娱乐、影视文化旅游产业是一种形式多样、内容丰富的旅游活动，可以联合这些韩流明星们的访渝活动期间，邀请他们前往重庆的知名旅游景区参观，不仅可以带来国内外游客的“追星”效果，也可以加大访渝韩国游客的“明星效应”更加促进重庆旅游市场的发展。

图7:（ 韩国组合—少女时代重庆演唱会）

图8:（韩国 RUNNING MAN重庆粉丝见面会）

旅游业与会展业，旅游业与演艺事业都是覆盖面广、带动性强的现代服务性产业，两者之间肯定有着内在联系和互动发展需求。一个大型会展、大型演唱会的举办，对当地旅游业的旅行社、酒店、交通、购物、娱乐等均会产生促进作用。会展、演唱会、粉丝见面会及旅游业结合起来，可以整合多元化的旅游服务，比如：把会展活动和旅游观光活动有机地结合在一起，使参会、参展客把会展之余的时间转向旅游观光上，提供多元化旅游服务，可以创造更大的旅游经济社会效益。

（三）完善产业配套设施及服务品质

当前，重庆正积极融入国家“一带一路”和“长江经济带”战略。重庆的区域位置在中国经济版图上交汇成Y字形大通道的连接点上，具有承东启西、转接南北的区位优势；重庆水陆空综合交通方式齐全，港口枢纽、铁路枢纽和空港枢纽功能齐备，结合内陆地区唯一拥有“水、陆、空”国家一类口岸和保税区的优势，构建了独具重庆特色的“三个三合一”开放“大平台”；重庆是我国西部地区唯一的直辖市和国家中心城市，是全国唯一的省级统筹城乡综合配套改革试验区，具有继上海浦东新区、天津滨海新区之后的第三个国家级新区—两江新区。

近年来，重庆与韩国经贸往来更趋频繁，重庆市外经贸委的统计数据显示，截至2014年，全市累计批准韩国外商投资企业及机构达140家，如LG、SK、浦项制铁、锦湖韩亚、GS、韩泰轮胎等一大批韩国企业来渝投资设厂。实到外资额达7.78亿美元，主要涉及制造业、房地产业、服务业等。随着两江新区卡房步伐的加快，与韩国的经贸往来日趋频繁，近几年，大量韩资西进两江，贸易额连年增长，新区已成为韩国优势产业全球布局的战略节点和中国西部地区布局的战略高地。

图9：北京现代重庆工厂开工典礼

图10：重钢—韩国POSCO合作项目协议

随着中韩两国贸易和投资的继续扩大，两江新区中韩产业园发展将再次提速。来自市外经贸委的数据显示，2015年，重庆进口前十强中，韩国排第三；出口前十强中，韩国排第六，足见重庆与韩国的经贸往来紧密。仅2014年，重庆与韩国进出口总额就高达460.5亿元，同比增长了2.9倍。其中，两江新区与韩国的贸易往来最紧密，两江新区与韩国进出口贸易达到356.2亿元，增长6.2倍，占了全市份额近八成（王莉，2015.）。

两江新区“中—韩产业园”，启动区面积7.9平方千米，拓展区面积6.4平方千米。重点发展汽车和电子产业，积极培育文化创意、数字娱乐等新兴产业，择机发展新能源设备等其他产业，打造以引进韩国优势制造产业和文化创意产业为主的高端产业基地，韩国优势产业全球布局的战略节点和中国中西部地区布局的战略高地；按照韩国的社会文化习俗及建筑风格建设相关的配套生活居住设施，营造韩国化的生活环境，打造韩国人在中国中西部地区的文化家园和第二故乡，成为功能现代、产业高端、总部集聚、生态宜居的中—韩产业重要平台。

随着重庆中韩产业园发展提速，会有更多的韩国人会到访重庆，近年来在渝常驻韩国人口也在逐步增加，据韩人商会的统计，目前在渝常驻韩国人达1500人，预计现代汽车项目正式启动会有更多的韩籍驻派员工常驻重庆。而且每年到重庆访学的韩国留学生人数也在稳步增加。这些数据和平台都足以给重庆旅游业创汇的重要渠道。

重庆高校韩国语专业方面，现有两所高校开设韩国语专业，一个是四川外国语大学，另外一个是四川外国语大学南方翻译学院，四川外国语大学2006年开设韩国语专业，2009年开设亚非语言文学硕士点，2012年开设翻译硕士点，是西南地区首家韩国语专业，2012年被评为四川外语学院重点学科（金日权，2016（47））。随着市场经济的多元化发展，对人才的需求也越来越多元化，为了适应这一需求，在兼顾韩语语言能力培养的同时，注重对学生“国际商务”、“国际关系”、“翻译”等附加能力的培养，学科积极推进跨专业、跨学科的交叉、集成和整合，发挥外语类应用型、复合型、国际化人才发展，辐射带动学科整体发展。学科还与“重庆大韩民国临时政府旧址陈列馆”、“ 驻重庆韩国贸易馆”、“两江新区中韩产业园区”等机构签署实习基地协议书，优化了校企合作的创新人才培养途径，从而提升重庆市韩国语人才的服务品质。

四、结语

目前中韩旅游合作还处在起步阶段，以市场互换为其主要模式，今后应加强如何实现要素协同发展、产品—市场共享、最终实现区域一体化发展的研究力度（马波，2007，22（5））。东北亚地区是世界上总体经济实力最大的地区之一，经济上互补性最强，但由于该地区各国的政治体制、经济体制、发展水平、开放程度和意识形态等方面存在着多元化和复杂性，至今没有形成由各国中央政府签订的制度化的经济合作组织（汤秀莲，2004(6)）。在这种国际背景下，以旅游合作促进区域经济发展成为各国政府的共识。中韩处在东北亚区域旅游合作的核心地位，中韩旅游合作的发展将会促进整个东北亚地区旅游合作的发展（胡文海，朱晓华，蒋文燕，2007，26(6)）。

西部地区唯一直辖市—重庆，是中国西部向东开放的前沿、国家“城乡统筹”发展的实验口，处于国家西部大开发战略的首选和经济龙头地位。重庆各方面的发展，无疑在整个西部地区都具有借鉴意义。目前重庆旅游产业的发展模式，还只是停留在传统旅游观光层面，产业结构待需调整，重庆拥有着得天独厚的地理条件和旅游资源，重庆应以市场需求为导向，结合重庆资源特色优势及有效整合，加强政府的管理和规划，着重打造创新旅游产品体系，推动重庆市旅游产业的全局、健全、稳步发展。

参考文献：

[1] 张广瑞. 旅游业：21 世纪中韩两国经济与友谊发展的桥梁. 当代韩国，1998，(冬季号).

[2] 邱菲. 亳州地区中韩旅游合作发展研究. 湖北经济学院学报，2016，13(1).

[3] 王继庆. 试析韩国旅游业的政府主导型发展模式. 东北亚论坛，2005，14(5).

[4] 甘露. 重庆与韩国的历史文化交流. 重庆与世界 学术版，2013，30(6).

[5] 王莉. 两江新区中韩产业园提档升级 - 韩资加速布局重庆. 重庆日报，2015.11.04.

[6] 马波. 旅游业的转型与区域旅游合作—兼论中、日、韩旅游合作的推进. 旅游学刊，2007，22(5).

[7] 汤秀莲. 东北亚经济发展中的“中、日、韩自由贸易区”. 南开经济研究，2004，(6).

[8] 胡文海，朱晓华，蒋文燕. 中国与周边国家国际旅游发展特征及其对比. 地理研究，2007，26(6).

[9] 金日权. 多维视野下的韩国学研究. 博文社，2016.

[10] 2015年中国旅游业统计公报，中国国家旅游局，中国旅游报，2015.

[11] 2015年重庆市商务统计公报，重庆市商业委员会，2015.

[12] 2015年重庆市旅游业统计公报，重庆市旅游局办公室，年度统计公报，2015.

（作者简介：金日权，男，四川外国语大学东方语学院，讲师，博士，研究方向：区域国别研究）

“一带一路”背景下重庆低碳旅游发展研究

呙小明

摘要：为了更好地融入国家绿色“一带一路”战略，打造中国西部区域旅游经济中心，重庆的旅游业急需向低碳发展转型，走可持续发展之路。文章首先阐述了国内外针对低碳旅游的概念，以期统一认识，然后分析了重庆低碳旅游现存的问题，并从政府、旅游企业和游客等方面对重庆低碳旅游的推进进行了对策研究，提出相关建议。

关键词：一带一路；重庆；低碳旅游

一、导言

中国正在积极推动“一带一路”的建设，其中“一带一路”提出的“互联互通”目标主要是指政策沟通、道路联通、贸易畅通、货币流通和人心相通等五个方面，这基本上已经达成共识。而旅游业作为“和平的使者”，能使不同地区的居民更加了解外界的文化传统和风俗习惯，在促进沿线国家和地区互联互通方面，旅游业能发挥以文旅商贸促进睦邻友好、和平邦交的新使命，为“一带一路”构想的落地开路导航，因此可作为实践“一带一路”的先导产业。

与此同时，中国也申明将同沿线国家一道携手打造“绿色、健康、智力、和平”四大指向的丝绸之路，可见，绿色和可持续发展是“一带一路”战略的重点。纵观各大行业，相对而言，旅游业是资源节约型和环境友好型的低碳产业，在应对气候变化、节能减排和产业替代方面具有明显优势，如中国统计年鉴数据显示，自1990年以来，我国工业能源消耗占全社会能源消耗的比例基本稳定在70%。然而，尽管旅游与其他产业活动相比，资源消耗、污染排放及对自然生态系统的干扰都较少，但这并不表示旅游业是“零碳排放”产业，旅游业是一个涉及食、住、行、游、购、娱等各部门的交叉性行业，由于高度的关联性并伴随产业规模迅速扩张，旅游业整体也消耗了大量能源，产生了大量的碳排放，尤其是旅游交通、旅游饭店等更是耗能相对较高的部门，对气候变化和生态环境的影响不可忽视，已引起相关国际组织和学者的广泛关注。例如，世界旅游组织和联合国环境规划署研究表明，2005年全球旅游发展所产生的CO_2排放量达到13. 07亿吨，占人类活动所有CO_2排放量的4. 95%。能源需求和温室气体排放问题成为旅游业的一个前沿问题。2008年我国国家旅游局发布了《关于旅游业应对气候变化问题若干意见》，旅游业节能减排首次出现在我国政府文件中。《意见》要求全行业增强责任意识，坚持绿色发展，积极推动旅游企业节能减排、大力推广新型能源、大力倡导文明旅游，自觉节能减排，主动减缓对气候变化的影响。可见，作为与环境密切相关的行业，我国旅游行业也已步入节能减排的时代。

重庆地处“一带一路”和长江经济带战略节点，也是我国19个主要旅游目的地城市之一，具备充分的区位优势将自身建设成为参与“一带一路”发展的区域旅游经济中心。在我国从高碳工业社会逐步向低碳服务型社会转变的关键阶段，重庆大力发展低碳旅游，实现旅游产业绿色生态化，无疑对于重庆更好的融入“一带一路”战略具有重要的理论意义和实践价值。

二、低碳旅游的概念

低碳（low carbon）指较低（更低）的温室气体（二氧化碳为主）排放，主要是指化石燃料燃烧产生的CO_2排放，建设基础设施、公用设施、以及住房和商业用房等都需要消耗各种能源，也必然会产生CO_2排放。如何在经济发展与控制CO_2排放之间找到出路，实现对两者的兼顾，国际社会提出了建立低碳经济的构想。“低碳经济”术语是2003年英国政府首先提出的，在2003年2月24日由英国时任首相布莱尔发表的《我们未来的能源——创建低碳经济》的白皮书，在《能源白皮书》中指出，英国将在 2050 年将其温室气体排放量在1990 水平上减排60%，从根本上把英国变成一个低碳经济的国家。2006 年10 月，由英国政府推出、前世界银行首席经济学家尼古拉斯·斯特恩牵头的《斯特恩报告》呼吁全球向低碳经济转型（Stern，2007）。2009 年，中国环境与发展国际合作委员会（CCICED）报告把低碳经济界定为“一个新的经济、技术和社会体系，与传统经济体系相比在生产和消费中能够节省能源，减少温室气体排放，同时还能保持经济和社会发展的势头”（CCICED，2009）。随着低碳经济在全球的快速推广和实施，低碳旅游也被越来越多提及。2009 年世界旅游组织联合其他组织结构在哥本哈根举行的"气候变化世界商业峰会"上，正式呈递了《迈向低碳旅游业》的报告。但什么是低碳旅游，低碳旅游如何实现，学界并未形成统一的观点，大家从各自的角度赋予了低碳旅游不同的含义。

比较占据主流的观点认为，低碳旅游就是节能减排旅游，这种观点强调在旅游的各个要素、环节实施节能减排，从而实现旅游全过程的低碳化。如蔡萌等（2010）认为，低碳旅游是指在旅游发展过程中，通过运用低碳技术、推行碳汇机制和倡导低碳旅游消费方式，以获得更高的旅游体验质量和更大的旅游经济、社会、环境效益的一种可持续旅游发展新方式。核心理念是以更少的旅游发展碳排放量来获得更大的旅游经济、社会、环境效益。谢园方等（2010）则强调在旅游过程中，尽量降低碳排放量，减少碳足迹。其核心是减少二氧化碳的排放量，使旅游发展与环境相协调，以保护旅游地的自然环境，保证旅游业的健康可持续发展。唐承财等（2011）以可持续发展与低碳发展理念为指导，采用低碳技术，合理利用资源，实现旅游业的节能减排与社会、生态、经济综合效益最大化的可持续旅游发展形式。但这些观点也具有一些局限性，将低碳旅游的概念定义太狭窄，把低碳旅游片面地认为是"节能减排"旅游，要求旅游者尽量降低CO_2排放量，实现低能耗、低污染。低碳旅游的实现途径可以是多样化的，不仅仅是减排、降低能耗，如果把低碳旅游局限于"节能减排"，旅游发展与节能减排的矛盾必将凸显，可能成为约束旅游行业低碳发展的障碍。

还有部分观点认为，低碳旅游就是要通过控制旅游活动中的奢侈消费行为，实现低碳发展，比如减少一次性用品的使用、少做长距离飞行等等。但如果仅仅为了降低碳的排放，而使原有的服务打折、改变或降低旅游者的消费体验，有违低碳旅游的原则。有消费就会有排放，没有旅游发展当然也不会有排放增加，但单纯抑制消费来减少排放的做法，不符合发展规律，也不是旅游行业所需要追求的低碳。

因此，综合而言，低碳旅游是低碳经济的组成部分，与低碳经济一样，低碳旅游的实现途径是多样的，包括降低能源消耗、提高能源利用效率、增加使用可再生能源、转移二氧化碳排放、碳抵消以及提高社会节能意识等等，这些手段都是为了维持和提升现有的消费和生活体验，并以相对更低的排放获取这些体验。低碳旅游理念是发展低碳旅游的基础及出发点，只有低碳旅游的理念得到充足的认识、推广和普及，低碳旅游的行为才能被付诸实践。

三、重庆发展低碳旅游存在的问题

重庆是中国西部地区唯一的直辖市，是中国内陆的、中西部地区的重要交通枢纽，以“美女、美食、火锅、温泉”闻名于世界，具有三千多年的悠久历史和丰富的旅游资源，有集山、水、林、泉、瀑、峡、洞等为一体的自然景色，也有汇熔巴渝文化、民族文化、移民文化、三峡文化、陪都文化、都市文化于一炉的文化景观。重庆丰富且各具特色的旅游资源为其打造低碳旅游创造了客观基础条件，然而，近年来伴随着重庆市旅游业的蓬勃发展，其能耗不断提高，温室气体排放加剧，自然生态环境也遭到了破坏，景区内部的污染情况有所加剧，这给重庆市旅游业的健康可持续发展带来了严峻的挑战。

1. 从消费的角度看，低碳旅游的观念和意识不够深入人心。社会公众的低碳旅游消费观念和意识是决定低碳旅游发展的重要因素。重庆地处中国西部，经济水平较东部沿海地区落后，人们的收人水平和消费水平还比较低。因此，在部分人的眼里，旅游应该是豪华享受的体验，自己花了钱就应该满足自己的一切要求，自己就是上帝，这样的一种仅追求个人享受与满足的观念势必造成不少能源浪费与污染环境的行为。在重庆，低碳旅游的消费意识还没有真正深入人心，如在仙女山、金刀峡等著名景区经常看到不少游客乱扔垃圾，特别是节假日景区人流量大的时候，垃圾随处可见，更不用说农家乐了，在交通出行上，重庆游客偏爱自驾游等高能耗出行方式，且重庆人爱购买的家用汽车大多比较耗油。可以说，旅游者在旅游中缺乏低碳环保的意识，是制约重庆低碳旅游业发展的最大因素。

2. 从供给的角度看，低碳旅游的开发和管理滞后。许多旅游类企业在建设和经营的过程中，过于注重短期的经济利益，较少考虑或者基本不考虑资源与环境的承受能力，出现许多损坏自然资源、污染生态环境等恶劣情况。

在开发旅游资源时，很多企业没能做深入的调查研究和全面的科学论证，粗放式的开发 造成了旅游资源的损害与浪费。以重庆的北碚缙云山景点为例，最初开发缙云山的时候，并没有严格进行绿色规划，农家乐随意修建，农户随便乱砍乱伐，对缙云山的生态环境破坏十分严重；花大精力修建的缙云山索道，在修建和后期的运营中都需要耗费大量的能源，而以高能耗为代价的缙云山索道却没带来相应的经济利益，现在很少游客选择坐索道，索道几乎成了多余的摆设。更有甚者，有的企业为了追求商业利益破坏古迹，占道占地建设，这些都在浪费资源的同时对环境产生了极大的破坏。

在管理过程中，针对游客的吃、住、行、游、购、娱等环节，不少景点或企业仅提供非环保产品，例如餐饮企业所用的一次性的餐具等，一些旅游酒店的餐饮污水、洗浴用水以及住宿用电十分粗放，用量大，造成了能源资源的浪费，且对环境造成极大的损害。少数旅游企业甚至伪装式发展"低碳旅游"，只提口号不开展行动，反而加剧了能源损耗，对低碳旅游的发展起到负面影响。之所以出现以上行为，可能是因为企业缺乏开展低碳建设与运营的动力，以及相关部门没有按照低碳旅游的相关宗旨对他们进行规范和管理。

3. 相关政策和标准制度的缺失。虽然重庆市人民政府在《关于促进旅游业改革发展的实施意见》等文件以及其他场合提及生态旅游或旅游业的可持续发展，但是并没有出台关于具体如何促进低碳旅游发展的细则，无法对旅游企业落实执行低碳旅游的发展做出正确指导和支持。此外，低碳是一个具备一定技术规范的名词，发展低碳旅游需要相关的衡量标准来进行规范与推进。虽然《重庆市人民政府办公厅关于贯彻落实国家应对气候变化规划（2014—2020年）的意见》对于全市整体节能减排规定了目标：到2020年，全市单位地区生产总值二氧化碳排放比2005年降低45%以上，非化石能源占一次能源消费的比重达到15%。遗憾的是，具体针对重庆旅游业的低碳发展并没有设置目标，也没能安排为达到目标而需逐步开展的行动方案。因此，重庆缺乏低碳旅游业的标准规范，低碳旅游可能更多只是一种停留在人们脑海中和口头上的概念，没有具体的衡量标准和制度，政府推动低碳旅游业的动力不足，旅游企业和游客也缺乏践行低碳旅游的主动性和目的性，低碳旅游的科学推进自然将面临困境。

四、重庆发展低碳旅游的措施

（一）政府方面

政府主管部门应在政策、资金、规范标准等方面对低碳旅游发展提供必要的引领和支持。①市政府牵头，制定具体的全市低碳旅游行动方案，为旅游相关部门提供发展低碳旅游的行动纲领；④制定低碳旅游的技术标准和规范，设定低碳效益量化考核指标，加强低碳发展在旅游规划评审中的份量；如2014年底重庆市城乡建设委员会发布的《绿色低碳生态城区评价标准》，为重庆市工程建设设立了推荐性标准，虽然不专门针对旅游行业，但对旅游业而言也是一个很好的借鉴；②提供专项发展资金，引导旅游企业走低碳发展之路；针对重点旅游景区和旅游企业开展低碳旅游试点示范工作；③加大对公共交通工具的投资力度，降低新能源、环保型运输车的生产成本，鼓励旅游企业购买节能环保型运输车辆，开发低碳旅游交通，如长江三峡低碳航运交通，增强游轮旅游的吸引力；⑤加强低碳旅游技术支撑体系建设，增加低碳旅游发展的应用基础科研项目立项，为发展低碳旅游提供技术创新的平台。

（二）旅游企业方面

旅游相关企业如旅游开发公司、旅游景区、旅行社、旅游酒店等，由于直接接触消费者，在低碳旅游发展中发挥着核心作用。如旅行社，从出游方式、旅游路线的选择，到旅游目的地的确定、旅游活动项目的组合，大都是由旅行社来进行确定的。如果旅行社在规划游客出行的时候就充分考虑节能环保的因素，便可有效地帮助游客践行低碳旅游。如重庆冬季阴冷，旅行社可以加大对沿海城市的宣传力度，比如三亚，引导游客前往这些城市避寒旅游；同时也可多鼓励游客多参加低能耗的旅游项目，如重庆温泉旅游，从而降低能源消耗。如素有重庆“主城肺叶”之称的铁山坪，曾主推“低碳登山健康游”，根据市民的年龄和体质差异，分为“中、东、西”三条不同健身强度的步游路线，让游客体验登山、骑行等低碳旅游，也是很不错的尝试。

据统计，在星际酒店能源消费中，有50%左右的电力消费用于空调设施（石培华等，2010）；而旅游过程中游客 90% 的能源消费用于住宿和交通（UNEP，2008），因此，住宿酒店、农家乐等必须重视游客在住宿过程中的能耗问题，可以利用太阳能照明、太阳能热水器、地源热泵等节能设施，也可以考虑使用可再生能源提供的燃气、热力供应等方式替代电能以及煤、天然气的使用，可以通过改造客房门窗、墙体、屋顶、建筑朝向提高冬季取暖效率，通过选用具备变速变频风机、高能效与高性能的冷热机组等高节能的空调设备提高空调能耗利用率等。如希尔顿全球酒店集团做出过一个五年承诺，承诺从2009年到2014年间，能源消耗减少20%，碳排放量减少20%，垃圾排放量减少20%，用水量减少10%。这些都是旅游相关企业可以做出的努力。

如果部分企业面临常规减排方式如节能、提高能效等成本过高、实施困难的情况，可以考虑通过抵消碳排放的方式实现低碳发展。碳抵消的方式可以非常多样化，如通过自身挖潜，寻找区内减排项目如植树造林等，也可以通过购买市场上通过认证的碳减排量实现抵消。

（三）游客方面

要发展低碳旅游，大力提升公众的低碳旅游意识非常重要，因为意识决定行动。低碳旅游本质上是一种低碳化的生活方式，因此，人们需要首先在日常生活中就培育起低碳的观念，意识到低碳行为会造福环境，惠及子孙后代，这需要大量的宣传工作。

在宣传中需要向大众强调：低碳旅游并非遥不可及，可以随手而为。游客可以通过多种方式和途径来践行低碳旅游，如在出游交通方式的选择上，游客可以考虑优先选择徒步、自行车、公共交通工具等相对低碳的方式；在选择住宿酒店时，游客尽量选择节能环保型酒店，不一定为了面子选择豪华型酒店，理性消费，减少浪费行为；在旅游参观过程中，游客也应持环保理念，不乱丢垃圾，在不牺牲旅游舒适性的前提下尽量减少消耗能源和资源。例如，重庆希尔顿酒店于2013年3月23日晚8:30至9:30举行了"地球一小时"运动，"地球一小时"始于2007年，由世界野生动物基金会（WWF）发起，旨在告知大众，只要简单的行动，即可对减少温室气体排放及应对气候变化产生巨大的影响。

参考文献：

[1]蔡萌，汪宇明. 低碳旅游：一种新的旅游发展方式[J]. 旅游学刊，2010，25(1)：13-17.

[2]谢园方，赵媛. 国内外低碳旅游研究进展及启示[J]. 人文地理，2010，(5)：27-31.

[3]CCICED. 中国发展低碳经济途径研究[R]. CCICED政策研究报告，2009.

[4]石培华，冯凌，吴普. 41号文件解读之三：关于低碳旅游发展机制[N]. 中国旅游报. 2010-09-20.

[5]唐承财，钟林生，成升魁. 我国低碳旅游的内涵及可持续发展策略研究[J]. 经济地理，2011-5:862-867.

[6]Stern N. Stern Review on the Economics of Climate Change[M]. UK: Cambridge University Press，2007.

[7]UNEP，University of Oxford，UNWTO，WMO. Climate ChangeAdaptation and Mitigation in Tourism Sector: Frameworks，Tools and Practices[M]. UK: Oxuniprint，Oxford University Press，2008: 15-77.

（作者简介：冯小明，女，四川外国语大学国别经济与国际商务研究中心，副教授，博士，研究方向：国际旅游经济）

阿尔及利亚罗马遗址旅游资源研究

潘雷　闵敏

摘要：阿尔及利亚是非洲和阿拉伯世界面积第一大的国家，拥有丰富的旅游资源，其中尤以六大罗马遗址最为出名，这六大罗马遗址是：帝巴扎、杰米拉、蒂姆嘉德、沙赫沙、伊波内、提迪斯。中国对于阿尔及利亚旅游资源的了解极为有限，本文从历史、文化、食住行等各个方面研究了阿尔及利亚的六大罗马遗址，为中国了解该国旅游资源提供了有价值的资料。阿尔及利亚现正在逐渐开放旅游业，该国的旅游业拥有巨大潜力，也是中国游客潜在的旅游目的地之一。

关键词：阿尔及利亚；旅游资源；罗马遗址

阿尔及利亚位于北非，地中海的南岸。总面积2,381,741平方千米，是非洲面积第一大国。古罗马时期，罗马人曾经统治阿尔及利亚的部分地区，在当地建立城市，有些城市的遗迹成功地保存了下来，成为阿尔及利亚重要的旅游资源。

阿尔及利亚最著名的罗马遗址有六个，也是官方所宣传推广的六个罗马遗址，在每个罗马遗址公园的大门口，都悬挂着六大遗址的宣传图册，一共有六本，每一本既是宣传手册，也是一本考古书籍。书不厚，薄薄的一本，里外全部彩色印刷，一本售价600阿尔及利亚第纳尔[①]。

这六大罗马遗址分别是：1.帝巴扎（Tipasa）(تيبازة)，2.杰米拉（Djemila）(جميلة)，3.蒂姆嘉德（Timgad）(تيمقاد)，4.沙赫沙（Cherchell）(شرشال)，5. 伊波内（Hippone）(هيبون)，6.提迪斯（Tiddis）(تيديس)。

一、帝巴扎

名胜之所以为名胜，原因之一是名胜自身的质量，原因之二就是文人墨客浓

① 根据2016年8月7日最新汇率，1人民币=16.4903阿尔及利亚第纳尔。

墨重彩的描绘，就好像李白之于庐山，杜甫之于泰山，范仲淹之于岳阳楼，崔颢之于黄鹤楼……加缪之于帝巴扎。

法国诺贝尔文学奖获得主加缪对帝巴扎这个地方有着深厚的感情，他有两篇文章描写帝巴扎，其中一篇名为《帝巴扎的婚礼》，加缪在这篇文章中写道："在春天，帝巴扎住满了神祇，他们说着话儿，在阳光和苦艾的气味中，在披挂着银甲的大海上，在深蓝色的天空中，在铺满了鲜花的废墟上，在沸滚于乱石堆里的光亮中。"另一篇名为《重回帝巴扎》，在这篇文章中加缪写道："战乱的那些年耗尽了我的青春。而打战争结束不久，我就曾回到过帝巴扎。我想，我还是希望在帝巴扎重获那难以令人忘怀的自由的。二十多年前，就在那个地方，我每日清晨都在断壁残垣中游荡着，呼吸着苦艾草的味道，倚着石头给自己取暖。"。

在帝巴扎罗马遗址公园里，有一个专门为加缪立的纪念碑，碑上用法语写着"Je comprends ici ce qu'on appelle gloire : le droit d'aimer sans mesure"，翻译过来就是"在这儿我领悟了人们所说的荣光，就是无拘无束地爱的权利"，这句话选在加缪的《帝巴扎的婚礼》。

从首都阿尔及尔坐出租车前往帝巴扎需要一个小时，单程费用2000第纳尔左右，不打表，和司机谈价格；也可以选择长途公交车，时间需要两个小时左右，单程费用不超过100第纳尔，但是长途公交车下午4点钟即收班，首都有两个长途汽车站，是位于市中心（وسط المدينة）的那一个；阿尔及利亚还有一种往返于各省之间的长途出租车，但是没有前往帝巴扎省的长途出租车。帝巴扎罗马遗址公园门票80第纳尔，毛里塔尼亚皇家陵墓也属于帝巴扎文化遗产的一部分，需要单独购买门票，60第纳尔。

（一）帝巴扎的历史

帝巴扎是阿尔及利亚的一座城市，位于地中海边的帝巴扎省，在首都阿尔及尔以西75公里。腓尼基人建造了帝巴扎，作为他们众多贸易殖民地之一，在当时，帝巴扎有显著的地位。帝巴扎在腓尼基语中的意思是走廊，因为这个城市曾经是人们来往于伊库兹（阿尔及尔）（إيكوزيم）和伊瓦尔（沙赫沙）（إيول）之间的通道和走廊。在那之后，帝巴扎又变成了迦太基人的城市。帝巴扎作为腓尼基人的殖民地，历史可以追溯到公元前5世纪，那时候她有另外的一个名字——提帕萨（تيباسا）。当罗马人来到这个地方的时候，他们把它变成了隶属于古罗马拉齐奥地区的一个殖民地，在罗马皇帝克劳狄乌斯时期（公元54年—公元41年）（كلاوديوس），帝巴扎变成了隶属于罗马的殖民地。

在公元二世纪和三世纪，这个地方还被称作提帕萨的时候，它有着重要的贸易地位，但是这个地方并不以艺术或是教育而著称。在公元三世纪，提帕萨是基督教僧侣的大本营之一，圣女撒尔沙（السالسا أو الصلصا）将伪上帝雕像之首扔到了大海里，但是崇拜这个雕像的民众用石头将她砸死。但是更神奇的是相传圣女的身体又从大海里回来，被埋葬在港口山丘上的小教堂里，这个小教堂后来发展为巨大的宗座圣殿（البازيليكا）。城市的规模也扩大了，在公元四世纪末，城市的人口达到两万人。

在公元484年，提帕萨处于汪达尔人的统治之下，汪达尔人的国王温德里·亨里克（الملك الوندالي هينريك）派了一个阿里安教派（المذهب الأريوسي）的主教到提帕萨。那个时候，大量提帕萨的居民都通过海路逃到西班牙去了。而阿里安教派的主教则残忍地迫害留下来的人。据一些古代文献记载，那些居民的右手被砍掉，舌头被拔掉，但是他们仍然可以讲话。在公元523年之后，当年逃往西班牙的提帕萨居民逐渐回归。在公元534年，拜占庭人来了，占领了沙赫沙和提帕萨。在那之后，提帕萨逐渐淡出了历史的舞台。当穆斯林阿拉伯人来到这里的时候，他们并没有选择在提帕萨定居。

（二）帝巴扎的地理

古罗马提帕萨城建在地中海边上三个连绵起伏的小山丘上，民居建在中间的山丘上，但是已经没有遗址了。剩下的遗址是三个基督教教堂：在西边的山丘上有大宗座圣殿和亚历山大宗座圣殿；东边的山丘上是圣女撒尔沙宗座圣殿。

大宗座圣殿被当作采石场用了几个世纪，但是至今仍能看出它的大概样子，有七个配殿。大宗座圣殿的下边发现了一些坚硬石头组成的墓地，其中有一个圆形墓地，直径有60英尺，能容下24口棺材。至于圣女撒尔沙宗座圣殿里面，依然保存有马赛克，发现它的人是史蒂芬·厄齐尔（ستيفن غزل），神殿由主殿和两个配殿组成。在帝巴扎也有博物馆，虽然博物馆不大，但是里面的文物很丰富。

提帕萨城以前有高大的城墙，城墙有几公里长，整座城被37个碉楼所围绕，由于害怕被侵略，警卫工作无时无刻不在进行。但是当地严苛的自然环境毁掉了这些高大的城墙，蚀掉了整座城市，有一部分城市沉入了海中，但是水下的搜寻工作还没有进行，因为这一工作需要众多科研机构的参与。

（三）帝巴扎特殊的丧葬风俗

腓尼基人建造和发展了提帕萨，他们将橄榄树带到了这个地方，同时，这个地方的人对于死亡有着特殊的风俗，有一些墓地专门用于埋葬富人，另外一些坟墓则专门用于埋葬宗教人士，而孤儿则不被埋葬，他们的尸体被扔给要塞中的狮子吃。

有一些文献中记录，存在着一种双子棺，富人们会为他们的坟墓购置这种棺材，放在夫妻合葬墓里面，希望在另一个世界的旅程中夫妻也能够同行。还有一些一般的坟墓是专门埋葬仆人的，仆人坟墓中间簇拥着一个大的坟墓，是这个贵族家庭的坟墓，这些仆人都是为这个家族服务的。这个城市里最奇怪的殡葬风俗之一，就是死者要带着一个小玻璃瓶和一些陶制的容器，玻璃瓶里装上眼泪，是对现世生活的证明；陶制容器里装上香料，在通往阴间的旅途上使用。

在帝巴扎遗址中还保存着一定数量的石棺，游客可以近距离地观看。

（四）帝巴扎遗址中的重要景点

1. 罗马剧场

罗马剧场位于遗址公园一进大门的右边，损毁比较严重，勉强还可看出剧场的大概形状。在东西两边各有一扇正门，东边的正门已完全倒塌，西边的正门还保留至今。

2. 毛里塔尼亚皇家陵墓

毛里塔尼亚皇家陵墓还有另外一个名字，帝巴扎当地人称它为“罗马女人埋骨之地（قبر الرومية）”。之所以叫这个名字，是因为很多研究罗马遗址的专家相信，这个陵墓的主人是国王尤巴二世（يوبا الثاني），他的妻子是埃及艳后克丽奥佩脱拉（كليوباترا السابعة）的女儿克丽奥佩脱拉·西里妮（كليوباترا سيليني），克丽奥佩脱拉·西里妮是埃及艳后和罗马将领安东尼的女儿，父亲是罗马人，女儿自然是罗马女人，故陵墓有此称呼。陵墓位于帝巴扎省的一个地方，叫做“赛迪·拉什德（سيدي راشد）”，距离帝巴扎罗马遗址公园有些距离。陵墓位于一条公路左侧的山丘上，非常显眼，从公路上经过的时候就可以看到，这条公路连接首都阿尔及尔和沙赫沙。陵墓下半部分成圆柱体，上半部分成圆锥体，圆柱体底部圆形周长为185.5米，圆形直径为60.9米，整座建筑高32.4米，四面各有一扇巨门，每扇巨门高6.9米，巨门上刻有类似十字架的巨大图案，由此一些研究者便认为这是基督教的建筑，但是很多考古学家认为这座建筑和基督教没有什么关系，因为在罗马帝国占领此地之前，陵墓就已经建成了。陵墓既是一处景观，又是一座建筑，还有些人喜欢将它称为“蜂巢”（خلية نحل），这反映出这一古代建筑高超的工艺技术和卓尔不群的艺术品位。陵墓海拔261米，公元1865年，奉拿破仑三世之命，法国考古学家“阿德里安·比利布鲁格尔”（أدريان بيربروجر）在陵墓的东侧发现一道暗门，暗门后有一个像密道一样的廊殿，殿顶很低，人无法在其中直立行走，必须弯下身子。廊殿右边的墙上刻着公狮子和母狮子的图案，所以这座廊殿被称为“狮子厅”(بهو الأسود)。穿过这座廊殿，又是一座廊殿，第二座廊殿长141米，高2.4米，成盘旋状直接到达陵墓的中心，中心部分面积80平方米。

3.神庙

神庙在罗马剧场的附近，无名神庙现在就只剩下基座和部分台阶了，是谁建造了无名神庙现在已无从考证。新神庙在无名神庙对面，面积和无名神庙相同，只是新神庙的地板砖与无名神庙不同。

二、杰米拉

杰米拉，罗马人称它为库威库尔（كويكول），位于阿尔及利亚东北部塞提夫省(ولاية سطيف)。从首都阿尔及尔前往塞提夫省的省会塞提夫城，乘坐长途大巴的话需用时3个小时，票价500阿尔及利亚第纳尔。塞提夫城是阿尔及利亚第五大城市，以红绿灯而出名，因为这个城市的红绿灯是阿尔及利亚城市中最多的。阿尔及利亚反法独立战争胜利初期，国家的意识形态就是凡是西方的都要反对，红绿灯是从西方传进来的，所以也要反对，所以在一些老的城市如首都阿尔及尔，你都看不到太多的红绿灯，反而是在一些新兴城市如塞提夫，红绿灯更多。从省会塞提夫城再花费一个小时乘出租车前往遗址公园，费用单程2000阿尔及利亚第纳尔左右，遗址公园票价60阿尔及利亚第纳尔。1982年，联合国教科文组织将其列为世界文化遗产之一。杰米拉遗址公园的大门看起来颇为有气势，在阿尔及利亚的罗马遗址公园里算是最豪华的一个了，原因大概是因为现任总统贝特福利卡曾经到访。进入遗址公园大门，可以看到一座石碑，上面刻着总统贝特福利卡于某年到访此地，别的罗马遗址里并没有见到类似的石碑。每年，在杰米拉遗址还会举办阿拉伯歌曲国际音乐节。

（一）杰米拉遗址的地理

杰米拉建立于公元一世纪末，位于比巴尼山脉（سلسلة البيبان）东部，被群山所围绕，遗址地处高原，海拔920米，距离最近的城市尔玛（مدينة العلمة）32公里，尔玛是位于杰米拉遗址和塞提夫城之间的一座小城，如想从塞提夫城坐长途大巴前往杰米拉遗址，必须先乘坐大巴前往尔玛，再从尔玛乘坐小巴士前往杰米拉遗址，塞提夫没有直达杰米拉遗址的巴士。遗址所在地区大约50%都是山地。杰米拉的气候是夏天炎热，冬天寒冷。之所以在环境如此严酷的地方建造城市，是因为这里的地形易守难攻，可以有效地监视和管理周边地区。

（二）杰米拉遗址的布局

1.浴室

罗马人酷爱洗澡，这一点也体现在杰米拉遗址中。在进入杰米拉城的南大门之前有一些浴室，这些浴室呈东西走向，总共有十二间浴室。罗马人从大厅进入，进入地下室，地下室作为健身房。人们通过更衣室，进入冷水浴室，冷水浴室很大，充满了马赛克和大理石的装饰，冷水浴室里有两个小池子和一个大池子，大池子和两个小池子中间被一些粉红色的大理石柱子隔开。冷水浴室后边是桑拿房。桑拿房的边上是两个出口，通往常温浴室和一个小的热水池，常温浴室和按摩房相连。最后是厕所。在浴室建筑群里游客还可以看到用石头镂刻成的下水道地漏，有现在的井盖那么大，雕刻工艺十分精美。

2.广场

在杰米拉遗址里有两个广场，老广场被一群公共建筑所围绕，建筑已经残缺不全了，目前只有一部分保存了下来，老广场是在公元二世纪建立的。在公元二世纪末三世纪初，老广场已经成为了杰米拉城的中心，变得拥挤不堪。于是建了第二个公共广场，命名为南广场。南广场的设计没有按照传统的套路进行，面积比老广场要大出不少，也没有老广场那样拥挤，同时，新广场并非步行街，车、马亦可通行。新广场周围有两座标志性的建筑，其中之一是凯旋门，建于公元216年，当时正值罗马皇帝卡拉卡拉（كاراكلا）统治时期。另一座标志性的建筑是大神庙，建于公元229年，为了彰显西弗勒斯王室家族（أسرة سيفيروس المالكة）的神圣地位。

新广场的设计具有里程碑式的意义，新广场再也不是经典的长方形平坦广场，广场的周围也没有了装饰和雕刻对称的雕像和石碑。新广场建在一个斜坡上面，从卡拉卡拉凯旋门开始，斜坡的坡度越来越大，广场的北边和东边是笔直的，另两边则不是。广场的西边矗立着卡拉卡拉凯旋门，经过了重新修葺，以前是广场的入口。

3.宗教

罗马人所留下的遗迹，足以证明基督教在阿尔及利亚存在过一段时间，比如杰米拉遗址当中两座拥有精美石刻和丰富马赛克的基督教堂，还有一座小型基督教堂，还有基督教神职人员的住所。

除了基督教之外，遗址中还保存了专门祭祀朱庇特（جوبيتر）、朱诺（جونو）、密涅瓦（مينيرفا）这些神的场所，位于遗址的东北部。

4.市场和商店

杰米拉的商店和蒂姆嘉德的商店非常相似，但杰米拉的商店里陶瓷制品更多。杰米拉的市场有一个大门，由六根柱子支撑，有水池、称重房、市场建立者的雕像，还有诸神的雕像。

5.罗马剧场

罗马剧场呈半圆形，座位呈阶梯状向上排列，剧场保存非常完整，朝向北边的森林。通过广场的拱门可以到达剧场，剧场可以容纳3000名观众，观众根据他们的社会地位被安排座位，比如元老院成员坐在前排，而老百姓则坐在远离舞台的最高处。

6.住宅

在杰米拉遗址中还存在着一些豪宅，我们能够知道一些豪宅主人的名字，比如，卡斯图里尤斯（كاستوريوس），他的豪宅占地1600平方米，此人是当地两位总督之一，另一个总督是鲁修斯·库鲁德修斯·布鲁图（لوسيوس كولوديوس بروتو），在卡斯图里尤斯的豪宅中还发现了私人游泳池和私人浴室。

7.杰米拉博物馆

博物馆位于杰米拉遗址公园内，由一处院落和三间房屋组成。博物馆中陈列了众多出土于杰米拉遗址当中的文物，有一些文物是独一无二、举世无双的，尤其是铺陈在博物馆墙上和地面上大片大片精美的马赛克图画，这些马赛克图画的主题都是神话传说，比如根据古罗马神话中的巴克斯（باخوس）——也就是古希腊神话中的酒神狄俄尼索斯（ديونيسوس）——的传说故事所制作的马赛克图画。

（三）蒂姆嘉德

蒂姆嘉德古时候被罗马人称为塔姆高迪（تاموقادي），遗址位于阿尔及利亚东部的巴特那省（ولاية باتنة），距离巴特那省省会巴特那城36公里，在巴特那城的东边，距离首都阿尔及尔418公里。巴特那省是一个被奥雷斯山脉（جبال الأوراس）所环绕的省份。罗马皇帝图拉真（تراجان）于公元100年下令建立塔姆高迪城，建城是出于军事目的。一开始，这个城市所起的是防御作用，但是后来这个城市变成了一个人口大城，慢慢地变成了一个文化中心。塔姆高迪城的面积只有11公顷，城市的设计非常精妙。蒂姆嘉德遗址是非洲最大的罗马遗址，也是非洲保存最完整的罗马遗址，遗址完整体现了罗马城市的建筑风格和布局。1982年，蒂姆嘉德遗址被联合国教科文组织列入世界文化遗产名录。

从首都阿尔吉尔驱车5个小时或乘飞机1个小时到达巴特那，再乘车1个小时到达蒂姆嘉德遗址所在地。遗址中有大量刻在石柱头的浮雕，内容取材相当丰富，有当地生长的野草，有刀剑，有葡萄藤蔓，雕刻工艺细腻，在今天看来依然精美绝伦。罗马车辆的痕迹也留在了圆形拱门地面上两条深深的车辙当中。

1. 蒂姆嘉德的建筑风格和历史

蒂姆嘉德是一座配套设施完备的城市，整座城市几乎是一个正方形，长354米，宽324米，总面积大约11公顷，整座城市设计巧妙，布局犹如象棋棋盘，南北走向和东西走向各有一条罗马大道从城市中间穿过，作为城市的主干道，由这两条主干道又衍生出众多的支路。每一条支路的起点处和结尾处都有两座石头砌成的拱门。道路修好之后，罗马人就开始修建一系列的住宅和其配套设施，就像他们在其他城市中做的那样。整座城市被高大的城墙所包围保护。在两条主干道相交汇的地方，有一片边长为20米的正方形区域用来修建房屋，这片地区是蒂姆嘉德城最古老的地区，最先来到这里的人们都居住在这片区域。随着时间的推移，城里的人口越来越多，老的城墙被拆掉了，在城市的东边，新的居住区建立了起来。

遗址当中的设施还保存得很完好，游客可以清晰地看出它的样貌。主要的设施都围绕着公共广场，比如政府机构、罗马皇帝的神庙、法院、公共市场、贸易商店，还有离广场不远处矗立着的罗马剧场。

是什么使得蒂姆嘉德成为世界上独一无二的城市呢？因为这座遗址至今还保存着建城时的最初设计方案，也就是说通过这座遗址，你可以全面了解罗马城市的设计、构造和布局。由于蒂姆嘉德遗址的面积广大，它又被人称为努米底亚①的孟买。笔者认为之所以有这个称呼，其一是因为蒂姆嘉德遗址位于当年努米底亚国的疆域内，其二，孟买是印度最大的城市，而蒂姆嘉德又是非洲最大的罗马遗址。

从公元2世纪后半叶开始，蒂姆嘉德城原有的面积已经不能满足需要，城市的扩建开始了，新的居民区出现了，新的神庙被建成，14座新的公共浴室被建成。到公元3世纪，扩建的浪潮到达顶峰，一系列新建筑应运而生，如新的公共图书馆、市场，更宽敞更奢华的民居。到公元5世纪，汪达尔人（الوندال）占领了蒂姆嘉德城，在城中过着腐朽的生活，对城市大肆破坏，正如他们对其他阿尔及

① 努米底亚是一个古罗马时期的柏柏尔人王国，存在时间为公元前202年-公元前46年，位置在今天的阿尔及利亚东北和突尼斯的一部分，以出产精锐骑兵而闻名。

利亚的罗马城市所做的那样。汪达尔人对于蒂姆嘉德的占领持续了大约一个世纪，直到拜占庭人（البيزنطيون）取代了他们的位置。拜占庭人大肆劫掠了蒂姆嘉德一番，破坏了巨大的神庙，在离蒂姆嘉德城不远的地方建造了拜占庭式的城堡，但是比起罗马建筑的艺术性来，拜占庭式的城堡就差远了。

到了公元七世纪，伴随着伊斯兰的开疆拓土，拜占庭的时代结束了，蒂姆嘉德城的居民逐渐移居到其他伊斯兰开拓者新建的城市中去了。又过了几个世纪，泥土渐渐覆盖了这座城市，人们渐渐将它遗忘。直到公元1880年，一群法国人重新又踏上了这片土地，对蒂姆嘉德城遗址进行勘探，对遗址的研究工作一直持续到阿尔及利亚独立战争胜利，当时，75%的遗址已经重见天日。

1962年的夏天，遗址最原始的部分——罗马皇帝图拉真命令建造的部分也成功出土。法国人建了一座博物馆，将大批有价值的文物放进博物馆加以保护，其中有陶艺工具，镶嵌在私人住宅地面上和公共浴室中的精美马赛克壁画，刻有文字和图画向我们讲述塔姆高迪人历史和信仰的雕像和石碑，石碑实际上是墓碑，墓碑前边还会摆放盘子，因为罗马人相信逝者的灵魂会起来吃东西。这一习俗和中国人祭祀时在先人的墓前或灵位前摆上食品以祭奠先人的习俗非常相似。

（四）沙赫沙

沙赫沙是帝巴扎西边的一个小城市，这里所说的沙赫沙指的是位于沙赫沙城附近的罗马引水渠遗址。如果你乘车从首都阿尔及尔前往沙赫沙，在快要到达沙赫沙的时候，在高速公路的左侧，两座山丘中间，横亘着一座巨大的桥梁似的古老建筑，但它并不是什么桥梁，而是一座巨大的引水渠。引水渠有两层，每一层都由并排的拱门组成，一个拱门连着一个拱门，延伸向另一座山丘。阿尔及利亚并没有为这个遗址建一座公园，也就是说这个遗址就这么矗立在荒野当中。当然，没有遗址公园，游客也就不用付门票。但是游客如想近距离参观，就得通过一条勉强可以过汽车的羊肠小道，穿过一片树林才能到达。游客可以选择在帝巴扎市雇佣一辆出租车前往，往返费用在2000阿尔及利亚第纳尔左右。从首都阿尔及尔可以乘坐中巴前往帝巴扎市，费用大约几十阿尔及利亚第纳尔。这个遗址并不好找，因为不管是在沙赫沙还是帝巴扎，当地人很多人不知道这个地方。

（五）伊波内

伊波内罗马遗址位于阿尔及利亚东部临近突尼斯的安纳巴省（ولاية عنابة）的

省会安纳巴城。安纳巴城以圣奥古斯丁[①]教堂（الكنيسة المسيحية سانت أوغستين）而闻名，还以拥有柔软细腻沙子的黄金沙滩而闻名。伊波内罗马遗址位于一座山丘脚下，山上正是圣奥古斯都教堂。遗址残破不堪，但是遗址内有博物馆，博物馆内保存有马赛克壁画和文物。安纳巴城治安情况欠佳，偷盗、抢劫事件时有发生。

（六）提迪斯

提迪斯罗马遗址位于阿尔及利亚东部第三大城市康斯坦丁（قسنطينة）西北30公里的地方。关于提迪斯遗址的相关文献少之又少。相对来说，历史名城康斯坦丁比提迪斯名气要大得多。康斯坦丁是一个建筑在峡谷两岸的城市，很多建筑建在悬崖峭壁之上，看了就让人不寒而栗，更不要说住进去了。因为城市修建在峡谷两岸，桥梁成为了沟通两岸交通的重要通道，因此，这个城市也以众多历史悠久的桥梁而闻名。

总结

阿尔及利亚旅游资源丰富，其中又以罗马遗址最为著名，有些罗马遗址还是世界文化遗产，而且这些遗址公园的门票都是非常的便宜，阿尔及利亚国内的交通费用也不高，住宿旅馆的价位和中国的相当，并不便宜。总体来说，在阿尔及利亚旅游的价格相对低廉。现在，阿尔及利亚出口石油天然气的收入锐减，急需寻求其他经济来源途径，阿尔及利亚已经开放了旅游签证，现在正是阿尔及利亚发展旅游业的最好时机。从长远来看，阿尔及利亚旅游业发展的潜力和空间都很大，阿尔及利亚也将成为中国游客潜在的旅游目的地之一。

参考文献：

[1] Charles Thomas-Stanford.About Algeria: Algiers, Themcen, Constantine, Biskra, Timgad.Kessinger Pub Co, 2009年9月15日.

[2] Hephaestus Books.Articles on Roman Sites in Algeria, Including: Lambaesis, Tebessa, Hippo Regius, Timgad, Djemila, Tipaza, Khamissa, Icosium, Mesarfelta, Diana veteranorum, Altava, Uzinaza, Roman Roads in Africa, Quiza cenitana.Hephaestus books, 2011年9月28日.

[3] Hephaestus Books.Articles on Archaeology of Alaeria, Including: Lambaesis,

① 圣奥古斯丁（公元354年-公元430年），天主教圣师，古罗马帝国时期天主教思想家。

Tebessa, Hippo Regius, Timgad, Djemila, Tipaza, Khamissa, Icosium, Mesarfelta, Diana Veteranorum, Altava, Uzinaza, Roman Roads in Africa, Quiza Cenitana, Partenia, Tassili N' Ajjer.Hephaestus Books, 2011年9月30日.

[4] Niek Yoan.Cherchell.Miss Press, 2011年10月12日.

[5] Reinhold Urmetzer.Tipasa.Tredition Gmbh, 2012年7月5日.

[6] 赵慧杰.阿尔及利亚.社会科学文献出版社, 2006年1月1日.

[7] 赵霁宁.阿尔贝·加缪笔下的阿尔及利亚.北京:首都师范大学, 2011年.

（作者简介：潘雷，男，四川外国语大学东方语学院，讲师，硕士，研究方向：阿拉伯社会文化；闵敏，女，四川外国语大学东方语学院，讲师，硕士，研究方向：阿拉伯社会文化）

“一带一路”背景下提升我国邮轮旅游竞争力初探

邹思晓

摘要：在“一带一路”战略中，我国政府明确提出要推动海上丝绸之路的发展，其中就包括邮轮旅游产业。邮轮旅游在我国尚处于起步阶段，借助这一政策的东风，发展潜力受到各方关注。我国最具代表性的海上丝绸之路重要枢纽——海南，凭借先天的资源优势，成为我国邮轮旅游发展的先头部队。本文通过对海南的邮轮旅游产业现状做出分析，找出能够提升地区邮轮旅游竞争力的对策建议，对今后重庆等地发展内河邮轮旅游产业也具有参考价值。

关键词：“一带一路”战略，邮轮旅游，竞争力

一、“一带一路”与邮轮旅游

2015年3月，国家发改委、外交部、商务部联合发布了《推动共建丝绸之路经济带和21世纪海上丝绸之路的愿景与行动》，其中明确指出要“推动21世纪海上丝绸之路邮轮旅游合作”这一重要方向，也标志着“一带一路”战略落地实施的大幕被拉开。

“丝绸之路经济带”和“21世纪海上丝绸之路”，简称“一带一路”。“一带一路”战略包含了从地区到产业（涉及贸易、金融、文化、旅游、交通、基础设施等多元产业）发展的多种设想，为相关地区和产业带来新的发展机遇和合作方向。

“海上丝绸之路”是古代中国走向海洋、走向世界的主要通道，中国的陶瓷、香料、茶叶就是通过海上丝绸之路运送到了亚洲、欧洲及非洲其他国家。凭借着得天独厚的港口优势和文化特质，“海上丝绸之路”为现代邮轮旅游航线的设计和开发提供了资源。

邮轮旅游（cruise travel/tourism），是指以邮轮为目的地的新型旅游方式。与传统旅游不同的是，邮轮旅游是以船上活动和岸上休闲观光为主要内容的高端旅游活动，是一种多功能、复合型、高度现代化的旅游产品，拥有“海上流动度假村”的美誉。旅游的主体部分是以船上的娱乐设施及服务为主要目的，上岸观光则仅为旅游的一部分。

随着“一带一路”战略的提出，我国沿海地区的一些地方政府和部分旅游企业也将邮轮旅游产品的设计和开发同“海上丝绸之路”结合起来，例如《三亚市邮轮旅游发展专项规划（2012—2022）》就率先提出要开辟“海上丝绸之路”的邮轮航线，途径越南、马来西亚、斯里兰卡、印度等国家。广西北海市政府也表示：“北海将借助海上丝绸之路发展邮轮经济”。

二、邮轮旅游市场现状

从国际上看，邮轮产业主要集中于欧洲和北美地区，邮轮市场相对较为成熟，也比较饱和。而亚洲则是后起之秀，香港、新加坡和巴生港邮轮产业的发展也具有一定规模。并且，随着市场的不断扩大，各大公司开拓新市场的愿望越来越迫切，大家都纷纷瞄准了潜力巨大的中国市场。

从国内看，中国经济的发展和人民生活水平的提高，都使得邮轮旅游的推广变得更加容易接受。近十年来，上海、天津、青岛、大连、宁波、厦门、海口、三亚的港口都陆续开始接待国际邮轮的登陆，其中，上海、天津、厦门和三亚是目前我国所拥有四个国际级的邮轮母港。邮轮旅游近十年的平均增速超过30%，也给当地经济带来一股活力。尤其是在2014年，中国邮轮旅游出现“井喷式”发展，出入境游客数量达到120万人次[①]。

随着中国经济的增长，未来几年中国就将成为继美国之后的第二大邮轮消费市场。据交通运输部预计，到2020年，中国邮轮旅客将达到450万左右[②]，成为亚太地区最具活力和最大的邮轮市场。

三、我国邮轮旅游的优势和存在的问题——以海南为例

海南作为我国邮轮旅游重点发展地区，除了具备先天的历史、地理优势以外，还有国家和地方政府的政策扶持。但是尽管如此，海南目前邮轮旅游发展仍

① 《2016—2021年中国港口行业发展前景与市场竞争力分析报告》

② 网易财经：http://news.163.com/14/0604/10/9TT0KKC700014JB5.html

然还处于初级阶段，与其他国外知名港口相比，存在不小的差距。

（一）优势

1. 地理位置优越

海南地处亚太经济带中心，是古代“海上丝绸之路”重要枢纽，即使航线屡次变更，海南依然是国际海运的必经之道。而海南的三亚市，其经纬度类似于“世界邮轮之都”迈阿密。而对比迈阿密，海南具有更有利的地理位置。在最早发展邮轮旅游的中北美洲，邮轮旅游被分成两种市场：可常年开车邮轮旅游活动和只能开展季节性活动。而海南作为我国唯一热带海岛，是可以常年开展邮轮旅游的。

2.基础设施建设情况势头良好

港口城市便利的陆地和航空交通设施是发展邮轮旅游的重要因素，海南目前的公路网络建设受到政府重视，连接旅游景区和景区之间的主干道正在加速建设。

航空交通运输方面，海南目前拥有7个机场，对外开放的只有三亚的凤凰机场和海口的美兰机场。海南另外还计划新增和在建的机场有4个，另外还有一个直升机场用于满足交通需求。

就港口本身而言，海南省拥有两大重要港口——海口港和三亚港。海口港从2012年起成为了北部湾经济带中心枢纽港。另外，海南省政府还将三亚凤凰岛国际邮轮港建设成亚洲最大的邮轮母港，预计2016年底完成。

以上这些都为海南邮轮旅游发展提供了坚实的基础设施和服务平台。

3.政策支持、发展前景良好

邮轮旅游产业链长，涉及的部门多，需要投入的资金量大。我国政府近期宣布将出资400亿美元成立丝路基金，为“一带一路”沿线国家基础设施建设、资源开发、产业合作等有关项目提供融资支持。国际邮轮协会（CLIA）发布的“亚洲邮轮行业发展趋势”指出，2015对于亚洲尤其是中国市场是一个蜕变之年，2015年将有26个邮轮品牌，52艘邮轮在亚洲为最多217万名游客提供1065次邮轮游览和航行[①]。而与之紧密相关的，则是邮轮停靠的母港的整个服务水平和城市形象。这是一个提升港口城市邮轮旅游水平的最佳时机。

（二）存在的问题

虽然近年来海南邮轮旅游发展取得较大的进步，但是就带动当地旅游经济的作用还不明显，主要是受到以下几个原因的影响：

---

① Travel Weekly China：http://www.travelweekly-china.com/32547

1.邮轮经济产业链尚未形成

海南邮轮经济发展到现在，并没有掌握整个邮轮产业最关键最核心的环节。邮轮母港产业链的核心在于邮轮公司，整个邮轮经济都是以邮轮公司作为主导，连带港口码头、旅行社、景区、船舶企业、政府机构等共同协作运行的。海南目前仍未有国际邮轮公司总部驻扎。而整个港口的收益还局限在港口服务、旅客消费和船票代理等方面，并且在整个邮轮经济直接收入中占的比例非常小。而邮轮制造、邮轮公司运营、邮轮港口运营、邮轮商贸等环节上，处于低技术、低附加值的处境。

2.邮轮旅游配套不足、服务欠缺

港口经济效益依赖旅游相关设施和食宿条件。因此，除了提升港口承载邮轮的能力以外，还需要同当地的旅游资源和产业链上的其他环节共同作用。尤其是腹地的旅游资源和配套设施。例如四通八达的交通网络、丰富的传统文化资源、引人入胜的节庆活动以及配套完善的购物中心等。

而目前海南境内的交通网络虽初步形成，但景区与景区之间互通仍有困难，县级公路及以上还需要提高通行能力。尽管海南已有两个对外机场，但是对比另一个国际旅游岛——台湾，其拥有的12个机场，有一半都对外开放。海南的机场数量远远没有达到国际标准。

另外，虽然海南的自然旅游资源非常丰富，但是大部分都属于旅游海岛具备的基础条件，人文旅游资源则相对欠缺。

3.开通航线少，游客选择不多

目前，以海南三亚为邮轮母港开通的固定国际航线班次较少，通往较为短途的海上丝绸之路沿线国家新加坡、马来西亚、泰国的东南亚航线尚未开通。而距离较长的延伸至太平洋、大西洋的远洋航线则更是言之尚早。海南的邮轮线路全球化格局尚未成型。

4.污染问题无法避免

伴随邮轮旅游发展，不可避免地会出现海洋污染问题。一个能承载3000人左右的中等大小的邮轮，每天产生的污染物相当于成千上万的汽车柴油机废气排放量。而与之对应的是，我国尚未建立完善的海洋生态补偿机制，与以生态系统为依据的科学综合海洋管理还存在差距，对邮轮等海洋污染治理缺乏力度。

（三）提高邮轮旅游竞争力对策建议

前面提出的几点问题，既有阻碍海南邮轮旅游发展的因素，也有伴随海南邮轮旅游发展而出现的负外部效应。其他地区的港口城市也有类似问题出现。想要从根本上解决这些问题，需要依靠多方面的途径来协同作用。

1.依托鼓励性政策，完善配套

丝路基金的出台为“一带一路”沿线国家基础设施建设和资源开发等项目提供了融资支持。相对于其他几个港口城市，海南的基础设施建设相对比较缓慢，更是需要争取丝路基金的支持。作为我国邮轮旅游发展的第一梯队，海南三亚港是交通部认定的邮轮运输试点港口。国家旅游局在设立丝绸之路旅游基金的基础上，考虑设置定向可控的海南邮轮旅游专项基金，积极引导企业和民间资金共同参与海南邮轮旅游建设。重点改善交通、旅游集散中心、购物中心等港口经济环节。

并且在构建配套设施的过程中，注入文化元素，以三亚为核心，向周边地区覆盖，增加旅游资源含金量，丰富资源内涵，逐步形成一个邮轮经济综合体，让游客不仅仅是在港口附近游览观光，更有兴趣往腹地走走。实现从基础的邮轮港建设到综合的邮轮城市建设。

与此同时，政府部门也应出台相应的便利措施作为软性支持。例如，允许国外邮轮公司在海南注册和建设经营机构，制定更多国家的免签入境、延长入境时间、离岛免税和落地签证等。这些便利条件都会提升了海南作为邮轮旅游目的地的吸引力。当地政府也可以为邮轮旅游的游客提供了更加便利快捷的通关手续，对外省游客从海南乘坐邮轮出境简化办证程序等。

2.以海上丝绸之路建设为契机，深化区域旅游合作

在国际方面，海南既处于亚太经济圈内又处于东南亚经济圈内，东盟是海南的第一大贸易伙伴，参与海上丝绸之路建设，海南需要东盟各国的支持。以东南亚为基础，依托几大重要国际组织（中国——东盟自由贸易区、APEC、博鳌亚洲论坛组织等），组建海上丝绸之路邮轮旅游联盟，增加与沿途国家的合作，更好更多地开发邮轮旅游项目。并且，海南也已经成功加入全球首创的“亚洲邮轮专案”，目的是拓展邮轮旅游区域合作，资助邮轮公司开发推广包含合作港口的邮轮旅游产品。

在国内，邮轮市场资源争夺日益激烈，海南与广东广西邻近，通过整合三地旅游资源，亦可推进琼粤桂三省联合开展丝路邮轮旅游发展。

通过区域合作，海南可以吸引更多的消费者选择邮轮旅游，也使得亚洲邮轮旅游选择更加丰富，提升吸引力。

3.利用自身特性，获得竞争优势

人们的刻板印象通常认为海南适合冬天旅游，而夏天太热，但事实上海南具备常年邮轮旅游的气候条件。因此，海南还应加大宣传力度，塑造海南常年都适合邮轮旅游的形象。现时有不少旅游景点通过提供影视剧或电视节目的拍摄场地等方式打响知名度，利用粉丝效应获得旅游收入，海南三亚在一定程度上已经取得了不少的收获。但邮轮旅游旅游发展很容易受到政策限制。借助已经奠定的良好群众基础，加上“一带一路”战略的大背景，海南可以将自己的定位做得更加明确。例如申报“XX旅游特区”或是“XX运动指定景区”来获得国家发改委、交通运输部、商务部、甚至体育总局等政府部门的特殊优待，便于更有效地提高在同类型港口城市中的竞争力。

4.完善环保政策，保证环境质量

港口环境评价应该设置更加严格的标准，尤其是在前期港口建设中，就该强调使用新技术、新工艺和节能环保材料，防止污染。而对事后已经造成污染的邮轮和相关单位，要采取更具有操作性的惩治手段。完善港口管理条例和相应的而惩治办法是唯一途径。

（四）海南模式对重庆内河邮轮旅游的借鉴意义

上面对海南三亚提出的提升竞争力的意见同样也可以适用于像重庆这种内河港口城市。重庆虽不属于海上丝绸之路经济带的一环。但是却是陆上丝绸之路的重要节点，并且特殊之处在于重庆还拥有非常良好的水路运输资源。重庆以特有的长江三峡邮轮旅游闻名于世，甚至在国际上都具有一定的知名度和游客基础。“来重庆，必坐船游三峡”的印象深入人心。

近年来，重庆把发展豪华邮轮作为建设长江三峡国际黄金旅游带的重要举措。通过乘坐豪华邮轮的方式游览，在将三峡两岸风光尽收眼底的同时，还可以弥补沿线五星级酒店相对不足的问题。在重庆市政府的大力推动下，重庆五星级邮轮在2014年已经达到30艘以上，接待游客40万人次[①]。

参考海南模式，重庆同样可以利用自身的优势获得优惠政策，并且反之作用于当地各个相关产业联动发展，产生良性循环。吸取海南的教训，从港口建设初期就重视相关地区条例的制度，完善政府管理，避免过度污染。同时，改善城市环境，提升旅游城市形象。加速基础设施建设，联通各个景区之间的要道，做到畅通无阻。还要同长江上游和下游地区的其他兄弟城市做好配合，使整个长江沿

① 新浪新闻：http://news.sina.com.cn/o/2013-03-20/023926581139.shtml

线的邮轮旅游各个环节都能尽善尽美。甚至，重庆还有海南不具备的一项优势，那就是重庆本土民营企业具备制造海华邮轮的能力。重庆的新世纪邮轮公司是国内唯一的上市邮轮公司。

（五）总结

从目前整个邮轮产业来看，欧美国家的邮轮产业更重要的收益是集中在邮轮修造方面，而我们国家由于技术层面原因，自主研发设计制造邮轮尚处于起步阶段。因此，更多的偏重于较为低端的接待环节。但这是我国整个行业发展的必经阶段。我们先从基础的邮轮旅游环节入手，提高国际影响力和竞争力，再依靠“一带一路”政策优势，和其他地区政府以及企业合作，将邮轮经济从下游延伸至上游环节，从根本上提高邮轮产业对整个经济的贡献度，从这一点来说，对我国的传统船舶制造业向高端发展转型也具有现实意义。

参考文献：

[1] 刘卫东.“一带一路”战略的科学内涵与科学问题[J].地理科学进展，2015(5): 538-544.

[2] 郭鹏等.丝绸之路经济带旅游业格局与国际旅游合作模式研究[J].资源科学，2014.36(12): 2459-2467.

[3] 王柏玲等.对当前我国发展邮轮旅游产业的认识和思考[J].中国商贸，2010(10).

[4] 田言付.国际邮轮游客对三亚港口旅游接待的挑战[J].港口纵横，2010(1).

[5] 齐静文等.着力提升邮轮旅游竞争力[J].今日海南，2015(4).

[6] 梁晓杰.邮轮产业—上海国际行业中心建设新的增长领域[J].世界海运，2010(3).

[7] 潘勤奋.国际邮轮经济发展模式及对我国的启示[J].科技和产业，2007(10).

[8] 韩宏涛.上海发展国际邮轮经济研究[D].上海：上海海事大学，2005.

[9] 中国(海南)改革发展研究院.2020年的海南[M].北京：中国经济出版社，2011.

[10] Ross K. Dowling. Cruise Ship Tourism[M]. Wallingford: CABI, 2006.

（作者简介：邹思晓，女，四川外国语大学国别经济与国际商务研究中心，讲师，硕士，研究方向：国际旅游管理）

阿尔及利亚撒哈拉沙漠旅游资源研究

闵敏　潘雷

摘要：撒哈拉沙漠是全世界面积最大的沙漠，但是这片不毛之地中却有着不同寻常的旅游资源。本文主要研究阿尔及利亚撒哈拉沙漠中的珍贵旅游资源——双重世界遗产塔西里高原，塔西里以奇特的沙漠地貌和史前人类留下的石刻和岩画而著名。笔者在阿尔及利亚期间曾亲自到访该地，获得大量第一手资料，本论文中所谈论的撒哈拉沙漠旅游过程中的交通、饮食、住宿、行程安排等均来自该第一手资料。

关键词：阿尔及利亚；撒哈拉；塔西里；阿杰尔；世界遗产

阿尔及利亚位于非洲北部，地中海南岸，是非洲面积最大的国家，但是其总面积的百分之85%都是撒哈拉沙漠。在撒哈拉沙漠中有独一无二的旅游资源，吸引着世界各地的游客前往撒哈拉沙漠探险。目前，前往撒哈拉沙漠旅游的游客多数还是西方人，但是中国人的面孔已经越来越多地出现在撒哈拉沙漠了，他们多是在阿尔及利亚工作居住的中国人，随着阿尔及利亚逐步开放旅游业，前往撒哈拉沙漠探险的人将越来越多，当然这其中也包括中国游客，因此，我们有必要更全面地研究了解撒哈拉沙漠的旅游资源。

一、撒哈拉沙漠的历史

远在新石器时代，即公元前9000年到公元前2500年期间，撒哈拉地区的气候湿润，这个地区的广大土地上覆盖着植被，人类和多种动物在这里生活，例如鸵鸟、长颈鹿、大象、羚羊。当时撒哈拉地区还有几个大的湖泊，水源很充沛，所以还生活着各种鱼类、鳄鱼、河马。这些有利的条件使得狩猎部落定居于此，之后是牧民，他们在各个高地和土壤肥沃的地区定居下来。

到公元前1200年，除了尼罗河周边地区之外，撒哈拉地区全部变成了不毛之地，人类再也不适合在此居住了，但是过去的时光却通过前人所绘刻的分散在撒哈拉沙漠各个角落的石刻和岩画立体地保存了下来。那些岩石变成了一幅幅的图画，记录着古代北非居民如何适应改变的自然环境，如何获得工具，如何形成新的习惯。撒哈拉沙漠中超过一半的石刻和岩画都集中在阿尔及利亚的塔西里·阿杰尔（طاسيلي ناجر أو تاسيلي نعاجر）（在图阿雷格语中，意为众峡谷平原），其他的石刻和岩画分布在利比亚沙漠和尼日尔北部。到目前为止，被发现的石刻和岩画超过三万处。这些石刻和岩画可以划分为四个时期：

（一）消失时期（狩猎时期，公元前5000年以前）

在这一时期，石刻中的动物体型都比较大，这些动物当时在当地都已经灭绝了，这些动物有野牛、大象、犀牛、长颈鹿、羚羊、河马。岩刻当中并没有被驯服动物的记载。石刻中还反映出人的形象，他们是武装着棍子、长矛和斧子的。这一时期岩刻的经典作品位于杜杰拉山谷（وادي دجيرات），长颈鹿的岩刻位于尼日尔的埃尔（أير بالنيجر），还有一些位于利比亚。

（二）牧人时期（公元前4500年—公元前2500年）

在公元前4500年到公元前4000年，牲畜群出现在了北非地区，这一时间段和牧人时期的时间段相吻合。绝大多数的石刻和岩画都追溯到牧人时期。岩画中有些情景是一些人在专注地从事自己每天的工作，有一些则是被驯化的牲口：绵羊、山羊，有时候放牧的人就站在自己牲口群旁边。这些岩画看上去更美，因为有了颜色：红色和白色。有人认为作画的人就是这些放牧的人，他们描绘部落的生活场景，这些部落就好像现在苏丹的努巴部落（قبائل النوبة في السودان）和尼日尔的弗拉尼部落（القبائل الفولانية في النيجر）。牧人时期的岩画多分布在塔西里和利比亚的阿卡库斯山（جبال أكاكوس في ليبيا）。

（三）马匹时期（公元前2500年—公元前1200年）

这一时期的岩画所反映的是装备了小型武器的人类和马拉的车子。所以人们认为马匹开始在撒哈拉地区被使用是在这一阶段。和前一时期的岩画比起来，这一时期的岩画中，人显得更矮，体型更瘦削。

（四）骆驼时期（公元前1200年）

到这个时期为止，北非已经完成了沙漠化的进程，作为“沙漠之舟”的骆驼取代了马出现在人们的生活中和石头上的画里。但是由于撒哈拉沙漠面积太大，当地的政治情况又极其复杂，所以关于石刻和岩画的研究还非常有限，人们还不能很好地理解石刻和岩画的内容。

二、撒哈拉沙漠旅游资源的分布

阿尔及利亚撒哈拉沙漠最著名的旅游资源位于塔西里高原，阿拉伯语直译为“塔西里·阿杰尔”，阿拉伯语的意思是拥有众多河流的高原。塔希里高原实际上是位于伊犁基省（ولاية إليزي）的一连串山脉的组合，高原位于阿尔及利亚最南部靠近利比亚、尼日尔边境的撒哈拉沙漠腹地，高原海拔2000米，总面积达到12000平方千米。塔西里高原是阿尔及利亚国家自然公园，也是自然和人文双重世界文化遗产，1982年被联合国教科文组织列入世界遗产名录，自然遗产指的是当地奇特的地貌特征，长期风化后奇形怪状的岩石组成的石林，好似一座座被时间遗忘并被风沙严重侵蚀的古老城市遗址；人文遗产指的是史前人类留下的诸多石刻和岩画，描绘了当时人们舞蹈、狩猎的情况，还描绘了很多动物的形象，如长颈鹿、牛等，除了现实当中存在的人和动物，岩画中还有一些现实中不存在的生物，有人说那是想象中的生物，有人说是外星生物，有人说是来自未来的生物。塔西里地区有两个主要城市接待旅游者，一个是伽奈特（جنات أو جانت أو جانات)，另一个是塔纳拉塞特（تامنغست أو تمنراست)。塔纳拉塞特最著名的旅游景点是塔希里高原的最高峰——海拔2700米的哈格尔峰（أهقار)，爬到哈格尔峰去看日出是当地一个传统的旅游项目；而伽奈特最著名的则是石刻“哭泣的牛”和被印在1000阿尔及利亚第纳尔钞票上的著名岩画“卧牛”。需要指出的是，不管是奇特地貌还是史前人类痕迹，都是星罗棋布、零零散散地分布在面积为12000平方千米的土地上，一个景点与一个景点之前往往有数小时车程，旅行者更不要期望在几天内将所有的景点都看完。笔者个人以为塔纳拉塞特更侧重于自然文化遗产，也就是奇特的地貌，而伽奈特更偏重于人文遗产，即史前人类留下的痕迹，因为从阿尔及利亚本国出版的地图上来看，史前人类的岩画标志基本上集中在伽奈特地区。

三、适合撒哈拉沙漠旅游的季节

撒哈拉沙漠地区自然环境极其恶劣，夏季白天温度太高，不适合开展旅游活动，事实上夏季也没有人去撒哈拉沙漠旅游，撒哈拉沙漠的旅游在夏季是处于停滞状态的，就连沙漠腹地的常住民有些人在盛夏时节也要搬到沙漠边缘的城市去“避暑”。撒哈拉沙漠地区的旅游活动一般在冬季进行，一般是从11月份到第二年的3月份。如果游客在晚秋或是早春季节前往，白天的温度已经不低了，游客会感受到撒哈拉沙漠极大的“热情”，但在这个季节出游的好处是晚上并不太寒冷。如果选在严冬季节出行，比如在十二月底或一月初前往，游客一点儿都不会感到沙漠的炙热，因为冬季的沙漠即使在白天也是寒风凛冽，比较寒冷，需要穿羽绒服；到了夜间，气温会降到更低，就算穿上羽绒服也会感到异常寒冷，如果选择在旷野中搭帐篷露营，就算和衣而睡再盖上两张羊毛毯，早上太阳升起之前的那段最寒冷的时段依然很可能被冻醒。

四、前往撒哈拉沙漠旅游的方式

在阿尔及利亚首都阿尔及尔和其他城市有当地旅行社组织旅行团前往撒哈拉旅游，但并不是每一家旅行社都有能力有资质组织团队前往撒哈拉沙漠的。还有的旅行社会告诉你，外国人是不允许前往撒哈拉地区的，但事实上阿尔及利亚政府并没有这种强制性的规定。有一些能够组团去撒哈拉沙漠的旅行社，比如在首都的贝尼·买苏斯（بني مسوس）区，有一家私人旅行社组织去塔纳拉赛特，为期8天，其中6天在撒哈拉沙漠中露营，费用6万阿尔及利亚第纳尔；在首都市中心的帝督市大街（Didouche）还有一家名为ONAT的旅行社，是一家国有旅行社，组织去伽奈特为期6天的旅行团，其中有4天在撒哈拉沙漠中露营，费用为5万5千阿尔及利亚第纳尔。笔者曾于2014年底到2015年初参加ONAT的旅行团前往伽奈特，在沙漠中露营，本文中所提到的饮食、住宿、行程安排等信息均是笔者参加这个旅行团的第一手真实资料。

以上所说是第一种方式，从首都或是其他城市报团，然后前往。也可以采用第二种方式，即首先自己前往伽奈特或是塔纳拉赛特，然后在当地再寻找当地旅行社。如果游客采用第二种方式，必须提前和当地旅行社沟通好，确认当地旅行社是否还有名额接待你。伽奈特和塔纳拉赛特当地从事旅游业的旅行社并不多，接待能力有限，游客行前务必和当地旅行社沟通确认好。

五、交通

从首都前往伽奈特一般乘坐飞机，有两个航空公司执行这条航线的飞行任务，一个是阿尔及利亚航空公司，另一个是塔西里航空公司。如果飞机中途不经停的话飞行时间在2个小时左右，如果经停，4个小时左右。阿尔及利亚航空往返票价接近3万阿尔及利亚第纳尔，如果在首都报好旅行社，旅行社会为游客买好票，只需要1万5千阿尔及利亚第纳尔左右。

航空公司	航班号	起点	起飞时间	终点	降落时间	是否经停
阿尔及利亚航空	AH6292	阿尔及尔	周三22:00	伽奈特	周四00:15	否
	AH6312		周四22:00		周五00:15	否
	AH6486		周六9:30		周六14:10	一站经停
	AH6292		周六22:00		周日00:15	否
	AH6233	伽奈特	周一03:15	阿尔及尔	周一05:30	否
	AH6313		周五01:15		周五04:55	一站经停
	AH6233		周六03:15		周六05:30	否
	AH6313		周六15:00		周六18:30	否
塔西里航空	SF2360	阿尔及尔	周一12:00	伽奈特	周一15:50	一站经停
	SF2361	伽奈特	周一16:20	阿尔及尔	周一20:10	一站经停

①

在撒哈拉沙漠旅行必须要依托一个团队，要么是在其他城市报好的团，要么是在撒哈拉当地报的团。如果自己租一辆车，找一个向导去沙漠旅行是很危险的，因为这辆车一旦出了故障，没有同伴可以支援你。旅行团一般都会组织5、6辆车一起行动。伽奈特和塔纳拉赛特当地的越野车都是九十年代初日本生产的丰田兰德酷路泽或是日产的途乐，车况比较差，有的车尾气排放口一直排放着黑烟；有的车前引擎盖盖不上，用安全带一边固定在引擎盖上，一边固定在前保险杠上，借助安全带的锁扣将引擎盖盖上；还有的车电池没有电，启动车的时候打不着火，需要借助别的车上的电池才能发动汽车。诸如此类的问题如果发生了，身边又没有别的车可以帮忙，沙漠中手机是完全没有信号的，那么生命都可能会受到威胁。

六、撒哈拉沙漠的餐饮

（一）早餐

冬天的撒哈拉沙漠，清晨时分异常寒冷。早餐仍旧是阿尔及利亚的传统内容：法式长棍面包，这种面包刚烤出来的时候又香又脆，吃起来非常可口，但过了一天左右就会变得很硬、很有劲道、很有嚼头，咬下一块儿来很费力，吃在嘴里需要用力咀嚼很长一段时间也嚼不烂，最后勉强下咽。沙漠里的长棍面包尤其如此，再加上低气温的冷冻，吃起来更是费力，而且冰冷难以下咽。阿尔及利亚人吃法棍面包常搭配的黄油也被冻住了，用刀切起来都很困难。早餐的饮品有热

---

① 数据来源于阿尔及利亚航空公司官方网站www.airalgerie.dz和塔西里航空公司官方网站www.tassiliairlines.dz。

水冲调的奶粉和现煮的咖啡，热饮在那种寒冷的环境下变成了异常珍贵的稀缺资源，成了众游客追捧的对象。在沙漠露营期间，每天的早餐无一例外，都是这样的安排。早餐时间早上七点。

（二）午餐

在沙漠露营期间的午餐都是冷餐沙拉，由随队的厨师现场制作，一大盘蔬菜金枪鱼肉米饭沙拉，沙拉最底层由米饭摆成一个金字塔型，在上面铺上多种蔬菜，番茄、生菜、胡萝卜、甜菜、土豆、洋葱……，最上面摆上切成一半一半的煮鸡蛋和金枪鱼肉，金枪鱼肉是现成的金枪鱼罐头，蔬菜除了生菜和洋葱外其他也是煮好的。还有水果，苹果、橙子、橘子。主食还是法国长棍面包。

午餐一般在十二点、一点钟，第一天的时候由于赶路，直到下午四点才用午餐。

（三）晚餐

每天的晚餐都有餐前汤（شربة），是一种用库斯库斯（سكسك）和胡萝卜、土豆、肉类、香料熬制的汤，在夜晚寒冷的环境下喝下去起来非常舒服，主食是法国长棍面包。有一天吃的是库斯库斯，是一种北非当地特有的食物，黄色的，像小米一样，蒸熟之后浇上炖好的肉汤来食用。有一天食用当地图阿雷格人用传统手法烧制的囊，在沙地上挖一个坑，将面粉制成的囊胚放进去，将坑里堆满木头，使木头燃烧起来，就这样将下面的囊胚烤熟。等囊烧熟之后，掰成小块儿拌在咖喱焖饭里食用，囊吃起来非常脆，味道鲜美。沙漠露营期间的最后一顿晚餐是烤全羊。

晚餐时间和中国不同，很晚，有时晚上九点，有时晚上十点。

（四）饮水

和几辆越野车同行的还有一辆皮卡作为补给车，补给车上装载有一路上所需的食物和水，这辆车一般都是提前到我们要去的目的地安营扎寨做饭，等我们到了饭也差不多做好了。水装在两个大塑料桶里，桶里有水舀子，用水舀子取水来喝，或者游客自己带有杯子、瓶子，用水舀子从桶里舀水倒入瓶中或杯中喝。沙漠地区风沙大，水中难免会混有沙子，喝水的时候喝到沙子，吃饭的时候饭里面有沙子也都是很正常的事情。沙漠中是买不到水的，所以只能喝补给车上的水。

在沙漠中除了能喝到水，还能喝到咖啡和茶。撒哈拉的茶在阿尔及利亚是很有名的，把茶叶放到黄铜壶里，放上水，放在火上煮开，煮开后将茶水倾倒入一个敞口铝壶当中，一共有两个这样的铝壶，将茶水在这两个铝壶中来回反复倾倒数十次，直到茶水表面飘起一层厚厚的泡沫，泡沫的厚度和茶水的厚度相当。到这个时候，将茶水倒进小酒盅大小的玻璃茶杯当中，分给游客享用。喝撒哈拉沙漠的茶有讲究，一只玻璃茶杯里的茶上一半是泡沫，下一半是茶水，三口将泡沫和茶水喝光：第一口，甜的，像爱情一样甜；第二口，苦的，像生活一样苦；第三口，淡淡的，像死亡一样平淡。这句话反映出撒哈拉居民现实生活的艰苦，还反映出他们的世界观、人生观和对于死亡的态度。

七、撒哈拉沙漠的住宿

由于飞机晚上夜里到达伽奈特的时候已经是三点了，到达旅馆差不多凌晨四点了，在旅馆睡了一晚，第二天早上十点钟集合。宾馆位于伽奈特城区，条件比较简陋，共有两层，没有电梯。房间里用油漆粉刷的墙面，有电视，有空调。到伽奈特的第一天晚上在这家宾馆住一宿，最后一个白天从沙漠返回伽奈特城后在旅馆洗澡休息，乘坐夜里的航班返回阿尔及尔。

有四天的时间是露营，两个人用的那种露营帐篷，帐篷比较小，仅够两个成年人睡下，一个人一张海绵垫子，两张毛毯。晚上都是和衣而睡，但早上还是会被冻醒，自己如果带一个睡袋的话，情况应该会有所好转。

四天露营，其中有一天是住在图阿雷格人的村庄里，房子的墙是用形状不规则的石头垒起来的，所以石头之间会有缝隙，石头之间并没有粘合剂。房子中央有一根椰枣树干，房顶是用椰枣树枝和树叶铺成的，也有缝隙。风会从石头间的缝隙和屋顶的缝隙中刮进来。房屋的地面是沙子地，门是用椰枣树枝编成的栅栏门。睡觉的时候将海绵垫子铺在沙子地上，盖上两张毛毯。

八、行程安排

第一天夜里坐飞机到伽奈特，入住旅馆。

第二天上午出发前往撒哈拉沙漠，一路上行，海拔一路攀高，高原上都是黑色支离破碎的石块，远处的山体外侧岩体都碎裂垮塌了下来，堆积在山脚下，而中心的山体依然屹立着，仿佛几亿年前这里发生了巨大的地震或是爆炸将这些山都炸碎了。四个小时之后来到一个图阿雷格人的村庄吃午饭，这时已经是下午了。在这个村庄休息，吃晚饭，过夜。这个村庄里的电能是靠太阳能供给的，白天太阳能电池板充电，到晚上使用，这个村庄里的人没有什么电器，消耗电能的就只有电灯。电能也不能无限使用，从天黑到晚上八、九点钟，太阳能储存的电能就会耗光。在撒哈拉沙漠仰望天空，满天的繁星，天顶周围的星星最多最密集，越往地平线星星越稀疏。

第三天去看史前人类留下的石刻，那是一块平铺在地上的巨大岩石。在这块岩石的表面上刻有各种动物的图案，其中最大的一幅图案是一头巨大的牛，牛的身体上布满了螺旋状的花纹。还有其他小图案也是牛的造型，阿尔及利亚面值1000元货币上的卧牛图案就来源于这里，除了牛之外，还有长颈鹿等动物的造型。游客可以登上这座巨大的岩石，但是不能穿鞋。然后驱车在布满碎石的戈壁旷野中驰骋，来到一处峡谷的入口。这里有阿尔及利亚军人检查游客的身份证和护照。峡谷中的河床上布满了沙子，车子开在上面尘土飞扬，这时候才发现图阿雷格人长长的头巾把嘴也遮了起来，有效地阻挡了尘土。沙漠中日照强烈，风沙大，图阿雷格人的头巾能有效地遮挡太阳并阻止沙尘进入口鼻，防止自然界对人体的侵害。峡谷两侧峭壁高悬，峭壁是一层一层的，仿佛是摆放得歪歪扭扭摞起来的盘子堆，这里凸出来一块儿，那里凹进去一块儿，有许多块儿巨石看起来摇摇欲坠，如果来一场地震，这些摇摇欲坠的峭壁土崩瓦解的话，就会将峡谷全部掩埋。当地的图阿雷格人说不用担心，撒哈拉沙漠从来都没有地震，那些“危岩”也绝对不会掉下来。但是在峭壁的底部堆满了大大小小的碎石块儿，明显是从岩体上脱落下来的，这些石头又是什么时候脱落下来的呢？车子开到峡谷腹地停了下来，晚上在峡谷中露营过夜。

第四天，徒步进入峡谷深处。在隆冬时节，撒哈拉沙漠腹地的峡谷深处，长满了各种各样的植物，有的植物还点缀着硕大的花朵，沙地上到处都是鹅卵石，证明这里曾经有丰沛的水资源。峡谷的深处道路变得极其狭窄，峭壁高耸，阳光被峭壁所阻挡，还可以看到水塘，在峡谷的尽头有一处较大的水塘。离近了仔细观看，就会发现峭壁上的岩石实际上就是由一粒一粒的沙子构成的，我猜测，由于长期的风化作用，山体中的沙粒被一粒一粒地剥离下来，沙漠慢慢地便形成了。在我们露营处不远，还有图阿雷格人居住，几户人家，政府还为他们打了水井，可见峡谷地区还是有地下水资源的。徒步进入峡谷后又徒步走出，然后驱车前往黄沙漫漫的地区。塔西里地区的沙漠并不是一望无际的黄沙，而是交叉了多种地形的沙漠，有戈壁，有黄沙，有峡谷，有山峰。在一望无际的黄沙中露营，傍晚欣赏沙漠中的落日。站在高高的沙丘上，可以看到远处的戈壁上有植物生长，沿着植物生长的轨迹，可以判断那是一条地下河。

第五天前往各个零散的地点去看史前人类留下的石刻和岩画，其中最有名的一幅石刻叫做“哭泣的牛”。据笔者观察，凡是能够完整或部分保留下来的石刻和岩画，均是绘于或刻在避风的地方，比如两块巨大岩石相交且凹陷进去的地方，这样的地方风吹不到。撒哈拉沙漠的风很大，壁画和岩刻如果绘在或刻在迎风的一面，久而久之会被风刮掉。这一天露营的这个地方风尤其大，所有游客将帐篷搭成一排，就好像一排沙丘一样，这样可以防风。晚上是新年晚会，食物是烤全羊，还有图阿雷格人乐队伴奏，但风是在是太大了，天气实在是太冷了，穿了羽绒服再披上两床毛毯还是很冷，脚都被冻僵了。刚烤好的羊肉送到手里的时候肉的脂肪就已经凝固了。

第六天，从沙漠返回伽奈特城，到达第一天夜里下榻的旅馆。因为已经六天没有洗澡、刷牙了，所以返回旅馆后的第一件事情就是洗澡。洗完澡后步行前往伽奈特城边的图阿雷格人村庄用午饭。伽奈特城非常小，走路的话二十分钟就可以把全城逛遍。村庄的房屋都是用椰枣树的树枝和树叶搭成的，村里面种满了高高的椰枣树，上面缀满了沉甸甸成熟的椰枣，椰枣是真主给沙漠居民的馈赠，椰枣里含有丰富的维生素，以至于阿尔及利亚有种说法，一天吃三颗椰枣就能满足一天身体所需要的维生素。午饭后在伽奈特城里的市场里转转，有很多当地特色的产品可以购买，比如图阿雷格人长长的缠头巾，当地人还会教你如何将头和嘴都裹得严严实实的；还有质地粗糙但非常厚实的宗教隐士修炼服，衣服很长，到脚踝，穿上后马上增加了宗教的神秘感；还有撒哈拉沙漠的特产沙漠玫瑰石——一种主要成分为含水硫酸钙，形状酷似玫瑰的石头，有很高的观赏价值。晚餐地点和午餐地点一样，晚餐过后前往机场乘飞机返回首都阿尔及尔，到达首都的时间是第七天凌晨五点左右。旅行结束。

总结

撒哈拉沙漠的旅游资源是丰富的，独特的，在世界其他地方很难看到相同的景色。撒哈拉沙漠旅游方兴未艾，可开发的空间还很大。但是在撒哈拉旅游条件较为艰苦，不管是露营还是旅馆，所以想去撒哈拉旅游的游客一定要做好充分的心理准备。

参考文献：

[1] http://lexicorient.com/algeria/tassilin.htm

[2] http://www.el-mouradia.dz/arabe/algerie/Histoire/tassili/ALG-tassili.htm

[3] http://www.fjexpeditions.com/tassili.html
[4] 赵慧杰.阿尔及利亚.社会科学文献出版社，2006年1月1日.

（作者简介：闵敏，女，四川外国语大学东方语学院，讲师，硕士，研究方向：阿拉伯社会文化；潘雷，男，四川外国语大学东方语学院，讲师，硕士，研究方向：阿拉伯社会文化）

“一带一路”战略下开展国际旅游合作的策略选择

姬妍婷

摘要：在2013年9月7日，习近平总书记在哈斯克斯坦演讲时提出了丝绸之路经济合作的建议，同年，习近平总书记在印度尼西亚会议中在此强调发展“21世纪海上丝绸之路”的构想，提出了“一带一路”的基本战略。本文主要介绍了一带一路的历史及战略意义，并进一步分析了“一带一路”开拓国际旅游合作战略的必要性以及实现“一带一路”战略下开展国际旅游合作的影响。

关键词：丝绸之路；“一带一路”；基本战略；国际旅游；合作

一、“一带一路”的历史及战略意义

“一带一路”指的是丝绸之路。丝绸之路起源于我国古代时期，它连接了亚非欧三个区域的贸易，丝绸之路也分为海上丝绸之路与陆上丝绸之路。最初，丝绸之路是用来运输丝绸等产品，是中国输出产品的一种渠道，最后，它逐渐演变成为了一条连接中国与西方贸易的交通纽带，成为一种中国对外贸易的载体。

陆上丝绸之路，由汉代的张骞出使西域开始，从西汉的长安穿过了中西亚，直到罗马帝国。丝绸之路有着不同的走向，可以分为北方丝绸之路与南方丝绸之路这两种。北方丝绸之路也可称为草原丝绸之路，途经河西走廊和新疆一代，然后划分为北、中、南三条路线。所谓南方的丝绸之路，也被称为“茶马古道”，它起源于今天的四川，途经云南达到印度，是中国国际通道中最为古老的一条。

海上丝绸之路，是中国与世界打开海上贸易的交通通道，也被称为“陶瓷之路”，这条道路可以分为东南西三个航线，其中，东洋航线主要是打开日本与朝鲜的市场，南洋航线主要打开的是东南亚各国的市场，西洋航线主要是打开欧洲各国以及东非地区市场的航线。

丝绸之路作为一个集政治、经济、文化为一体的交流载体，在开启这条通道之前，中国通常都是以“军事征服”为主，我们可以看到，秦始皇修万里长城就证明了此观点。

随着汉武帝派遣张骞出使西域，以往的“军事制服”对外策略改变了，成为了“广地万里，重九译，威德便于四海”的交流方式，体现出了我泱泱大国对外的融合。除此之外，丝绸之路的开辟，将中国从单一的朝贡关系多元化，形成了集市舶贸易、朝贡贸易、官方及民间交往的多重贸易体系。

由于贸易体系走向了多元化，丝绸之路的作用已经不简简单单地只是服务于经济贸易，同时也超出了这个范畴，文化的影响可以说更为浓重。从玄奘取经到意大利的马可·波罗，中西方的文化在不断相互往来，世界的文化交流也在不断发展。不仅如此，南洋人口的迁移使得儒家文化在全国范围内初具规模，以这样一种文化圈的构建，逐渐使得儒家文化成为了国家精神文明传播的纽带。

所以，丝绸之路它构建的不是简单的一种贸易关系，而是一种对外的智慧体系，它和单方面的殖民以及军事制裁不同，它体现的是一种和平共处的原则，它向往的是平等、友好，而不是暴力和欺压掠夺，从中我们可以看出中国人自古以来的外交态度，对国外人民的尊重和包容，无论我们处在什么样的环境下，这一点始终都没有变。

古代的丝绸之路并不是单纯的海权或者陆权的经济，而是实现海陆联动的一个综合性通道系统，力求在良好的外部环境作用下，实现各国之间的相互往来，通过海陆通道，弥补各个国家之间资源短缺的问题，使得国家对外贸易的道路更加畅通无阻。

在唐朝末期之前，陆权经济的优势明显要高于海权经济，陆地上的丝绸之路，发展要明显快于海上的丝绸之路。汉武帝派遣张骞出使西域，是从中国的最高政府层面出发，建设了良好的开端。经过了魏晋时期的荣辱跌宕，到了隋唐时期，丝绸之路又再次进入繁荣达到了全盛时期。不断有新的商路被开辟，到达亚洲的各个角落以及欧洲地区。唐末因为政治方面的“安史之乱”使得中原政权再度不稳定，阻碍了亚欧大陆的友好往来，陆上丝绸之路陷入了一个低谷。

随着唐末的到来，陆上的丝绸之路也渐渐衰败，海上丝绸之路渐渐崛起，再次使得中国的对外贸易壮大了起来。

在张骞出使西域之后，他虽然开辟了陆上贸易，但是海上贸易方面，汉朝的商人在一点一滴地探索，直到东汉时期，海上的丝绸之路真正地形成了。但其真正的崛起是在唐末宋初，随着通航国家的数量不断上升，宋代时期有58国，到了元代时期已经有了200多个国家和地区都已经实现了通航，然而郑和下西洋的范围已经达到了东非。到了明末时期，国家开始实行海禁，官方贸易逐渐退出历史舞台，但是民间的贸易却愈演愈烈。到了鸦片战争之后，中国的海权丧落他国手中，海上的丝绸之路归给了西方的殖民者。

从历史的角度来看，海上丝绸之路和陆上丝绸之路是并肩发展的。古代时期西北战事频繁，东南沿海也有倭寇侵扰，海陆的兴衰主要取决于国家的实力，国家的军事、外交实力是对外贸易的最佳保障。南方丝绸之路的发展，也告诉了我们海陆联通始终是我国对外贸易不能缺少的一个部分。与此同时，海陆通道的共同开辟，为我国打开了多个对外交流的窗口，海上丝绸之路主要面对的是东南亚地区以及儒教、佛教盛行的地区，陆上丝绸之路主要面对的是中亚地区的伊斯兰文明国家。

古代的丝绸之路的存在和发展，不仅为中国对外贸易的格局改变划上了浓重的一笔，同时也使得我国城镇的内部格局在不断变化。海上、陆上的丝绸之路使得长江黄河一线的城镇格局逐渐向外拓展，促进国家产生沿线城镇的居住模式，更进一步使得我国城镇从政治、农业中心逐渐走向了手工业和工商业的道路，实现城镇功能的转变。

海上丝绸之路有效地推动了西北地区人口的聚集和发展，通过丝绸之路，成功地将中原地区的农耕技术传向了一些军事地区、宗教文化传播地区以及少数民族的聚集地区，以此促进了更多地区的发展，逐渐形成构造复杂的城镇布局。在隋唐时期，沿海城市的经济逐渐增强，呈现出商业、手工业以及交通运输业聚融的特性。与此同时，复杂的政治军事、民族特色文化、佛教文化以及戎装要地，都被发展得极具特色。

海上丝绸之路推动了中国港口的开发与手工业城镇的雄起。在汉代时期，就有了琅琊港、褐石港、徐闻、合浦、南海港这几个港口坐落边远地区的格局，也就是现今的青岛、烟台、湛江、防城港市以及广州这些地区的雏形。到了唐代，又有了东来、永宁、梁安等港口，成为了温州、泉州的雏形，总的来说，广州港的规模最大。到了宋元时期，沿海地区形成了东、南两条航线，其中泉州就凭借位于东、南两个航路之间的优势，逐渐成为了最具贸易优势的港口。在广州和泉州，政府分别设置了市舶司。除此之外，景德镇等内部手工业城市也因海上丝绸之路的繁荣而得到了相应的发展。

二、“一带一路”开拓国际旅游合作战略的必要性

（一）落实战略思想的实践需要

专家认为，旅游业就是促进经济与文化交流，不同地区间人民友好交流的一种重要方式，

作为一带一路的先导产业，我们要重点落实共享和共建的原则，有效地开展国际旅游路线，进而提升区域之间的经济、政治方面的交流与合作，增强政治信任，实现经济互补，以地势优势和经济优势最终转化为具有实践意义的合作方式，这就是一带一路的战略目标。国际旅游项目的推出正好符合当下一带一路战略思想的需求，所以，实现二者的合作十分有必要。

（二）落实发展的需要

合作作为发展的主体，在一带一路项目中，合作是基石。所以，我国一贯奉行和平友好合作、开放包容、相互借鉴、互利共赢的方式，重新塑造丝绸之路对我们生活的影响，在未来的发展过程中，共同构建新的历史篇章。国际旅游项目也应该紧紧跟随发展的需要，学会与沿线国家相互协作，否则就会被时代抛弃。

（三）国际旅游发展的需要

国际旅游本身就是一个具有合作性质的产业，要想切实有效地提升自身发展的成效，就需要从合作开始，没有良好的合作理念就不可能充分地壮大国际旅游的项目。在当下，国民生活物质水平在显著提升，人们对于文化的追溯、对风景名胜的向往已经成为一种大众趋势，所以，国际旅游不能放弃这样一个机会，要牢牢把握时代特色和发展的契机，营造出一个更广阔的发展空间。“一带一路”将从多边和双边各个层面推进命运共同体建设。“一带一路”和人类命运共同体均是合作、发展的理念和倡议，不是一个实体和机制，将充分依靠中国与有关国家既有的双边多边机制，借助当前行之有效的区域合作平台形成互动。通过与60多个国家、40多亿人口建立广泛的沟通和协作机制，形成推动人类合作共赢发展的新格局。

三、实现一带一路战略下开展国际旅游合作的影响

（一）加速亚洲经济一体化进程

一带一路的国际旅游合作，有效地成为了经济连接的翅膀，实现了东南亚、

南亚和东北亚地区的发展，尤其改善了整体的互联状况和商业环境。亚洲作为世界经济发展不可或缺的重要部分，在世界经济中的力量不容小觑，但是也面临着诸多的问题。例如，亚洲一体化的整体水平和欧洲、北美洲的实力水平相比，还存在着一定的差距。在2015年的博鳌亚洲论坛中我们曾提到，在经济危机的影响下以及经济复苏状况不堪的情况下，亚洲在全球经济一体化的进程中要面临着更加艰巨的挑战。在2013年，亚洲对自身的贸易依存度由以往的59.49%下降到了53.01%，亚洲内部的贸易增长率由原来的8%降到了5%，亚洲在世界价值链上的区域依存度从原来的61.1%下降到了60.1%。亚洲国家有着巨大的生产效力，如果可以扩张到亚洲区域的市场内部环境，则可以有更多的投入品从发达地区转向亚洲地区，亚洲可以获得新的增长动力。与此同时，亚洲区域之间存在着发展不平衡性，缺乏紧密有效的联系，交通设施没有连接，或是及时连接了也有不通的现象，通了也多有不畅，这些问题的突出性，已经成为了深化区域合作的障碍。实现一带一路的旅游国际合作，涵盖了亚洲的26个国家地区，包括了44亿人口以及20多万亿美元的经济规模。一带一路在国际金融危机时，发挥了自身的产能、技术与资金优势，有效地将经验规模转化为了市场动力，将市场与合作的优势最大化，通过一带一路，有效地促进亚洲国家的改革，分享发展红利，实现多个国家的对话、合作，建立更为平等、均衡的利益关系，实现亚洲经济一体化，一同处理经济问题，并开创良好的未来。

一带一路战略有效地化解了亚太地区经济发展进程中的诸多难题，当下，亚太经济一体化主要要解决的问题是经济水平的差异性。在亚太地区，不仅有美国、日本和新加坡这些发达国家，同时也有越南、菲律宾这些相对落后的发展中国家。其中，不同领域的人均GDP就已经反映了不同成员对于利益的需求。一个统一的方案是难以满足这些不同区域、不同发展程度的成员的需求的，所以，在亚太经济合作发展中，很多贸易自由化的方案得不到根本性的落实，最终导致项目的落空，其中“茂物目标”作为著名的发展事件，因为发达国家的实验导致目标最终没有得到落实。除此之外，亚太经济成员在社会制度和政治格局中也存在着一定的差异，为经济一体化带来了重重挑战。在一带一路国际旅游合作项目的开展下，未来亚太地区也将走向辐射性的发展路线，以自身的影响力来散布贸易网络。共建一带一路的国际旅游合作有助于促进亚太国家之间的相互交流，实现互利共赢，进一步增强亚太国家在政治、经济文化方面的交流程度，切实有效地促进亚太合作一体化。

（二）打破亚欧大陆长期封闭的状态

亚欧大陆作为世界上面积最大的陆地版块，面积共有5000万平方千米，占据了世界版图的1/3，其中横跨度超过了1万千米，囊括了100多个国家和地区，有着世界上80%以上的人口，在全球经济影响力高达60%，在世界范围内拥有着跨度最广的经济长廊。所以，这条经济纽带是十分具有发展潜力的。陆路不畅始终制约着亚欧大陆的发展。在古代地区，海运不发达，所以有了丝绸之路，进一步实现了亚欧大陆的交通畅通和贸易往来。但是后来随着中国政治和其他因素的影响，古代丝绸之路渐渐落寞，亚欧大陆始终处于一个封闭的状态。亚欧大陆从人口、经济规模以及政治的发杂程度上来看，在世界范围内是大陆之首，国家之间矛盾之多，缺乏相互信任，严重阻塞了国家之间交流的通道。

一带一路战略下开展国际旅游的策略，有效地打通了亚欧大陆的各个国家和区域之间的联系。一带一路横穿亚欧大陆，一边是经济活跃的东亚经济圈，另一边是发达的欧洲经济圈，中间的国家实力雄厚。根据一带一路的走向，陆上通道要依托国际要到，实现以沿线城市为支撑，以中心产业园为合作平台，通过"渝新欧"的铁路建设，实现中南北三个地区的方位打通亚欧大陆桥，最终形成中国——中亚——西亚三个国家的经济合作走廊，打通中国到俄罗斯到波罗的海地区以及中国向波斯湾、地中海的通道。在海上则从沿海港口出发，连接印度洋直接到达欧洲。中国积极推进中国与亚洲国家、欧洲国家的铁路合作，是实现进一步促进交通互联的措施，推动亚欧大陆之间的更深层次的合作，为亚欧经济的发展注入新鲜动力。通过这样的形式、方式，有效地打破长期封闭的亚欧大陆状态，促进不发达地区的经济得到有效的增长，改善区域经济发展的格局和活动方向，为区域发展做出更深层次的贡献。

一带一路的国际旅游合作项目，不仅打破了亚欧大陆封闭的状态，同时也推动了全球的经济发展，实现全球经济的均衡发展。以往全球发展以欧美国家为主导，经济中心主要侧重于西方世界，导致东方地区处于一个从属地位。实现一带一路，有效地打破了亚欧大陆封闭的状态，实现内陆国家的开放和均衡发展，改变以往丝绸之路只是进行贸易、文化交流的功能，让一带一路战略真正地成为可以促进国家与国家、区域与区域之间的共同发展，改变因为欧美主导全球化而带来的区域间贫富差距过大的问题，改善区域发展不平衡的问题，进一步推动世界经济走向新的格局，让全球人民真正地做到互利共赢。当前，世界经济仍处于深度调整期，低增长、低通胀、低需求同高失业、高债务、高泡沫等风险交织，气候变化、能源安全、粮食安全等全球性挑战不断增多，不仅发展中国家需要实现可持续性的经济转型，发达国家也需要促进经济转型，这需要世界各国携手打造利益共享的全球价值链，促进共同发展。

结语

实现"一带一路"的塑造，有利于加深各国之间的认知环境和政策帮扶，深入建设"一带一路"战略，实现国际旅游产业与一带一路战略的协调发展，为扭正世界格局做出贡献。在其中会有诸多的挑战，我们国家也需要承担诸多的责任，在这个过程中，需要不断努力与奋斗，最终实现丝绸之路在21世纪重现的伟大梦想。

参考文献：

[1]刘慧，叶尔肯·吾扎提，王成龙．"一带一路"战略对中国国土开发空间格局的影响[J]．地理科学进展，2015，05:545-553.

[2]申现杰，肖金成．国际区域经济合作新形势与我国"一带一路"合作战略[J]．宏观经济研究，2014，11:30-38.

[3]马胜春，黄基鑫．"一带一路"战略与中国区域经济发展——2015中国区域经济学会年会观点综述[J]．中国工业经济，2015，11:156-160.

[4]许和连，孙天阳，成丽红．"一带一路"高端制造业贸易格局及影响因素研究——基于复杂网络的指数随机图分析[J]．财贸经济，2015，12:74-88.

[5]孔庆峰，董虹蔚．"一带一路"国家的贸易便利化水平测算与贸易潜力研究[J]．国际贸易问题，2015，12:158-168.

（作者简介：姬妍婷，女，四川外国语大学国别经济与国际商务研究中心，讲师，硕士，研究方向：国际旅游管理）

谈俄罗斯文化的双重性

包淑萍

摘要：本文从比较东西文化的差异入手，探讨俄罗斯文化双重性形成的原因；俄罗斯文化的欧洲起源；俄罗斯文化欧亚双重特征的萌芽；以及俄罗斯文化双重性的特点。以期对俄罗斯文化有一个全面而深入的认识。

关键词：俄罗斯 双重性 东方文化 西方文化

俄罗斯是一个独特的民族，它兼具欧洲民族和亚洲民族的特点，它是西方人眼中的东方民族，东方人眼中的西方民族。俄罗斯地处欧洲和亚洲两大洲的中心地带，这一地理位置对俄罗斯的历史方面、文化方面、民族性格及民族精神方面都带来了一系列的影响。

几个世纪以来，世界各国的哲学家、思想家、历史学家等对俄罗斯文化进行了广泛而深入的研究，虽然得出的结论各有不同，但整体上形成了共识，认为俄罗斯一直处于东西文化的交融与碰撞中，文化上兼具双重性。俄罗斯著名哲学家、思想家、理论家别尔嘉耶夫曾这样概括俄罗斯文化的这一特点："俄罗斯是世界的完整部分，巨大的东方与西方，它将两个世界结合在一起。在俄罗斯精神中，东方与西方两种因素永远在相互角力。"（安启念，1994：112）

一、东西文化的区别

文化的核心是观念的共识，在当前的世界上，有两种不同的观念的共识，那就是东方文化的整体性和西方文化的个体性，它们是人类历史发展的结果。不同的政治、经济、社会环境造就了不同的文化观念，产生了不同特性的西方文化和东方文化。

西方文化从本质上看是个体文化。西方文化主要特征是具有个体性特性，其核心问题就在于西方强调个体自由度的发挥，所以，西方文化可称之为"个体文化”。东方文化从本质是上看是整体性文化，东方文化的主要特征具有整体性特征，其核心问题就是强调整体的作用，个人通过整体发挥作用，重视整体的价值，而不是个人的价值。具体表现在以下几方面：

首先是人与自然的关系方面：在中国古代占主导地位的哲学思想派别道家、儒家都提倡人与自然的和谐相处，告诉人们要怀着对大自然的敬畏之心。老子《道德经》共81章，通篇强调的道理是人处天地间要以谦卑之心对待大然、对待身边的人与事。如：“江海之所以能为百谷王者，以其善下之，故能为百谷王，”又如：“天之道，利而不害；圣人之道，为而不争。”《论语》中有很多类似的思想，例《论语·雍也篇》子曰：“知者乐水，仁者乐山。知者动，仁者静。知者乐，仁者寿。”西方文化则强调人类战胜大自然，征服大自然的力量与智慧。尤其在文艺复兴时代，把人的价值提高至极致，认为人是万物之灵长，在天地间是高高在上的，甚至高于神的地位。由于过于抬高的人的价值与力量，人类肆无忌惮地利用大自然、破坏大自然，时至今日，人类与自然的关系越来越紧张，人类在征服大自然的同时，也在自掘坟墓，将人类推向万劫不复的深渊。

其次在家庭观念上，东方文化有着强烈的宗法情结，在古代个人利益服从家族利益，要有自我牺牲精神。个体依存于大家族中，需要家庭的庇护才能有所发展。个人奋斗不仅是追求个人价值的实现，更是为了“光宗耀祖”，而现代东方国家家族观念不再那么浓重，现在更多强调集体的利益、国家利益。而西方文化更重视个体，有着强烈的个体本位观念。强调通过个人努力、奋斗争取个人的幸福与成功，因此西方人更推崇英雄人物。

再次在宗教信仰方面：佛教在东方流传较广，信徒较多，佛教强调通过此生的苦难来修得来生的幸福，重视生死轮回，因果报应。而西方占导地位的基督教则奉上帝为神明，主张人是有原罪的，要通过今生的努力来赎罪，而不是寄托在来生方面。总体上基督教更积极入世，佛教则消极避世。

最后在文学创作方面：东西方文学无论在文体类别还是文本内容方面，都有着明显的差异。东方没有西方意义上的史诗，西方文学史诗文学发达，有很多名垂千古的创作，例如《伊利亚特》、《奥德赛》等，这些作品用神话、幻想、想象等方式，反映现实、征服自然、歌颂英雄人物。中国现存最早的《诗经》更多反映的是当时的社会现实，具有“诗史”的性质。文学作品内容方面，中国无论小说还是戏曲，更讲求花好月圆的美满结局，西文作品则不会刻意追求，尤其古典时期的悲剧，“将有价值的东西撕给人们看”，让观众在惊恐、悲痛中释放情绪，获得崇高感。整体文化和个体文化都是提高社会系统功效的重要因素，因此它们是互补的，是可以融合的。但东西方文化的互补和融合也是一个漫长的渐进的过程。

二、俄罗斯文化形成双重性的原因

俄罗斯之所以形成文化上的双重性主要受以下几方面因素的影响。

首先是地理位置的影响：俄罗斯横跨欧亚两大洲，这种独特的位置形成了俄罗斯国土自然环境方面别样的风景。正是俄罗斯的自然环境在某种程度上奠定了俄罗斯精神和民族性格的基础。俄罗斯拥有着广袤的平原和浩瀚的森林，纵横交错的河流和四通八达的运河网络，与西方人和东方人便利接触的机会等深深地影响着这个民族的方方面面。

其次是历史沿革:纵观俄罗斯千年历史演革，它一直在东方与西方之间摇摆。13至15世纪，蒙古人占领欧洲大片土地，俄罗斯的“西化”进程受到阻碍，受到更多东方文化的影响。18世纪，彼得大帝改革，俄罗斯走上了全面西化的道路。后来的叶卡琳娜、亚历山大一世等实施的政策使俄罗斯走上回归欧洲，融入西方文明的命运。19世纪中期以来俄罗斯资本主义经济受到封建农奴制的束缚，西方文化在俄罗斯缺乏广泛的社会基础，仅限于上层社会，19世纪末20世纪初俄罗斯革命运动风起云涌，尤其是十月革命，让其走上了社会主义道路。走上社会主义道路后，俄罗斯与中国等东方国家联系变得格外紧密，互相之间的交流与合作更加频繁，当时的俄罗斯作为“老大哥”在影响中国等东方国家的同时，也受到了东方国家多方面的影响，从政治模式，经济制度甚至文化作品的创作等方面都受到了影响。

最后是文明属性：俄罗斯文明属于农业文明或内陆文明，与欧美的海洋文明、工商业文明有着很大区别。统治俄罗斯人民上百年的农奴制得以实行的基础就是高度发达的农业文明。俄罗斯人有着浓重的大地情结，罗斯，就是大地的意思。居住在俄罗斯大地上的人，保卫它、耕种它、爱护它，享受它的恩赐，得到它的保护，当它的孩子，就成为русский(俄罗斯人)。也就是说，俄罗斯人是从属于罗斯的，俄罗斯人重土惧迁，吃苦耐劳，有着厚重的东方意味。

三、俄罗斯文化的欧洲起源

从种族起源上看，俄罗斯人属于欧洲人种，是东斯拉夫的一支。古俄罗斯人居住在西起德涅斯特河和喀尔巴吁山脉，东至伏尔加河流域，南抵黑海北岸，北达拉多加湖的地域。后来在基辅罗斯和莫斯科公国时期，他们的地域不断扩大，在沙皇凡四世时期俄国斯将其势力延深至亚洲，越过了乌拉尔山和乌拉尔河。

从语言文字方面看，俄语是印欧语系的一支，是希腊传教士为了便于在俄罗斯传教创立的，他们利用保加利亚文创立的俄语字母，因此俄语又被称为旧教会斯拉夫文或旧保加利亚文。18世纪彼得大帝改革时期又将其做了改变，成为现代俄语字母的基础。俄罗斯人在长期的社会实践中建立了自己的文字，同时受欧洲拜占廷文化影响，使文字形式和语法规则逐步成熟和规范化。

在宗教信仰方面，俄罗斯人最初信仰多神教，后来随着9世纪建立的基辅罗斯与拜占廷帝国交流的增多，基督教也由拜占廷进入俄罗斯成为东正教。伴随着基督教传入，拜占廷风格的建筑、雕塑、绘画风行于俄罗斯。但拜占廷文化不是俄罗斯文化的最初来源和唯一来源。当时俄罗斯部分地区有了自己的文字、口头文学等，同时也与周边国家进行着密切的联系，如一些天主教国家，因此吸收拜占廷文化前的俄罗斯文化并非一片空白，也不是照搬、照抄拜占庭文化，而是经过了结合自身需要的改造、过滤、消化和吸收的过程。比如，基督教的传入就经历了同俄罗斯原有的多神教相融合的过程，基督教中本没有太阳神，在俄罗斯基督教则结合了多神教，给上帝以太阳神的职能；还有基督教的某些宗教仪式也掺合了一部分多神教的内容；俄罗斯早期的宗教建筑多模仿拜占廷的建筑，但在后来的发展中，这些建筑的俄罗斯本民族风格越来越凸现出来。

从以上关于地域、种族、语言、宗教等方面来看，俄罗斯文化的最早起源是属于欧洲的。这种文化萌芽发展到13 世纪蒙古人入侵之前一直是沿着欧洲文化的发展轨道进行的，后来其文化中亚洲因素的出现并不是源自拜占廷，而是另有他因。

四、俄罗斯文化欧亚双重特征的萌芽

13世纪东方的蒙古人入侵俄罗斯，并统治达240年。蒙古人入侵时俄罗斯处在四分五裂的状态，是一个个独立的封建公国，人民生活在毫无屏障的平原上，不仅受到来自东方蒙古人的入侵，还不时受到西方瑞典人与日耳曼人、南方草原波罗维茨人的劫掠。这样的状况下俄罗斯急需要一个统一、强有力的集权政治的统治，因此专制王权应运而生。这些不同于西欧国家的情况。中世纪时期，西欧处于四分五裂状态，教会势力范围强大，王权、贵族力量受到了压制，直到16

至17世纪地理大发现，海外商业高速发展，专制王权势力稍有增强。

俄罗斯在封建专制制度方面发展无疑是当时历史的选择，同时也不可避免受到了东方蒙古人的影响。伊凡四世时期，俄罗斯在中央集权的基础上最终形成沙皇个人的专制统治。俄罗斯的社会政治、经济发展同亚洲国家有了很大的相似，而同时期的欧洲其他国家却在一点点摆脱君主专制走上了资本主义的发展道路。于是俄罗斯在西欧眼里成了一个“亚洲”国家。

蒙古人的统治无疑为俄罗斯文化注入了东方元素，但不得不说，俄罗斯受的影响是非常有限的，因为当时的经济发展状况、社会发展水平，俄罗斯明显高于蒙古人。恩格斯在《反杜林论》中说：“每一次由比较野蛮的民族所进行的征服，不言而喻地都阻碍了经济的发展，摧毁了大批的生产力。但是在长期的征服中，比较野蛮的征服者，在绝大多数情况下，都不得不适应征服后存在的比较高的经济情况；他们被征服者所同化，而且大部分甚至还不得不采用被征服者的语言。”

在东方蒙古人统治的两百多年时间里，俄罗期的经济、社会发展相对是缓慢的，但欧洲文化的影响并没有完全中断，一直在进行着各方面的交流和融合，并为俄罗斯文化的兴起、发展提供着源源不断的新因素。当时的建筑、绘画、文学、雕塑等绝大部分依然是欧式的。亚洲民族特色的东西少之又少，从历史的眼光看，蒙古人并没有在统治俄罗斯中文化方面占绝对优势。

五、俄罗斯双重文化的特点

德国文化史学家施本格勒将世界文化分为8种类型，分别是古典文化（指古希腊文化）、西方文化（指中世纪以后的文化）、阿拉伯文化、埃及文化、印度文化、中国文化、巴比伦文化。但他无法确定将俄罗斯文化归为这8种的任何一种，同时俄罗斯文化又不能自成一统，他认为俄罗斯文化及其灵魂未发展成熟。这正体现了俄罗斯文化在世界文化中是一种独特的存在，具有非单一性、不纯粹性和双重性的特征。

第一，在社会意识方面：俄罗斯人受西方文化影响更大一些。东方国家对政权、政府有一种敬畏和服从心理，尤其中国的官本位思想时至今日依然深入人心。俄罗斯自彼得大帝时期施行所谓“休克疗法”起，更注重人的民主意识，俄罗斯人创造了“无政府主义”一词，可见俄罗斯人对规范、制度、法律等一切约束人的自主能力的东西是持一种排斥态度的。他们对更推崇极权主义，致力于漫无边际的东西。

第二，在社会改革方面：俄罗斯人倾向于以一种“跃进式”的方式改变现状。俄罗斯经历的几次重大的社会变革可以准确地说明这点。

例如彼得大帝改革；十月社会主义革命；叶利钦的全盘西化等。在彼得大帝改革时期，彼得大帝亲自在西方国家参观学习，回来后俄罗斯进行全方位的改革，政治、经济、军事、教育、文化甚至生活方式方面全面向西方国家学习，这种改革使俄罗斯社会经济获得长足发展，整个国家出现了前所未有的新面貌，彼得大帝也成为俄罗斯历史上的千古明君。

20世纪初俄国十月革命，虽然性质上与彼得大帝改革完全不同，但在方式上以“跃进”方式变革社会，以最快的方法改变现状方面是一致的。叶利钦的全面西化更是激进，由于不顾现实，一味求快的方式，使苏联解体，引发整个社会的动荡与干戈。

第三，在民族关系方面：俄罗斯历史上既有中国封建社会式的“通婚”，又有西方式的侵略扩张。在俄罗斯沙皇统治时代，皇室子女与欧洲国家的王子、公主通婚的史实是非常多的。可见历代沙皇们还是懂得睦邻友好的重要性。

同时俄罗斯也有扩张的一面，纵观历史：封建专制主义和浓厚的军国主义贯彻俄国历史的始终。俄罗期历史也是一部军事扩张史。波兰籍的美国国际战略问题专家布热津斯基对俄罗斯民族性格中的扩张历史有过一段生动的解析，他认为“俄罗斯民族有一种争取生存的返祖本能，并因此驱使俄国人迫切地感到需要更多的土地，他们扩张是一种不断的向毗邻的领土渗透的过程，不安全感变成了持续不断的扩张。”俄罗斯持续数百年的扩张使俄罗斯周边的国家付出了巨大而又惨重的代价，这也使俄罗斯成为横跨欧亚大陆的大帝国。俄罗斯这一方面显然与欧洲国家是一致的。

第四，在宗教方面：俄罗斯是一个笃信宗教的国家，占主体地位是的东正教，其次是佛教。东正教于公元11世纪从基督教分离出来，与俄罗期原有的多神教结合成为东正教，是俄罗斯的国教，拥有众多信徒，占俄罗斯总人口的50%。佛教在俄罗斯也有相当长的传播史，在俄罗斯人心中占有重要地位。叶卡捷琳娜二世执政时期佛教尤其受到重视，专门设有大喇嘛职位，如今俄罗斯佛教协会是世界佛教协会的会员。在宗教信仰方面可以明显感受到俄罗斯文化的双重性。

第五，在家庭成员结构方面：俄罗斯在苏联时期“两代同堂”、“三代同堂”现象非常普遍，大的家庭结构，影响着人们的生活方式和思维方式。后来受西方影响，小家庭越来越多，家庭的稳定性也越来越差，现在俄罗斯很多年轻人推崇西方的生活方式，家庭观念越来越淡泊。

尽管在俄罗斯文化中具有上述种种东方或西方文化的特征，但是不能据此得出俄罗斯单纯属于某种文化范畴的结论。因为，在俄罗斯文化中还有大量东西方文化相互交融的成分，形成既矛盾、又统一的特殊的双重文化结构。

总之，俄罗斯文化的双重性并不意味着是东方文化与西方文化的简单相加，也不是两种文化成分势均力敌，平分秋色。而是在俄罗斯历史发展中不同时期发挥各自不同的作用，所起的影响作用也不同，俄罗斯的态度也是左右摇摆的。正如托洛茨基所说的那样："俄国不仅在地理上，而且在社会上和历史上都介乎欧洲和亚洲之间……在不同的时期、不同的方面，有时接近这一边，有时接近另一边。"(别尔嘉耶夫，1997：4-5)

目前的情况是追随西方，对西方文化有强烈认同感的俄罗斯现在意识到西方文明的没落，从而对富有生气、活力的东方文化开始给予更多的关注。其实笔者认为俄罗斯最为明智的做法是同时吸纳两种文化的优点，将积极因素融合为一体，为我所用，并努力创造出俄罗斯特色的文化，走自己独特的道路。

参考文献：

[1] 安启念.东方国家的社会跳跃与文化落后——俄罗斯文化与列宁主义问题.[M].北京：中国人民大学出版社，1994年版：第112页.

[2] 俄别尔嘉耶夫.俄罗斯思想，俄罗斯命运.[M].莫斯科：1997年版：第4-5页.

（作者简介：包淑萍，女，四川外国语大学东方语学院，讲师，硕士，研究方向：中外文学关系）

中国与“一带一路”沿线国家进行旅游目的地营销合作的分析

黄雅婷

摘要：针对我国日益严重的旅游贸易逆差和旅游目的地市场发展不平衡问题，本文提出了“一带一路”倡议背景下，我国与沿线国家进行旅游目的地营销合作的思路，并通过案例分析的方式，基于旅游目的地营销的基本原则，对我国和蒙古国进行目的地营销合作的方案进行了具体的阐述，同时对目的地营销合作中可能遇到的问题进行了讨论并提出了解决的措施。结果表明，旅游目的地营销合作是中国和沿线国家拓宽海外市场、吸引更多境外游客的有益举措。

关键词：目的地营销合作；一带一路；案例分析

一、引言

2015年5月5日，商务部发布了《中国对外贸易形势报告（2015年春季）》，其中明确指出，2014年，中国服务贸易逆差1599.3亿美元，其中旅游贸易逆差为1078.9亿美元，大幅增长40.3%，占服务贸易逆差总额的67.5%，是服务贸易逆差的最大来源。而国家外汇管理局发布数据显示，到今年3月，我国服务贸易收入1484亿元，支出2851亿元，逆差1367亿元，其中旅行项目依然逆差最大，逆差值达1243亿元。这组数据清楚地呈现了我国旅游行业面临的一个尴尬处境，即出境游年年增加而入境游增长放缓。除此之外，我国旅游业还面临另一个问题，那就是旅游目的地市场发展的严重不平衡。2015年，国内领先的入境旅游电子商务平台China Travel Depot与全球领先的旅游搜索网站Sky scanner对入境旅行和旅游在线搜索及预订数据进行整理和挖掘，共同发布2015中国入境（在线）旅游报告。该报告指出，2015年，位于入境游客旅游目的地前三位的城市分别为上海、北京和广州，到访这三地的入境游客数量占了总量的60%；而位于21世纪丝绸之路沿线的城市中，只有西安吸引了不足2%的境外游客。

可喜的是，随着“一带一路”战略的正式提出，各方都在积极参与，而旅游作为“一带一路”建设的重要组成部分，理应在其中发挥重要作用。可以说，丝绸之路本身就是旅游之路。习近平总书记在“加强互联互通伙伴关系”东道主伙伴对话会上说，“应该发展丝绸之路特色旅游，让旅游合作和互联互通建设相互促进。“一带一路”旅游合作具有很大的潜力，具体来说，可以开展沿线国家与我国沿线省份旅游目的地营销的合作。21世纪丝绸之路沿线国家中，尤其应该重视与新疆接壤的哈萨克斯坦、吉尔吉斯斯坦、塔吉克斯坦和与内蒙接壤的蒙古国之间开展合作。因为这几个国家与我国不仅地理位置相邻，而且文化相近，具备合作的天然优势。更重要的是，中亚各国以及蒙古国在实现独立发展之后，加强对国家品牌的塑造，积极推动旅游业的发展。世界银行数据显示，2014年，哈萨克斯坦入境旅游收入达到15亿美元，吉尔吉斯斯坦、塔吉克萨坦和蒙古国一共实现了近8亿美元的入境旅游收入。更值得关注的是，除蒙古国近两年入境旅游收入有所下滑外，前述三个中亚国家的入境旅游收入都呈逐年大幅上升态势。与之相对应的是，我国新疆和内蒙两省的旅游收入绝大部分来源于国内游客。因此，如何利用“一带一路”战略的契机，依托天时地利人和的优势，通过与上述国家开展旅游目的地营销合作，提升外国游客对我国丝绸之路沿线旅游目的地的认识，吸引更多来华游客，就是本文的目的。

二、目的地营销合作的基础

打造政治互信、经济融合、文化包容的利益共同体、责任共同体和命运共同体，是“一带一路”建设的重要目标。而我国的新疆维吾尔族自治区与哈萨克斯坦、吉尔吉斯斯坦、塔吉克斯坦，以及内蒙古自治区与蒙古国不仅地理相邻，而且文化相近，具备旅游目的地营销合作的天然优势。

（一）地缘基础

新疆与八个中亚国家接壤，其中，新疆的和萨克、维吾尔和塔吉克等民族更与哈萨克斯坦、吉尔吉斯斯坦和塔吉克斯坦三国的主体民族跨境而居，具有浓厚的民族、宗教、文化情结，形成了新疆与三国相关地区开展地方合作的独特、深厚的地缘优势。而蒙古国地处亚洲中部的蒙古高原，东、南、西三面与中国接壤，北面同俄罗斯的西伯利亚为邻，边境线总长8219公里，其中中蒙边境线长4676.8公里，同样具有深厚的地理优势。如此优越的地理优势为旅游目的地营销合作提供了良好的基础。事实上，这一地区的许多旅游目的地正是跨境存在的。其中，最著名的当然是“古丝路”。2014年6月22日中、哈、吉三国联合申报的陆上丝绸之路的东段“丝绸之路：长安—天山廊道的路网”成功申报为世界文化遗产，成为首例跨国合作而成功申遗的项目。此外，世界七大山系之一的天山，位于欧亚大陆腹地，东西横跨中国新疆和哈萨克斯坦、吉尔吉斯斯坦和乌兹别克斯坦。而著名的蒙古大草原更是占据了蒙古国85%的疆域和我国内蒙古自治区35%的土地。

（二）社会文化基础

新疆是多种少数民族的聚居区，这里生活着不少与中亚国家相同的民族。他们语言文字相同，风俗习惯很相近，宗教信仰一致，有着密切的血缘、心理、姻亲关系。而我国内蒙古自治区的蒙古族人民与蒙古国的主体民族蒙古族都起源于东胡的分支蒙兀室韦，虽然分隔多年，但仍然有共同的语言文字起源、相同的习俗和相近的生活方式。社会文化的相似性为合作开展旅游目的地营销提供了实践基础。

而更重要的是，相似的文化和习俗是合作进行旅游目的地营销时的关键。旅游目的地呈现给游客的不仅是自然景观，还应有独特的文化遗产。例如，我国内蒙古自治区与蒙古国合作进行目的地营销时，蒙古大草原和独特的草原文化都应成为营销的内容。

（三）制度基础

近二十年来，中国及中亚政治局势稳定。自1995年开始，中亚各国和中国建立了元首定期会晤制度；1999年，“上海合作组织”的组建，更是促使中亚诸国与中国舰队友好合作关系进一步发展。而2013年9月和10月，中国国家主席习近平在出访中亚和东南亚国家期间，先后提出共建“丝绸之路经济带”和“21世纪海上丝绸之路”的重大倡议，更是为我国与中亚国家多层次、全方位的合作画下了宏伟的蓝图。

三、目的地营销合作案例——以内蒙和蒙古国为例

蒙古地区由蒙古国和我国内蒙古自治区共同组成。蒙古地区的核心地带由170万平方千米的高海拔草原构成，占据了蒙古国85%的疆域和内蒙古35%的土地。蒙古大草原包括四个要素，即草原、牧群、骏马和蒙古包。居住其中的游牧

民靠着马群为他们在广袤的大草原上放养牲畜、迁移蒙古包。由木杆和毛毡搭建而成的蒙古包是蒙古人的居所，内里设有柴火炉，既可取暖、又可做饭，虽然大得足够容纳一家人居住，但是却可以方便地拆卸下来，搬迁到水草更为丰美的地方。数千年来，牧民就在草原上世代居住，生生不息。牧群既充当了交通工具，又为牧民提供了肉、奶以及毛毡。牲畜需要牧草，而牧草随季节枯荣。在逐水草而居的旅程中，人的双腿跑不过迅捷的牛羊，只能依靠马的帮助。蒙古马体型虽小，耐受力却很强，并且早已适应了蒙古草原的地形、气候和海拔。严冬寒风凛冽，蒙古包是生存之本，但单凭人力却是无法搬动。马群是最主要的运输工具，并且是财富的象征。

因此，草原、牧群、骏马和蒙古包四个要素互相依存，渗透到了蒙古人生活的方方面面，它们共同构成了蒙古草原的文化景观。文化景观不同于单纯的自然景观，也有别于纯粹的文化遗产，而是自然和文化的相互融合。人类文化和大自然共同塑造了独特的地形，而地形和人类一起共同塑造了独特的人类文化，文化和景观互相依存，成为密不可分的整体。对于蒙古国和我国内蒙古自治区来说，蒙古大草原的文化景观就是最具特色的旅游吸引物，也是这一地区有别于其他类似景观的竞争优势。在内蒙和蒙古国进行联合旅游目的地宣传推广的过程中，最重要的就是要将这一独特的文化景观形象传递给旅游者。

根据旅游目的地营销的4P原则，即推广（promotion）、产品（product）、渠道（place）和定价（price），同时为了便于讨论，下文将主要从宣传推广、产品设计和渠道选择三个部分进行分析。

（一）宣传推广合作

不论是蒙古国还是我国内蒙古自治区都已把旅游业作为经济发展的重要组成部分，而它们在进行旅游宣传推广时，也有意识地把茫茫的草原和游徙的牧民作为最大的旅游吸引物。这一点从现有的宣传资料中便可得到充分说明。

蒙古国的宣传册和网站上，草原和马背文化都被作为一个统一的产品，向亚洲以及全世界的游客进行宣传推广。比如一家旅行社的网站上写到：“无边的大草原、原生态的大自然、无上的神光。天空似乎触手可及，这片土地美得难以言喻。体验数百年来始终如一的牧民生活。这个顽强的马背上的民族曾经建立了世界上最强大的帝国，来到这里，你一定会为他们折服。来体验无尽的速度、无拘无束的自由和迷人的文化吧！”另一家旅行社将蒙古描述为“广袤无垠”、“驰骋在辽阔的大草原上”以及“牧民和他们的马群是大草原上唯一的人类活动”。还有一家旅行社提到了大草原、蒙古包、游牧民以及酸马奶、从古至今沿袭的生活方式，还提到了成吉思汗。这些语句都让人联想起南北朝时中国流传的一首民歌《敕勒歌》，其中写道："敕勒川，阴山下，天似穹庐，笼盖四野。天苍苍，野茫茫，风吹草低见牛羊。"

而目前内蒙古自治区共提出了六大旅游品牌口号，分别是品牌形象口号"祖国正北方，亮丽内蒙古"、旅游口号"内蒙旅游，马到成功"、线路口号"草原+风景道"、旅游服务口号"好客、自然、温馨"、旅游商品口号"内蒙古博乐歌"和自驾游口号"自由自在内蒙古"。从内容上看，这六大口号提到了"马"、"草原"、"自然"、"自由自在"，这些都是和蒙古国的宣传重点相一致的，也体现了内蒙古把草原和游牧文化作为旅游吸引物的宣传重心。但是，作为六大口号中心的品牌形象口号强调"祖国正北方"，说明内蒙古仍然是把国内市场作为其最主要的目标市场。由于这样的战略定位，2014年，内蒙古自治区接待国内旅游人数7414.88万人次，同比增长12.13%；而入境旅游者仅167.12万人次，同比增长仅为3.41%。也正是由于内蒙主要面向国内市场，而我国游客从学生时代开始，便在教材、书籍以及大量的电视电影节目中形成了对内蒙古大草原的原生形象，使得内蒙古在形象定位时没有再更多地传递其独特的草原文化。这一目标市场定位的差异，使得内蒙和蒙古国在形象定位和品牌塑造方面出现了侧重点的区别：内蒙更偏重纯粹的自然景观，而蒙古国将自然景观和文化遗产更好地整合起来。

从吸引国际游客的视角来看，蒙古国的形象定位无疑更为成功。对于国外游客来说，如果他们仅仅对草原自然景观感兴趣的话，他们还有更多其他的选择，比如东非大草原。东非大草原不仅幅员辽阔，更以其种类繁多的野生动物著名，一年一度的东非野生动物大迁徙都吸引了大量游客前往观赏。而蒙古大草原的竞争优势恰好在于其文化景观，即人类活动和自然景观在千百年的共存中互相依存、互相影响，最终形成了一个你中有我、我中有你的整体。因此，内蒙与蒙古国进行联合形象塑造和品牌推广时，应该将侧重点放在蒙古大草原独特的文化景观上，从而吸引更多的海外游客。

（二）产品设计合作

那么，如何将蒙古大草原独特的文化景观这一目的形象和品牌具像化呢？旅游产品设计是最重要的一个环节。蒙古国由于较早地定位并开始传播这一形象，因此他们的旅游产品设计也较为准确地反映了其形象定位。例如，一家总部位于美国的旅游公司，其蒙古国分公司曾于2005年推出了一系列旅游产品。该产品得到了蒙古当局的高度认可，并授予该公司负责人蒙古旅游大使称号，该公司也因其着力推广蒙古旅游的努力得到了蒙古政府颁发的奖励；而且该旅游产品系列还得到了美国国家地理杂志和纽约时报的专题报道，并在BBC电视台的纪录片中播出，其国际影响力可见一斑。该系列旅游产品中的旗舰产品是一款历时15天、长达150公里的骑马旅行产品。这趟旅程穿越库苏古尔地区，15天的行程中，游客宿在牛羊环绕的蒙古包中，吃的是当地食物，和当地人亲密接触，完全融入到当地人的生活中；另外，游客还能参与蒙古人一年一度的运动和赛马盛会——那达慕。

当年对游客反馈意见的调查证实，这款旅游产品得到了游客的广泛好评。游客认为，这款旅游产品主打的文化景观，确实是吸引他们到访这一地区的最大卖点；而且，能够有机会骑马旅行、参加那达慕、和当地人一起生活，这些都对外国游客有非常大的吸引力。

那达慕是蒙古人社会和文化生活中最精彩的部分。在蒙古国那达慕又被定为国庆节，是蒙古国最盛大的节日。在节日期间组织有蒙古传统的听雨声会、歌舞表演等，其中最负盛名的是被称为“男子三项”的摔跤、赛马和射箭。那达慕大会期间，蒙古国的领导人都要亲临现场并邀请许多外宾观看。尽管在蒙古国首都乌兰巴托举办的全国性那达慕大会已经被开发成了成熟的旅游产品，但是其他地区性的那达慕大会还没有得到同等程度的商业化包装，一定程度上还保留了其原汁原味。有趣的是，上文所提到的那家旅游公司还曾携带蒙古传统弓箭去到库苏古尔地区，以让游客观赏到那达慕射箭比赛。

而我国内蒙古自治区的旅游产品设计，则与蒙古国的旅游产品有较大的区别。不管是官方性质的内蒙古旅游网，还是国内最大的OTA之一的携程网，其网站上推出的内蒙古旅游产品都不是以文化景观的方式进行设计，而是自然景观和文化遗产相分离的方式。例如，携程网上一个报价2980元的名为“内蒙古+呼和浩特+希拉穆仁草原+库布齐沙漠5日4晚跟团游”的旅游产品，其标注的产品特色为“毕业游、博物馆、蒙古包、手把羊肉、6个景点”。在5天的行程中，游客主要游览希拉穆仁草原、参观成吉思汗陵、游览库布齐沙漠景区、参观呼市一所寺庙、参观内蒙古博物院，其间点缀一次时长为两小时的“蒙古男儿三艺”中的赛马及摔跤表演，一次酒店晚餐时的蒙古仪式敬酒和献哈达，以及一次时长为一个小时的蒙古风情园游览。这样的旅游产品设计或许满足国内游客的需求。大部分国内游客能用于旅游的空闲时间非常有限，主要集中在国庆黄金周，或清明、五一节小黄金周，时长最多7天，因此5天的旅游产品从时长上满足了国内游客的需求；另外，大部分选择跟团游的国内游客的旅游动机还停留在“到此一游”的阶段，主要的兴趣爱好为在景区拍照和购买纪念品，因此该旅游产品主要集中在自然景观的游览也从内容上满足了国内游客的需求。但是，正因为如此，这类型的旅游产品就不能满足以体验文化为主要动机的国外游客的需求。各大旅游网站上的旅游产品中，只有极少数提到了那达慕大会，这和蒙古国的旅游产品把那达慕作为一个重要组成部分实在是殊为不同。

因此，从吸引更多入境游客的角度出发，我国内蒙古自治区在与蒙古国进行联合旅游产品设计时，应更多地借鉴蒙古国的产品设计方式，即将草原自然景观与独特的草原文化作为一个整体来设计旅游产品。更为重要的是，文化体验应该成为产品设计的灵魂，而不仅仅是走马观花的浅尝辄止。而另一方面，我国内蒙各城市更为完善的旅游基础设施，比如酒店、交通工具等也可以作为蒙古国设计旅游产品时有益的补充，从而更好地满足不同需求的游客。

（三）渠道选择合作

旅游目的地营销渠道是指旅游产品从旅游生产企业向旅游消费者转移过程中所经过的一切取得使用权或协助使用权转移的中介组织或个人。简单的说就是旅游企业把旅游产品销售给最终消费者的途径。旅游营销渠道的发展经过了三个阶段，即互联网前时代的中介化、互联网时代早期的去中介化和移动互联网时代的再中介化。现在，旅行社和其他旅行代理机构在目的地营销中仍然占据着非常重要的地位，是营销渠道中不可或缺的一环。

如果蒙古国和我国内蒙古自治区进行合作营销，那就应该充分利用两地营销渠道的互补优势。我国的各大旅行社如国旅、中青旅以及各大在线旅游代理机构如携程、去哪儿等拥有庞大的国内客户群体，可以为蒙古国带去大量的中国游客；而蒙古国的各大旅行社和OTA一直以来都面向亚洲各国乃至全球游客，可以将内蒙古的文化景观传递给更多的外国游客。

四、我国与“一带一路”沿线国家进行目的地营销合作的注意事项

（一）价值观整合

“一带一路”沿线国家的政治取向和价值观与我国有所不同，我们应尊重相关国家的体制政策，并且乐见其政治稳定和经济繁荣，不应让不同的政治经济制度成为双方合作的障碍。另外，进入21世纪以来，中亚国家越来越重视环境保

护，而旅游业恰好是和生态环境联系非常紧密的一个行业。例如，对于蒙古大草原的旅游开发来说，如果不重视生态旅游和可持续发展，就很可能对自然景观和草原文化造成无法逆转的损害。因此，与相关国家合作进行目的地营销时，要有环保意识，自觉遵守当地生态保护法，确保生态安全。在项目开展前宜对环境影响进行评估，对可能产生的环境问题提前预防。

（二）资源整合

要充分利用我国和沿线国家的资源互补优势，实现资源整合。我国改革开放以来社会经济发展迅速，“一带一路”沿线城市的基础设施建设都已较为完善，能够为旅游业提供完善的道路、交通工具、酒店和餐饮等设施；而中亚国家20世纪90年代才开始独立发展，其基础设施建设比起我国仍是比较滞后的。而另一方面，或许正由于中亚国家经济发展等相对滞后，其自然景观保存相对完好；又由于中亚国家的民族种类与我国相比较为单一，因此对于民族特色文化的传承也较为完整。那么，无论是基础设施资源，还是文化景观资源，都可以在目的地营销合作时加以整合。

（三）增强风险防范意识

我国与沿线国家进行旅游目的地营销合作时可能会面临法治障碍，主要表现为法制不健全、执法不规范，政策干预的随意性大。发生纠纷时，当地的司法仲裁体系运行不公、行政执法透明度较低，败诉的常常是外商，这极大地影响了市场的公平竞争秩序，也增加了外国企业的跨国营销成本。因此，针对中亚市场政策多变、社会动荡的情况，中国政府应不断完善政府服务体系，加强与我国驻中亚机构的联系，拓宽信息来源，从不同层次提供中亚市场政策、法规、经济等信息，建立起政策法律风险预警机制，切实保护中国企业。

参考文献：

[1] Cynthia Werner. The New Silk Road: Mediators and Tourism Development in Central Asia. Ethnology, 2003, 42(2), 141-159.

[2] Erica Marat. Nation Branding in Central Asia: A New Campaign to Present Ideas about the State and the Nation. Europe-Asia Studies, 2009, 61(7), 1123-1136.

[3] Hamira Zamani-Farahani, Joan C. Henderson. Islamic Tourism Development in Islamic Societies: The Case of Iran and Saudi Arabic. International Journal of Tourism Research, 2010, 12, 79-89.

[4] Kemal Kantarci. Perceptions of Foreign Investors on the Tourism Market in Central Asia including Kyrgyzstan, Kazakhstan, Uzbekistan, Turkmenistan. Tourism Management, 2007, 28, 820-829.

[5] Marlene Laruelle, Sebastien Peyrouse. Cross-border Minorities as Cultural and Economic Mediators between China and Central Asia. China and Eurasia Forum Quarterly, 2009, 7, 93-119.

[6] Michael Swaine. Chinese Views and Commentary on the "One Belt, One Road" Initiative. China Leadership Monitor, 2015, (47), 1-24.

[7] Nicola Palmer. Ethnic Equality, National Identity and Selective Cultural Representation in Tourism Promotion: Kyrgyzstan, Central Asia. Journal of Sustainable Tourism, 2007, 15(6), 645-662.

[8] Ralf Buckley, Claudia Ollenburg, Linsheng Zhong. Cultural Landscape in Monglian Tourism. Annals of Tourism Research, 2008, 35(1), 47-61.

[9] 苏祖梅. 中国企业在中亚五国经营环境的比较研究. 国际观察, 2013, (2): 66-72.

[10] 原帼力. 新疆与中亚国家发展区域旅游合作的优势及对策. 新疆广播电视大学学报, 2007, 11(37): 49-51.

（作者简介：黄雅婷，女，四川外国语大学国别经济与国际商务研究中心，讲师，硕士，研究方向：国际旅游管理）

泰国旅游资源概况与2015年旅游业发展形势分析

赵银川

摘 要：泰国旅游资源丰富，旅游业发达。本文分为两大部分，第一部分从自然、历史和文化旅游资源三个角度对泰国的旅游资源作了概括性介绍；第二部分着眼于泰国的旅游业发展形势，从境外旅游情况、旅游业发展战略及面临的挑战等方面入手，重点分析了2015年泰国旅游业发展状况。2015年泰国政局趋于稳定，旅游业经历了2014年的低迷期后开始复苏，游客数量、旅游收入、旅游从业者信心指数等都大幅增长，预计2016年泰国旅游业将持续增长。本文希望为赴泰旅游和进行旅游业投资的人士提供参考。

关键词：泰国；旅游资源；2015年；旅游业

泰国是中南半岛上一个美丽的国度。“泰国”在泰语中意为“自由之地”，素有“千佛之国”、“白象王国”、“微笑国度”等美称。泰国有极其丰富的旅游资源，是亚洲旅游业最发达的国家之一。得天独厚的地理位置、迷人的热带风情、独具特色的佛教文化、别具一格的民族风情和人文历史、高效便捷的交通运输网、日趋成熟的配套设施、舒适宜人的购物环境、相对低廉的消费，再加上高质量的旅游服务、和蔼友善的泰国民众，使得这块面积仅51万平方千米，人口仅6000多万的土地吸引了年均上千万的境外游客。泰国已成为东南亚最受欢迎的旅游目的地，曾获得“世界上最值得旅游的国家”称号（林秀梅，2014:60）。

一、丰富的旅游资源

泰国大大小小的旅游景点超过1000个。下面将从自然、历史和文化旅游资源三个角度对泰国的旅游资源做一个梳理。

（一）自然旅游资源

泰国位于东南亚的心脏地带，东南邻泰国湾，西南靠安达曼海，东与老挝和柬埔寨接壤，西部与缅甸相连。长达3000多千米的海岸线造就了风光旖旎的海滩、岛屿达936个，分布在19个府，攀牙府、甲米府和素叻他尼府的海岛数量最多，闻名世界的海岛有普吉岛、皮皮岛、苏梅岛和象岛等。

普吉岛位于泰国南部的普吉府，是泰国第一大岛屿。普吉岛以其洁白无瑕的沙滩和丰富的矿产资源，被称为“安达曼海上的一颗明珠”。除了盛产锡矿，橡胶、海产和水果也十分丰盛。

象岛位于达叻府，是泰国第二大岛屿。岛上景色秀丽，迄今仍有70%的资源未被开发，自然环境得到很好的保护。悬崖、瀑布、陡坡和野生动物遍布岛屿，非常适合探险，被誉为“探险家的乐园”。

苏梅岛位于素叻他尼府，为泰国第三大岛屿。岛上的椰子树随处可见，素有“椰岛”之称，近年来发展成为泰国最受欢迎的岛屿之一。20世纪80年代起，旅游成为岛上的一个新兴产业，并逐步取代了传统的农业和渔业，是岛上的主要经济来源。由于旅游业的发展，当地政府十分重视基础设施建设，交通也非常便捷，设有苏梅国际机场，每天有直飞首都曼谷以及周边国家和城市的航班。

皮皮岛位于普吉岛和甲米府之间的海域，于20世纪90年代被泰国政府开发。虽然开发较晚，但是其优美绝伦的风光吸引了年均上百万的游客。政府十分重视海岛旅游活动的多样化，因此岛上的观光活动十分丰富，包括潜水、悬崖跳水、海上航行、捕捞、水疗等。

泰国北部和东北部多为山地和高原，山区林地十分密布，拥有许多奇花异木和珍禽异兽。泰国政府把一些天然森林划为自然保护区，并设置国家公园。迄今，泰国共设立国家公园148个，以更好地保护自然资源和珍稀物种。保护区空气清新，气候宜人，拥有瀑布、河流和山峰，吸引了一批批旅游者前来观光。因他暖山国家公园因其为泰国最高峰的所在地而闻名海内外。该公园位于清迈府，占地482.4平方千米，海拔2565米。园内景色秀丽，遍布郁郁葱葱的亚热带雨林，有上千种花卉、鸟兽和昆虫。园内河流湍急且清澈见底，在崇山峻岭间构成了大大小小的瀑布。

（二）历史旅游资源

泰国历史悠久。1238年泰族建立起第一个王朝至今，历经四个王朝，均以当时首都的名字命名，分别为素可泰王朝、大城王朝、吞武里王朝和曼谷王朝。王朝的更迭，历史的变迁给这几座都城打上历史的印记，从而使如今的素可泰府、大城府、吞武里府和曼谷等有许多历史文化遗址。

素可泰是泰族建立的第一个国家的都城，也是泰国文化艺术的摇篮。1911年被列入《世界遗产》名录（高关中，2013:58）。许多重要遗迹包括兰甘亨大帝雕像、兰甘亨纪念碑、素可泰王宫、玛哈泰寺及其他20多座寺庙就在古城内。兰甘亨大帝是素可泰王朝的第三位国王，在他统治时期，国力空前鼎盛，国土不断扩张，使素可泰王国成为中南半岛上的一大强国。他还创造了泰文字母，兰甘亨纪念碑的原碑就是泰文字母创立以来刻写的第一块石碑。玛哈泰寺是素可泰最大且最重要的寺庙，占地4万平方米，拥有200多座佛塔和多个宫殿。佛塔形式多样，其中一座佛塔四周雕刻着168位佛陀弟子的形象，神态各异，弥足珍贵，体现了素可泰时期佛教的繁荣和高超的建筑艺术。

大城府，又名“阿瑜陀耶”，是泰族建立的又一个王朝的都城，位于泰国中部。大城作为大城王朝的都城长达417年，历经33位君主，是泰国迄今为止最古老的都城。14世纪，大城王朝的文化、艺术、宗教在中南半岛产生极大影响，国际贸易和对外交往也十分发达，中国明朝航海家郑和7次下西洋，有两次访问过大城。大城占地2556平方千米，历史遗迹分布很广，有3座王宫、375座寺院、94座城门和29座要塞。1991年被列入《世界遗产目录》，与泰国史前时期的挽昌谷物文化村落、素可泰并称为三大古遗迹（杨靖筠，2006:23）。三宝公庙、挽巴茵行宫、帕西桑伯特寺院、大猜空蒙寺是重要的历史遗迹。

吞武里是大城王朝灭亡后，华裔郑信建立的吞武里王朝的都城，虽然只存在了15年便被曼谷王朝取代，但仍留下了郑信纪念碑等历史古迹。吞武里位于湄南河西岸，与湄南河东岸的曼谷相对，是曼谷的50个区之一。

曼谷是曼谷王朝的都城。曼谷王朝于1782年建立至今，历经9代君主，现正值曼谷九世王时期。曼谷位于泰国中部，湄南河在市中心穿过，距离泰国湾仅40公里。曼谷既是一座历史久远的古都，又是一座富有现代气息的国际大都市，是全球最有吸引力的城市之一。曼谷的建筑艺术高贵典雅，处处散发着古都文化和佛教文化的气息，大皇宫、玉佛寺、四面佛、唐人街、卧佛寺、黎明寺等都是著名的历史旅游景点。

（三）佛教文化旅游资源

公元4—6世纪，佛教已在泰国流传。迄今，佛教在泰国流传时间至少已有1500年（戚盛中，2013：32）。佛教是泰国的国教，佛教徒占总人口的95%，全国有僧侣30万人，佛寺4万座。佛教在泰国的影响十分深远和广泛：男子上至国王下至平民百姓，一生中要到寺院剃度出家一次，否则不被社会所接纳；国家庆典、阅兵仪式、皇家典礼、商户开张、学校开学毕业仪式等，都要邀请僧人主持佛教仪式和诵经；平常人家的衣食住行、生老病死或婚丧嫁娶等无一不受到佛教的影响。佛教已经成为维系家庭和社会的纽带，成为衡量道德规范的标准。

在佛教文化的长远和广泛影响下，泰国的建筑、手工艺品、音乐、舞蹈、绘画甚至饮食中都可以看到浓厚的佛教色彩；政治、社会、教育、风俗甚至思想观念都被佛教打上了深深的烙印。作为旅游业发达的国家，佛教文化资源无疑是吸引游客的重要因素。据统计，全国有4万座佛寺，10万座佛塔，4000万尊佛像，每一个村庄就有一座寺庙，可以说是寺院遍地。泰国佛寺高贵典雅、雕刻精美，再配上精致的富含佛教元素的壁画和金碧辉煌的塔尖，使泰国佛寺别具一格，吸引着大批游客前来观赏。观光人数较多的寺庙有玉佛寺、素贴寺、清曼寺、卧佛寺、金佛寺、帕辛寺等。此外，传统节日包括宋干节、万佛节、佛诞节、水灯节、春耕节等颇具佛教色彩的节日已经发展成为宝贵的佛教文化旅游资源。

二、2015年泰国旅游业发展状况

泰国旅游业于20世纪60年代开始起步。自始，泰国政府就十分重视旅游业的发展，1960年开始成立旅游管理和促进机构，有计划、有目的、有组织地发展本国旅游产业。仅1960年泰国就接待外国游客8.1万人次，创收890万美元（陈晖、熊韬，2012:279）。80年代泰国旅游业迎来黄金期，90年代泰国经济遭受亚洲金融风暴的冲击，但旅游业也能一枝独秀，成为稳定泰国经济的重要产业。经过五十多年的发展，泰国旅游业已形成一定规模，成为泰国经济的重要支柱。目前旅游业收入占泰国GDP的7.1%，平均每年有1 200万境外游客来到泰国观光旅游，旅游业成为泰国最大的外汇收入来源（李瑞霞，2006:53）。

2015年泰国经济形势整体增长缓慢，但与经济面临多种问题的2014年相比，可谓是黑暗中的一道曙光。2014年，拉动经济增长的内部动力，如政府支出和投资因国内政治因素而处于停滞状态，一向发展势头良好的旅游业也出现了负增长。2015年泰国经济增速2.8%，旅游业是促成经济增长的主力因素（刘素兰，2016:55）。泰国旅游业对政治、社会稳定和经济形势等较为敏感，2015年泰国政局趋于稳定，东盟经济共同体正式成立，势必给包括泰国在内的各成员国乃至亚洲经济带来一番新气象。在这样的背景下，2015年泰国旅游业发展状况良好。

（一）2015年泰国境外游客概况

2015年赴泰的境外游客达到约2988万人次，同比增加约507万人次，增长20.44%（见表一）。2014年由于泰国国内政局不稳，再加上曼谷及其周边地区实施的60天紧急状态令给旅游市场带来沉重打击，有50多个国家向本国赴泰游客发出安全预警，部分国家甚至要求国民暂停赴泰旅游，这些使得旅游业发展处于低潮，导致游客数量较2013年减少6.54%（见表一）。泰国旅游与体育部数据显示，政局不稳导致2014年游客数量减少310万人次，旅游业损失达到1410亿泰铢（กก.2558）。因此2015年政府实施了多项旨在刺激旅游业增长的计划，如继续施行“泰式风情”旅游营销理念、大力发展廉价航空，加上稳定的政局使得游客数量在2015年年初便开始复苏，并大幅增长。

对2015年1月到12月的数据进行分析，从地区和国别来看，赴泰游客最多的来自东亚，同比增长36.7%。中国、日本、韩国、马来西亚、老挝、印度等国占到游客总数的54.93%（ททท.2558），成为赴泰游客的主体。中国赴泰游客数排名第一，2011年到2015年中国赴泰旅游数量不断上升，对旅游创汇贡献也最大，始终处于泰国境外游客的首位。2015年游客数量排在前三的分别是中国、马来西亚和日本。中国游客最多，占游客总数的26.55%，共计约793.48万人次；马来西亚游客342.34万人次，占11.46%；日本游客138.17万人次，占4.62%。

从旅游收入方面分析，与2014年相比增长较快，增幅排在前三的地区分别为：东亚，同比增长50.65%；南亚，同比增长22.55%；中亚，同比增长15.82%；从创收总值来看，东亚对泰国旅游创汇贡献最大，达到约7595.836亿泰铢，其次是欧洲4084.4794亿泰铢和美国901.8138亿泰铢（见表二）。尽管欧洲赴泰游客数和创汇排第二，但较2014年相比，游客数递减8.56%，创汇降低3.75%，这和欧盟经济不景气以及赴泰的俄罗斯游客大幅缩减关系较大。

泰国旅游业协会、泰国国家旅游局和泰国朱拉隆功大学的联合调查报告显示：2015年第四季度泰国旅游从业者的信心指数为103，高于正常值，而2014年信心指数仅为96，为近三年来首次低于正常值。

与2014年相比，无论是旅客数量、旅游创汇还是旅游从业者信心指数方面，都表明2015年泰国的旅游业开始走出低迷期，并实现跨越发展。

（二）2015年泰国旅游业面临新挑战

泰国旅游与体育部颁布的“2015—2017年旅游发展战略”中指出，2015年泰国旅游业正处于迅速发展阶段，面对的是多变的市场和社会政局。

首先，赴泰欧洲旅客数量和旅游支出大幅锐减，泰国主要客源国：英、法、美、德、澳、西以及意等发达国家的经济、政治、社会等方面发生变化，导致出境旅游的需求降低。再加上这些国家赴泰旅游的市场基本饱和，是泰国旅游业面临的首要挑战。

其次，东盟经济共同体的正式建立，意味着泰国将面临一个更大的、更具竞争力的旅游市场。泰国旅游业如何在经济、政治、社会文化一体化的背景和趋势下，转变自身功能、调整发展方向并成功转型，能够在与其他成员国的激烈竞争中保持原有优势，并扩大市场占有率，是政府和旅游从业者不得不面对的挑战。

第三，“金砖四国”的经济正在迅猛发展，2013年，中国、俄罗斯、巴西、印度等国家的境外旅游支出总额排名全世界前十，中国境外旅游支出总额更是居全球之首（กก.2559）。这些国家赴泰游客数量每年以惊人的数字增长，令泰国旅游从业者措手不及。如何保持这些国家的客源量，让旅游市场长期、稳定、健康地发展，并在发展壮大的同时提高旅游服务质量，是泰国当下面临的又一个全新的挑战。

（三）2015年泰国旅游业发展战略及目标

针对上述问题和挑战，泰国旅游与体育部制定了未来旅游业的发展目标和战略。

泰国旅游业近期的发展目标分为两部分，第一，预计2016年境外游客数量达到3254万—3407万人次，增幅1.56%—1.64%，境外旅游收入1.6万亿泰铢（สกก.2559）；第二，促进旅游业稳定、繁荣和可持续发展。即在发展旅游业的同时，必须在游客满意度、环境承载力、旅游收入、开发新景点和旅游设施等方面保持平衡。可见，泰国已经充分重视旅游业的健康、可持续性发展，不再片面地追求旅游经济效益。

在发展理念方面，2015年泰国旅游局还将延续前两年的“泰式风情、创汇创收”思路，所谓“泰式风情”就是注重展示泰国的独特文化和风土人情，尤其在东盟经济共同体成立后，这样的思路能体现出区别于其他成员国的特点。该思路着眼于旅客的深度旅游，提升旅游价值和观光享受，如让游客亲身体验泼水节、水灯节、春耕节等代表泰国风俗文化的活动，目的是让游客更深层次地体验到“泰式风情”，从而自发、主动为泰国旅游做宣传，为的是让游客以后还会到泰国旅游。2015年境外游客对赴泰旅游的满意度为4.13分（总分5分），为八年来最高。可见该思路十分成功，展现了泰国文化的魅力和泰国人智慧，提高了泰国知名度。

在市场方面，着力于开发文化体验区，以提高旅游享受，从而代替传统旅游以金钱衡量“物有所值”的思想，彻底改变泰国游等同“低价游”或“穷游”的旧观念。致力于让“泰国生活”、“泰国体验”、“泰国文化”贯穿旅游的始终。为此，2015年泰国政府积极开发地方文化旅游区，如泰北兰纳文化、泰东北手工艺文化、泰南穆斯林文化、边境地区跨境民族多元文化以及湄南河、湄公河沿线风俗文化等。这些发展成熟的文化旅游区风格各异，充分呈现了泰国由南到北的文化民情差异，让游客印象深刻，流连忘返。

旅游市场的开发方面更注重质量，打破低价促销。一方面，针对中高层次的消费群体和专项旅游市场在国外市场大力推广和宣传，同时提高服务质量，做到真正迎合游客需求，培养游客继续赴泰旅游的忠实度。诸如蜜月旅行、养老休闲、会务和展览、医疗保健、高尔夫和游艇体验更要做到高质量，赴泰进行这些活动的游客主要来自中东国家，其消费能力较高，将大大增加旅游创汇。另一方面，坚决打击扰乱旅游市场的“零元团”或“低价团”，这些表面看起来“很划算”的旅游背后，实质上严重损害了游客利益和泰国形象。越来越多的不法机构为了吸引游客而打出“零元团”或“低价团”的诱饵，一旦游客上钩之后，这些不法机构往往通过向游客高价出售假珠宝、皮革、保健药品等来谋取高额利润。2015年，泰国政府已下令国家旅游警察署严厉打击违规操纵旅游市场的“害群之马”。

在服务方面，着眼于为游客提供便利。提高签证申请效率，推出电子签证、继续实行对中国游客实行落地签政策；在旅游区增加中、日、韩、俄等多国语言的指示牌，扩大无线网络的覆盖范围；在机场、关卡、景区、酒店、医院、商圈、警察局等区域派遣语言志愿者，为游客免费提供中、日、韩、英等语种导游和翻译服务。

在基础设施方面，注重游客出行的方便、快捷和安全。增加从景区到市区、从主要景点到周边景点的车次、路线；拓展府与府之间的交通路线，铁路、轮船、航空、汽车等形成网络，满足游客多样化需求。

（四）2015年旅游业发展困境

2015年8月发生在曼谷四面佛附近的爆炸案，直接导致第三季度的游客数量同比降低12.58%。爆炸事件发生后，作为赴泰旅游的第一大主体，东亚已有9个国家向本国赴泰游客发出安全警告，中国的香港和台湾地区甚至禁止向泰国输送游客。这无疑给旅游业造成重大创伤，9月份泰国旅游业仅增长25.08%，环比降低52.54%，直接损失超过1401亿泰铢。

此外，2015年尼泊尔地震、韩国MERS病毒和巴黎恐怖袭击等事件导致全球境外旅游下滑，一定程度上打击了泰国旅游业。

为此，泰国旅游部门着手制定了各项计划挽回市场，重拾旅游从业者和游客信心。如邀请国外媒体和主要合作伙伴赴泰考察；赴中国各大城市举办旅游巡回展览；邀请人气明星拍摄旅游宣传片；与航空公司合作推出优惠促销活动等。这些措施使得游客数量在短期内得到回升，到2015年10月，旅游业恢复至正常状态，年底出现大幅增长。

三、结语

进入21世纪后的15年，泰国旅游业遭受过自然灾害、世界经济危机、国内政局混乱等多重打击，但政府和旅游从业者始终一如既往地分析形势，制定措施，一次次从旅游萧条中迅速恢复，继续发展，推动旅游业比重占到泰国GDP的10%，充分显示了泰国旅游业的强大实力。2016年泰国旅游业将继续增长，持续壮大，呈现泰国独有的魅力。

参考文献：

[1] สกก.2559.ดัชนีความเชื่อมั่นผู้ประกอบธุรกิจการท่องเที่ยวในประเทศไทยไตรมาสที่ ๔ ปี ๒๕๕๘ [ออนไลน์] เข้าถึงได้จาก: http://www.thailantourismcouncil.org สืบค้น: 27 กรกฎคม 2559.

[2] กก.2559.รายงานภาวะเศรษฐกิจท่องเที่ยว. [ออนไลน์]เข้าถึงได้จาก: http://www.mots.go.th/ สืบค้น: 20 มิถุนายน 2559.

[3] ททท.2558.สรุปสถานการณ์นักท่องเที่ยวธันวาคมปี๒๕๕๘ [ออนไลน์]เข้าถึงได้จาก: http://thai.tourismthailand.org/home/ สืบค้น: 5 มิถุนายน2559.

[4] กก.2558.ยุทธศาสตร์การท่องเที่ยวไทย พ.ศ. ๒๕๕๘---๒๕๖๐. [ออนไลน์]เข้าถึงได้จาก: http://www.mots.go.th/ สืบค้น: 10 สิงหาคม 2559.

[5] 李瑞霞.再谈泰国旅游业的发展及其启示[J].东南亚，2006(1).

[6] 陈晖、熊韬.泰国概论[M].广州：世界图书出版广东有限公司，2012年12月.

[7] 林秀梅.泰国社会文化与投资环境[M].广州：世界图书出版广东有限公司，2014年2月.

[8] 刘素兰.2015年泰国经济形势分析与2016年展望[J].调查研究，2016(1).

[9] 高关中.泰国文化的发源地——素可泰[J].地理风物，2013(7).

[10] 杨靖筠.亚非旅游文化[M].北京：北京大学出版社，2006年10月.

[11] 戚盛中.泰国民俗与文化[M].北京：北京大学出版社，2013年8月.

附录：图表

表一　2012年—2014年泰国旅客人数

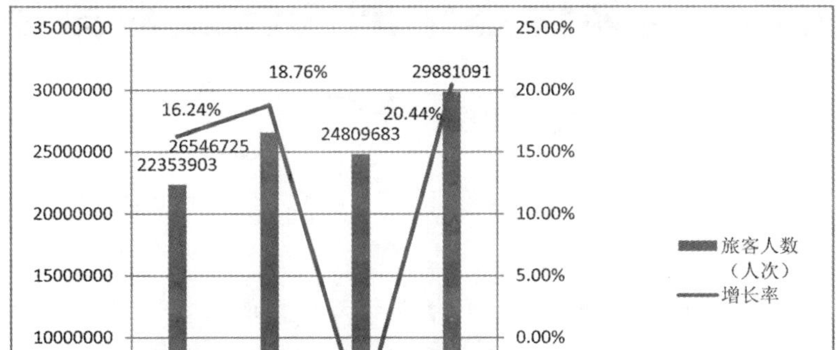

数据来源：泰国国家旅游局（Tourism Authority of Thailand）

表二　2015年泰国境外旅客人数及支出

地区	旅客人数（人次）			旅游支出（百万铢）		
	2015年	2014年	同比增长（%）	2015年	2014年	同比增长（%）
东亚	198,71,773	14,603,625	36.07	759,583.60	504,208.13	50.65
欧洲	5,629,122	6,161,893	-8.65	408,447.94	424,381.34	-3.75
美国	1,235,095	1,099,709	12.31	90,181.38	77,860.86	15.82
南亚	1,403,977	1,239,183	13.30	61,268.20	49,993.85	22.55
大洋洲	921,355	942,706	-2.26	70,992.02	67,033.79	5.90
中东	658,129	597,892	10.07	46,310.83	39,355.65	17.67
非洲	161,640	164,475	-1.72	10,374.08	9,966664.55	4.11
总计	29,881,091	24,809,683	20.44	1,447,158.17	1,172,798.17	23.39

数据来源：泰国国家旅游局（Tourism Authority of Thailand）

（作者简介：赵银川，女，四川外国语大学东方语学院，助教，硕士，研究方向：中国经典在泰国的翻译与传播、新闻翻译、泰国政治经济形势等）

中国旅游国际传播中的问题及对策研究

黄俊　李超

摘要：旅游国际传播兼具跨文化传播与经济传播的二重性，是提升旅游国际美誉度及境外游客吸引力的重要手段。中国旅游国际传播面临的突出问题在于以下几个方面，即信息流通能力较弱，受众指向模糊，传播手段陈旧单一，新媒体利用效能不足，搜索媒体引导乏力，传播话语生硬，叙事框架新颖性较差。要解决这些问题应明晰并细分受众，发挥逆向传播的强大舆论功能，充分发挥中外自媒体强大的舆论辐射及传播力，打造多元、鲜活、负责任的旅游大国形象。

关键词：旅游　国际传播　对策

一

旅游与传播本质上的一致性就在于都是人类对自由空间追寻的方式和手段，是人类精神解放的过程。[1]旅游国际化是旅游产业发展进入高层次阶段的表征，是一国（地）旅游享有较高国际美誉度及境外游客吸引力的重要指标。判断一国（地）旅游国际化的标准可以从旅游资源品质的国际化、旅游理念的国际化、文化传承及环保理念的国际化、入境旅游接待人数、旅游外汇收入等方面来进行判断。2014年和2015年，外国游客（非境外旅游，不包括港澳台地区同胞）入境人数的下降，表明中国旅游国际化的稳定性不足，旅游国际竞争力还不强。中国旅游国际竞争力的弱化除了政治、经济、市场、环境等多方面因素，还包括旅游国际传播力与影响力的低下。旅游国际化与国际传播密不可分。在罗伯特·福特纳看来，国际传播就是超越各国国界的传播，即在各民族、各国之间进行的传播。[2]改革开放以来，中国旅游国际传播步入了新的阶段，经过几十年的发展，取得了巨大成绩，不仅助推了中国经济的发展，传播了悠久的历史文化，还推动了国家形象的跃升。但随着人类进入网络时代（尤其是自媒体时代），中国旅游国际传播的滞后性及历史惰性逐渐凸显，与旅游产业发达国家的国际传播力及影响力还有很大差距。一方面，在国际受众接触率、旅游传播“走出去”能力等方面还有很大提升空间；另一方面，中国旅游国际传播效力不足，呈现出“传而不通”、“通而不受”的尴尬境地，并且在全球覆盖率、落户率上没有实质性的提高，旅游国际传播的影响力及引导力较弱。总体来看，旅游国际传播处于一种滞后状态，其为中国旅游国际化的推动作用还有待加强。本文拟从传播学视阈审视中国旅游国际传播面临的一些问题，并提出相应的对策及建议。

二

旅游国际传播兼具跨文化传播和经济传播的二重性质，具有特定异质文化融通的作用。跨文化传播要沟通的是传受双方的文化维度差异。文化维度差异具有价值判断的色彩，霍夫斯泰德（Geert Hofstede）认为文化维度差异的实质就是心灵程序的分歧和对立。“跨文化传播的目的不是追求认知和态度的改变，更不是影响和支配人的行为，意义共享是传播活动的前提”。[3] 美国传播学者汀·图梅（Stella Ting-Toomey）把跨文化传播定义为“分享意义的象征符号的交换过程”。[4] 经过几十年的发展，中国旅游国际传播的主体意识逐渐增强，跨文化传播与经济传播的本质得以回归，旅游国际传播开始卸下政治传播的沉重包袱。从传播媒介来看，中国旅游国际传播形成了传统媒体与新媒体双轮驱动的立体传播网络，形成了大众传播、人际传播、组织传播、自媒体传播等多种传播方式。从传播机制来看，旅游传播的路径逐渐优化，形成了主题旅游年会、视频游览、传媒会议、事件推广等传播机制。但中国旅游国际传播仍然面临着一系列的问题，这些问题制约了中国旅游国际传播效力，影响了国外游客的入境，主要包括以下几个方面。

第一，中国旅游国际传播受制于中国对外信息流通能力的掣肘，整体传播效力较低。信息流通能力是衡量一个国家传播能力高低的重要指标。总体上说全球信息的流通呈现出单向度的特征，即信息是从强势极往弱势极的流动与传通。造成信息流通呈现单向度的原因在于，信息流通能力与所在国综合国力成正相关关系，判断一个国家信息流通能力大小的标准主要取决于一个国家的经济硬实力及文化软实力。综合国力强的国家，其信息流通能力则较高，综合国力较弱的国家，其信息流通能力则较低。美国传播学者帕克斯（Parks）、斯皮伯格（Spizberg）和库帕克（Cupach）认为，传播能力包含着三个主题，即控制、合作和适应，优秀的传播者须具备控制能力、合作能力及适应能力。国际传播能力既是信息流通能力最终实现的目标，又是信息流通能力所呈现的结果，具有目标与结果叠加的二重性。中国经过多年的发展，经济总量已经跃居世界第二，但由于中国文化软实力的欠缺及西方传媒对中国的妖魔化建构，中国国家媒介形象整体欠佳，在国际信息流通中处于弱势地位。在此背景下，中国国际信息流通能力较弱，这导致中国整体对外传播能力较差。旅游国际传播属于整体对外传播的一个分支，因此其传播能力也相应较弱，这是中国旅游国际传播面临的最大问题，也是最难解决的问题。

第二，中国旅游国际传播受众模糊。从全球视野来看，旅游传播除了兼具文化传播与政治传播的功能，最根本的还是经济传播功能。从传播规律来看，要实现预期的传播效果，在传播行为展开之前，应对传播对象（受众）进行考量，作出严谨的分析与判断，精准把握期待受众。期待受众是指在进行旅游信息传播之先，传播主体在观念层面建构出的可能的接受群体，也就是信息传播的精确受众。传播发展史表明，传播行为与传播效果不是一一对应的关系。在传播学研究早期，筑基于宣传理念基础上的传播实践以“枪弹论”和“强效果论”为基础，把受众当作被动的信息接收者。随着对传播行为研究的深入，破除了传者中心论，转而强调受众的主体性，开始关注受众本身的意愿、喜好、需求、兴趣对传播效果的影响作用，如施拉姆就曾形象地把受众对信息的选择比作“自助餐厅就餐”。这一比喻表明，信息传播与信息接受共同构成动态的整体，任何一方如果出现问题都会对传播效果造成影响。旅游国际传播作为一种以文化传播为手段的对外经济传播，目的是发掘潜在的客户，实质是一种旅游营销。根据市场营销原则，针对顾客群体细分潜在客户是市场营销的重要手段。在大数据时代，旅游传播作为一种特殊的市场营销行为，应对顾客进行统筹与计算，把对游客进行的精确分析作为信息传播的起点。但目前，中国旅游国际传播面临的问题即是对受众信息的分析与掌握不到位，信息笼统而粗放，粗线条特征明显，使得传播地域和传播对象呈现出冷热不均的现象。受众方面，中国旅游的优势传播受众主要是欧美发达国家，传播区域集中在北美、东亚和欧洲，主要国家如美国、日本、韩国、德国、法国、俄罗斯等国。而对于欠发达地区的国际传播则显不足，造成旅游国际传播版图的丰满性不够。如海湾地区就具备极大的旅游开发潜力，其富裕程度保证了对其旅游传播的可能性及可行性。但中国旅游国际传播的覆盖率和到达率在这一地区都很薄弱。因此，作为旅游营销的一种文化方式，旅游传播首先应当发掘潜在旅游来源地客户，吸引经济实力较强的国家和地区的游客入境中国。

第三，中国旅游国际传播手段陈旧单一，新媒体利用效能不足。传播活动作为一种社会实践，受媒介技术环境影响巨大。媒介具有时代性，从结绳记事、鸿雁传书，到竹木、丝帛、纸张，到广播、电视、互联网、新媒体、超媒体等，每一次传播媒介的更新换代，都会带来传播革命。传播媒介的变更直接带来受众信息接收方式与体验方式的变更，并且发生受众的迁移。伴随着物联网时代的来临，云计算、大数据成为影响旅游市场发展的重要因素，新媒体成为沟通世界、从事实践的主要媒介。但目前中国旅游国际传播手段仍然采用的是电视媒体、纸媒等传统媒体，传播活动所增加的投入也主要用于这两大媒介。而对于日益占领年轻人市场的新媒体（如社交媒体）则利用效率不足。传播手段仍然主要采用的是传统的直白式广告形式，传播方式新颖性不够，传播技巧不足。美国社会学家威廉·盖姆森提出了著名的传媒包裹理论，他认为如果希望得到公众的关注，传播必须把握框架、象征、脚本三个因素。而目前，中国旅游国际传播的互联网思维体系仍未建构起来，还是采用老旧的传播者本位的立场，忽略了客体立场。

第四，搜索媒体引导乏力。当前的传播生态中，网络媒体已经超越传统媒体成为最为重要的媒体。网络媒体相对于传统媒体来说，其突出的优点就在于信息达到的及时与信息获取的便捷。以手机为主的移动终端加大了网络媒体的使用效率，推动了旅游市场的发展。携程旅行网发布的2015年旅行消费报告指出，2015年，共有2.5亿用户通过携程网预订机票、酒店、购买门票等。这个庞大的数据说明，网络媒体已经成为影响旅游行为的重要因素，为游客（潜在游客）提供方便、快捷、精准的旅游信息搜索至关重要。在此背景下，搜索引擎功能的发挥对于旅游国际传播起着巨大的制约作用。但目前，中国搜索媒体对于旅游国际传播的引导能力不足。其中一个重要的原因就在于搜索媒体在丛林法则下，以盈利为中心的定位扭曲了经济效益与文化效益的关系，用物质与金钱的获得感而剥夺了精神传承与文化传播的责任感。以国内最大的搜索引擎百度为例，输入“杭州旅游”，会获得9,850,000个搜索结果，但排在前四位的全是商业推广。另外，搜索媒体对精准化信息的投放能力较差，搜索引擎使用与贡献率不足，依靠搜索引擎获取信息的比例仅为44%。

第五，中国旅游国际传播话语生硬，叙事框架新颖性较差。怎么讲好中国旅游故事，将中国人文、历史、环境以及当代人的生活等融为一体，做好旅游文化大传播是摆在中国媒体人面前的一道难题。从传播内容上看，中国旅游国际传播呈现出几多几少的局面。首先是讲述中国历史文化较多，讲述现代中国人文较少。中国是一个有着几千年悠久历史文明的国家，中华文明具有连续性，这在世界文明史上是少有的，对于国外游客来说，中国古老的历史文明是旅游传播的亮点也是重点。但是随着中国国力的提升，中国往世界舞台中心的不断位移，西方受众同样关注中国现代人的生活、现代文明及精神文化，他们尤其迫切地希望了解今日中国的真实风情与面貌。其次，宏大叙事多，个人感受少。由于文化的差异，国外受众对于整齐划一的宏大文化叙事兴趣不足，更倾向于分享式的个体体验，但中国旅游国际传播正是在个体分享式体验上较少作为。周鸿铎认为，“文化传播是人民社会交往活动过程产生于社区、群体及所有人与人之间共存惯习之内的一种文化互动现象。……文化传播就是社会传播，是人对文化的分配和共享，沟通人与人的共存关系。”[5] 再次，自己讲得多，游客讲得少。这是中国国际传播传统思维惯性使然。以主体的视角遮蔽受众的视角，使得旅游国际传播成为以我为主的单向信息流动，缺乏主客体的交流与互动。

三

为提升中国旅游国际传播力，可以从以下几个方面入手，有针对性地对国外游客进行营销。

第一，明晰并细分旅游国际传播受众，尤其是要把握好期待受众。面对世界范围内受众在政治、经济、文化等方面的巨大差异性，旅游国际传播首先应该通过调研细分受众，如根据年龄大小，将其分为青年、中年、老年等，根据不同年龄层次，制作相应的传播内容，推荐相应的旅游产品，以提高旅游国际传播的针对性与有效性。尤其是在旅游产品推介前要提前预判期待受众，在把握期待受众的基础上，通过期待受众带动其他客户群体。

第二，发挥逆向传播的强大舆论功能，注重国际国内旅游传播的互动。“今天的国际传播，前所未有地受到国内舆论的影响。国内舆论对国际传播的影响，也从未像现在这么大。”[6] 由于历史原因及意识形态差异，西方媒体对我国官方媒体的喉舌功能普遍排斥，在采纳与中国相关的信息及舆论观点时，外媒的职业敏感性使其更倾向于来自草根的民间舆论场的声音，形成国内舆论影响甚至制约国际传播的局面。在这种大背景下，应该充分发挥逆向传播的功能。“所谓‘逆向传播’，即是指受众对媒体的信息传播和影响”。[7] 逆向传播对于信息的扩散，尤其是对于舆论的走向具有举足轻重的作用。在进行旅游国际传播时，应该积极发挥普通民众的传播作用，以其旅游体验为传播切片带动国际传播，做到内外并举，以内促外，以优化旅游国际传播。

第三，充分发挥中外自媒体强大的舆论辐射及传播力。进入自媒体时代，传统的传播渠道、传播方式与自媒体正面遭遇，但在时间的有效性、信息获取路径的多元化以及民意的通达上，传统媒体明显处于下风。而自媒体的发展，不仅拓展了个人的表达空间和自由限度，也与大众传媒产生了很好的互动效应。自媒体的传播具有强大的辐射能力及传播力量，国外著名的自媒体网站有Facebook，Twitter，Instagram，Flickr，Tumblr等，国内著名的自媒体网站有新浪微博、腾讯微信等。部分社会精英的自媒体在国际舆论场的引导力甚至强于大众传媒。社会精英作为意见领袖，他们的旅游观念及对旅游产品的评价很大程度上可以影响国外受众，甚至左右传媒观点。在汹涌的自媒体发展态势下，面对社会精英的自媒体表达，要重视自媒体的舆论辐射和传播力，充分展开和国内外自媒体空间意见领袖的合作。可以广泛收集整理这些意见领袖对于我国旅游行业的质疑观点与批评意见，进行梳理并仔细分析后，直面问题与分歧，放弃传统大而化之的宣传手段，以精细的交流与沟通获取意见领袖的支持。

第四，打造多元、鲜活、负责任的旅游大国形象，建构主动型传播模式。在今天的国际传播格局中，西方传媒拥有强势话语权。面对西方媒体对中国旅游的不利传播，目前，我们采用的是“哪里坏了缝哪里”的“补丁式”回应方式。这种回应机制看似合理，实则陷入一种“鸡同鸭讲”的悖论中。双方的平行信息很难相交，在反应时间与反应节奏上慢了半拍，处于非常被动的局面。加之我国传媒的国际影响力不强，回击与反驳的声音常显虚弱而乏力，这种防御性的传播策略使得在旅游国际传播中总是处于被动挨打的局面。因此，中国在旅游国际传播中，应该建立“主动型国际传播模式”，“通过转换话语体系，实现多元主体沟通，拓展公共外交和媒体公关，重视人际传播和文化传播，逐步改变部分国际公众一定时期内的思维定式”，[8]由被动变为主动，由自说自话变为合作对话，将国际传播的工作节奏提前，建构立体化的传播体系，打破国际舆论对中国旅游的刻板印象，如认为中国空气质量糟糕、食品安全性差等，通过事实与数据的传播有效减少旅游国际传播中的“噪音”和“误读”现象，打造多元、鲜活、负责任的旅游大国形象，建构主动型传播模式。

注释：

[1]王洁.试论一种特殊的传播方式——旅游传播.现代传播，2003年第1期：第53页.

[2][美]罗伯特·福特纳.国际传播.刘利群译.华夏出版社，2000年版：第5-6页.

[3]李景强.论跨文化传播的性质.新闻界，2010年第6期，第26-27页.

[4][美]Stella Ting-Toomey: Communication across cultures.上海外语教育出版社.2007年(英文版)：第16-17页.

[5]周鸿铎.文化传播学通论.中国纺织出版社，2005年第8页.

[6]周庆安.当代国际传播的三重困境与策略性突围.中国记者，2011年第8期.

[7]朱金平.受众对媒体你想传播之探析.军事记者，2003年第8期.

[8]崔守军.中国国际传播的逻辑困境与模式转换.国际展望，2010年第6期.

（作者简介：黄俊，男，四川外国语大学国别经济与国际商务研究中心，讲师，博士，研究方向：国际旅游管理；李超，男，重庆农村商业银行渝北支行工作人员）

沙特旅游业的现状和前景

黄婷婷

摘要：沙特的旅游业起步较晚，尚处于发展时期，主要有宗教旅游、文化旅游、生态旅游、购物旅游、商业旅游等类型。在发展中受到了社会文化习俗、国家政策法规、投资、人力资源和基础设施等因素的制约。针对这些问题，沙特在经济转型的过程中提出了发展旅游业的明确的规划，勾勒出了沙特旅游业的光明前景。

关键词：沙特 旅游业 问题 规划

众所周知，沙特的石油储量和产量均居世界第一，是名副其实的“石油王国”。石油是沙特国民经济的支柱，为沙特带来了惊人的财富，让沙特从二十世纪七十年代开始就成为世界人均国民收入最高的国家之一。然而随着国际原油价格的持续走低，沙特经济遭受重创，开始出现巨额财政赤字。为了摆脱对石油的依赖，实现经济的多元化，沙特政府提出了一系列经济转型计划和发展愿景，其中促进旅游业的发展成为发展非石油产业的重要一环。2000年，沙特成立了沙特旅游与民族遗产总机构，大力推动旅游业特别是境内游的发展。

一、沙特旅游业的类型

沙特并不是传统意义上的旅游目的地，其旅游业尚处于发展时期。但其独特的地理环境，丰富的生态面貌，璀璨的宗教文化，众多的历史遗迹为它发展多种类型的旅游活动提供了便利。根据世界经济论坛2015年旅游业竞争力报告，沙特在中东和北非的旅游竞争力排名为第5位，全球排名为第64位。[①]2015年约有5330万游客前往中东旅游，其中去往沙特的游客占总人数的33.8%，这一比例相

① 数据来源：世界经济论坛，https://cn.weforum.org/reports。

比于2004年的23.8%上升了十个百分点。[①]另外，沙特旅游信息与研究中心的统计数据显示，2015年沙特旅游业附加值达到855亿沙特里亚尔（约228亿美元），占国内生产总值的3.5%，占非石油行业产值的4.9%。创造了882900个直接就业岗位，占总劳动力直接就业岗位的7.7%，私有部门劳动力总数的8.3%，沙特本国人职位的27.8%。[②]

沙特主要的旅游类型有宗教旅游、文化旅游、生态旅游、购物旅游和商业旅游。

宗教旅游是指旅游者以宗教圣地、宗教名胜、宗教景观、宗教节事等为旅游对象物的旅游活动。宗教旅游是沙特旅游业的主要支柱，沙特是世界宗教旅游的中心。作为伊斯兰教的摇篮，沙特坐拥麦加和麦地那两大伊斯兰圣城和禁寺、先知清真寺等宗教名胜，吸引着全世界的穆斯林进行朝圣和参拜。朝觐是伊斯兰教的五功之一，《古兰经》中明文规定："为世人而创设的最古的清真寺，确是在麦加的那所吉祥的天房、全世界的向导"（3:96）"其中有许多明证，如易卜拉欣的立足地；凡入其中的人都得安宁。凡能旅行天房的，人人都有为真主而朝觐的天房的义务。"（3:97）[③]因此，身体健康、理智健全、有经济条件、自由的成年穆斯林，都会尽最大努力，一生至少前往麦加朝觐一次。据美国皮尤研究中心数据，2010年全世界穆斯林人口为16亿，占世界总人口的23%，这一数据到2050年将增长到28亿，约占世界人口的30%。[④]由此可见沙特宗教旅游的客源会一直呈上升趋势。2014年到沙特的穆斯林游客数达到1020万人，据沙特经济与发展事务委员会估计，到2020年朝觐人数将增长到1500万，到2030年将增长到3000万，这势必为沙特带来可观的经济收入。实际上，宗教旅游一直是沙特最重要的收入来源之一，也是最大的经济支柱之一。2015年宗教旅游为沙特创造了120亿美元的收入，占国民生产总值的2.7%，沙特计划在未来四年将这一收入提高到200亿美元。[⑤]

文化旅游是指以感知文化为目的，参观历史遗迹、博物馆、传统工业或参加展览、艺术节等文化活动的旅游。根据沙特旅游总机构的统计，沙特有4个世界

① 数据来源：沙特旅游信息与研究中心，http://www.mas.gov.sa/ar/Dashboard/Pages/default.aspx。

② 数据来源：沙特旅游信息与研究中心，http://www.mas.gov.sa/ar/Dashboard/Pages/default.aspx。

③ 马坚译《古兰经》，中国社会科学出版社，2003年6月第2版，第43页。

④ 数据来源：美国皮尤研究中心http://www.pewforum.org/2015/04/02/religious-projections-2010-2050/。

⑤ 沙特希望提高宗教旅游收入，BBC新闻http://www.bbc.com/arabic/business/2016/05/160524_saudi_arabia_religious_tourism。

文化遗产，超过12000个自然和文化景点，6300多个历史和文化遗迹中，其中有500个曾出现在阿拉伯古代诗歌中，另有400个出现在先知传记中①。沙特还有超过200家国有博物馆和非国有博物馆，其中最大的是坐落在首都利雅得的沙特国家博物馆，221间展室收藏了3700余件展品。此外，沙特每年都会举行大量的文化节活动，以2010年为例，沙特举办了600项文学文化活动，61项沙特传统艺术节，44项戏剧艺术节②。单是2014年夏季的45项文化节活动就吸引了超过1000万游客，创造了超过5000个临时岗位，实现创收超过100亿里亚尔。③在众多的文化节中，最负盛名的是“杰纳第利亚遗产文化节”，该活动从1985年开始举办，迄今为止已经成功举办了31届，每届参观人数超过800万人次。该文化节除了在位于沙漠中的永久展览区集中展示沙特各地和各部落的传统民俗文化，还每年邀请一个友好国家作为主宾国参展，以加强不同文明之间的交流和了解。中国曾在2013年受邀担任主宾国，进行了为期17天的中国传统与现代文化展示。

生态旅游是指以有特色的生态环境为主要景观的旅游。国际生态旅游协会认为其有保护自己环境和维护当地人民生活双重责任，是一种可持续发展的旅游。沙特坐落在亚洲西南部，面积约225万平方千米，约占整个阿拉伯半岛面积的80%，东临波斯湾，西邻红海，海岸线长达2437公里。地势西高东低，西部为希贾兹阿西尔山脉，中部为纳季德高原，东部为平原，沙漠约占全国面积的一半。沙特拥有延绵的海岸线，巍峨的高山，广袤的沙漠，多样的地形赋予了它多样的生态。沙特1986年建立了国家野生生物保护与发展机构，制定了战略计划来建立保护区，该计划计划建立108个保护区，其中56个陆地保护区，62个海洋保护区，总体面积达到沙特面积约8%。该机构在这些保护区恢复生态多样性，保护濒危物种，并在2002年与旅游发展最高机构合作召开沙特生态旅游国际研讨会，研究得出沙特有七个保护区适合开发生态旅游，可以在其中进行徒步旅行，观赏野生动物和鸟类，漫步沙丘，露营，潜水，参观小型生态博物馆展展览等等活动。沙特主要的保护区有红海西南海岸的福尔伞群岛保护区，鲁卜哈里沙漠西北部的阿鲁革·巴尼·姆阿里德保护区，萨尔瓦特山峦顶峰的里达保护区，纳吉德高原的马哈扎·绥德保护区，塔维格山一侧的瓦乌勒保护区等等。

购物旅游是一种以购物为主要目的的特殊旅游方式。在沙特各类旅游活动

① 数据来源：《观点报》，http://wejhatt.com/?p=1455。

② 数据来源：《利雅得报》，http://www.alriyadh.com/547957。

③ 数据来源：《今日报》，http://www.alyaum.com/article/3143484。

中，购物旅游占据了娱乐活动总消费的75%。沙特国内有民间市场、传统杂货店、大商店、现代化的购物中心以及国际商场，为游客提供手工艺品、家具、地毯、香水、香料、金饰、古董、工艺品、衣服等各类商品。每年夏季沙特首都利雅得市都会举行利雅得购物和娱乐节，该活动集文化、娱乐、购物于一体，是沙特全国性的盛会。2011年沙特国内游客在利雅得消费达到66500万里亚尔，超过了住宿设施消费的49700万里亚尔，饮食消费的40900万里亚尔，交通消费的37400万里亚尔，以及休闲娱乐消费的33700万里亚尔①。2016年第十二届利雅得购物和娱乐节从7月11日开始，持续三十天，吸引了10家商业娱乐中心中的2000多家公司参与活动。节日期间举行了150余项娱乐活动，设置500万里亚尔的现金奖项及100万里亚尔的社交网现金奖，吸引了众多沙特民众和游客参与其中。

商务旅游一般是以经商为目的，将参加展览、会议等活动与游览观光结合起来的旅游方式。商务旅游是沙特旅游市场的一个重要支柱，其规模占到沙特入境旅游的54%，占利雅得入境游的74%，商务人士在沙特的消费约占到沙特旅游总收入的21%。沙特每年约有超过十万项商业活动，有超过309万游客参与其中，平均消费总额超过42亿里亚尔。2010年沙特的商务旅游按照旅行次数排列分别是利雅得190万次，麦加地区98.2万次，东部地区69.4万次。该年沙特商务旅游消费达到68亿里亚尔，其中52亿来自国外游客。②根据沙特最高旅游机构预计，沙特商务旅游消费至2020年将达到80亿里亚尔。

二、沙特旅游业面临的问题

尽管沙特具有诸多发展旅游业的自然和人文要素，但由于政府对于旅游业长期的不重视以及社会环境的不开放，沙特旅游业的发展面临着诸多桎梏。2008年，沙特旅游信息与研究中心曾经从住宿业、旅行代理机构和吸引旅游的活动三方面对影响沙特旅游业发展的问题进行分析，排查出145条制约沙特旅游业发展的制约因素，经研究去除重复部分，依然还剩90条，大致可以归于以下几方面：

第一，与社会、文化和传统习俗有关的桎梏。作为伊斯兰教的发源地，沙特社会宗教氛围浓厚，社会生活的各个方面有很多需要遵守的行为规范；在对外开放旅游时，沙特社会普遍有受到外来文化影响的担忧；并且受传统的社会文化影

① 数据来源：http://www.aleqt.com/2013/01/31/article_728707.html。

② 数据来源：《利雅得报》，http://www.alriyadh.com/656200。

响，沙特人不愿从事旅游业方面的工作。

第二，与国家政策法规制度体系相关的桎梏。沙特政府官僚主义盛行，政策多变，缺乏透明度，执行力差且速度慢；签证政策严格；一些政策与国外投资政策相左，区别对待外资企业；税费较高，商业注册和关税豁免耗时长；担保制度和手续不够灵活；没有旅游产品质量标准及执行标准；旅游业工作系统不配套；没有海关保护等等。

第三，与投资相关的桎梏。沙特缺乏对投资的保护；外国资本难以直接进入旅游业；缺乏吸引适宜的外国资本的经济条件；旅游投资门槛高；投资服务和配套设施缺乏；投资回报慢，风险高等等。

第三，与人力资源相关的桎梏。沙特缺乏有旅游从业资格的劳动力；不允许使用临时劳动力；难以聘请到合格的外国劳动力。

第四，与基础设施相关的桎梏。沙特酒店价格总体较高；交通运输不够便捷；缺乏娱乐设施和场所；部分偏远景点的开发和保护不够；没有便捷的电子支付系统和电子商务系统等等。

此外，沙特还面临着旅游季节性强，监管力度不够等等问题。正是由于这些问题，长期以来，世界甚至是沙特国民本身对本国的旅游景点知之甚少。2012年的统计数据显示，沙特每年约有700万居民利用暑假出游，达到居民总数的40%，这700万人中约有80%的人选择境外游，旅游消费至少达到250亿沙特里亚尔。沙特的年出境游人数和消费总额占中东地区境外游总人数和消费的1/3以上，造成了沙特大量资金的外流。

因此，解决上述的诸多问题，促进旅游业的发展对沙特来说有重大的意义：第一，有利于沙特国家经济来源的多样化，减少对石油的依赖；第二，能为沙特青年提供更多的工作机会，帮助解决就业问题；第三，有利于减少本国国民出国游造成的资源流失，吸引外国资金流入；第四，有利于推动沙特各地区的基础设施建设，提高乡村地区和工业欠发达地区居民的人均收入，改善人民生活水平；第五，有利于保护自然文化遗产，增加国民爱国意识和归属感；第六，有利于改善沙特国际形象，加强国际交流。

三、沙特旅游业的发展规划

2001年沙特最高旅游机构总秘书处发布了《沙特国内旅游发展计划（2001—2020）》，提出了沙特发展旅游业的理念是：可持续原则；注重经济、社会、文化、环境利益分配的社会公平；遵循沙特崇高的伊斯兰价值观和热情好客的传统；让私营部门在投资建设旅游设施中发挥主要作用。这一理念具体体现在沙特旅游业的发展愿景上：沙特阿拉伯王国是伊斯兰的摇篮，沙特从伊斯兰价值观、古老遗产的纯正性和待客传统出发，致力于发展有价值、有特色，能带来社会、文化、环境、经济效益的旅游业。在这些理念和愿景的指导下，沙特确定的目标为旅游次数从2001年的6510次增加到2020年的14110次，其中包括12800万次的国内游，以及1310万的入境游。国内旅游平均消费从2001年的507亿里亚尔提高到2020年的783亿里亚尔，同时国外入境游客的消费从2001年的128亿里亚尔增加到2020年的230亿里亚尔。沙特政府将优先发展国内假期旅游市场，其次是朝觐之后的旅游市场，然后是以沙特自然文化遗产为基础的国外市场，主要客源预计为来自海湾国家、阿拉伯国家、其他伊斯兰国家以及重视环境游、沙漠游、潜水游、文化游的游客。

2016年4月15日，沙特阿拉伯副王储穆罕默德·本沙尔曼公布了沙特《2030愿景》，为沙特的经济转型和多样化勾勒出了一个雄心勃勃的蓝图。该计划分为四部分："生机勃勃的社会"、"繁荣昌盛的经济"、"雄心壮志的国家"以及"我们如何实现我们的愿景"。随后，沙特内阁会议于2016年6月7日通过了"2020年国家转型计划"，作为《2030愿景》的组成部分，该计划旨在通过经济结构性改革摆脱对石油的依赖，实现收入多元化和振兴经济。计划的主要目标中着重提到要增加旅游产业投资，大力发展旅游业，并提出了具体的指标：

第一，要建立和发展适于所有阶层家庭的新的旅游目的地及休闲城市，鼓励私有资本进行投资和开发。到2020年将有约1710亿沙特里亚尔（457亿美元）投入到旅游业，由此将新增37万新岗位。第二，保护、建设、发展和宣传国内遗址景点，鼓励私有资本进行投资和开发。到2020年将建设86家新博物馆，发展80个遗址，15个手工创作中心，新增6个在册的世界遗产、18个建筑遗址。第三，增加和发展旅游活动和节庆活动，吸引社会不同阶层。到2020年旅游业附加值要达到1188亿沙特里亚尔，游客数增长到8190万，实现旅游消费规模1748亿沙特里亚尔。

第四，增加和发展接待设施和旅游服务。到2020年要实现新增约17.5万客房，约2万多项旅游设施。由此可见，沙特政府已将旅游业视为能够有效推动实现经济、社会和国家发展目标的基础产业，并针对一系列问题制定了明确的发展计划，若能切实执行，必将为沙特旅游业的发展注入强劲动力，实现其战略目标，即在沙特价值观和特色的基础上发展均衡、可持续的旅游业，实现经济多样化、社会富裕、创造就业机会、保护环境及文化的正统性。

参考文献：

[1] 陈沫.沙特阿拉伯的经济调整与“一带一路”的推进.西亚北非，2016年第2期.
[2] 曹笑笑.沙特游客出境旅游动机的实证研究.浙江外国语学院学报，2014年9月第5期.
[3] 刘晖.阿拉伯国家旅游业发展一瞥.阿拉伯世界研究，2006年第2期。
[4] 刘晖.沙特阿拉伯旅游市场及其它.北京第二外国语学院学报，1999年第4期.
[5] 马坚译.古兰经.中国社会科学出版社，2003年6月第2版.
[6] 张桥贵，孙浩然.宗教旅游的类型、特点和开发.世界宗教研究，2008年第4期.
[7] 世界经济论坛，https://cn.weforum.org/reports，2016年8月6日.
[8] 沙特旅游信息与研究中心，http://www.mas.gov.sa/ar/Dashboard/Pages/default.aspx，2016年8月7日.
[9] 美国皮尤研究中心 http://www.pewforum.org/2015/04/02/religious-projections-2010-2050/，2016年8月10日.
[10] 沙特希望提高宗教旅游收入，BBC新闻 http://www.bbc.com/arabic/business/2016/05/160524_saudi_arabia_religious_tourism，2016年8月10日.
[11] 观点报.http://wejhatt.com/?p=1455，2016年8月14日.
[12] 利雅得报.http://www.alriyadh.com/547957，2016年8月16日.
[13] 今日报.http://www.alyaum.com/article/3143484，2016年8月23日.
[14] 利雅得报.http://www.alriyadh.com/656200，2016年8月30日.
[15] http://www.aleqt.com/2013/01/31/article_728707.html，2016年8月31日.

（作者简介：黄婷婷，女，四川外国语大学东方语学院，助教，硕士，研究方向：阿拉伯现代文学及中东问题）

中国大陆泰国文学研究综述
——以公开发表论著和CNKI网论文为中心分析

蒙昭晓

摘要：大陆学者对泰国文学的研究呈现出研究热点突出、研究角度多样化、不乏创新之作等特点。其中以泰国现代文学的研究居多，泰国古代文学的研究次之；而泰国近代文学的研究较少。泰国小说俨然成为研究热点，而影视文学的研究则有较强的时效性。

关键词：泰国；文学研究；特点

一、引言

随着译介传播，中国人越来越多地接触到泰国文学，从CNKI网看中国大陆对泰国文学的研究最早出现在1959年季羡林先生和刘板赢先生所著的《五四运动后四十年来中国关于亚非各国文学的介绍和研究》一文中。随着中泰两国合作交流的加深和“一带一路”战略的推进，大陆学者对泰国文学的研究无论是在深度上还是在广度上都有了进一步扩展。尤其是近年来随着“泰剧”热潮的掀起，大陆学者也越来越多地涉猎泰国影视文学。本文以公开发表论著和CNKI网论文为中心进行分析，试图从中归纳出泰国文学研究领域的研究特点，对研究状况有全面的把握，探索泰国文学研究空间，了解中国人对泰国文学的关注点。

泰国文学除传统意义上的诗歌、小说、散文、戏剧和民间故事外，还包括泰国影视文学和泰华文学。笔者将按照栾文华教授的泰国文学史分期法对大陆学者对泰国文学的研究分为古代文学、近代文学和现代文学三个时期进行分析，又因影视文学和泰华文学在时间上没有明确的分界线，所以另作一类进行分析。由于搜索条件有限，会议论文、本科论文以及港澳台学者的论著将不纳入分析范围。

二、大陆学者对泰国古代文学的研究

泰国的古代文学自素可泰王朝起至曼谷王朝四世王时期止（公元1257—1868），基本上是宗教文学、宫廷文学和经过宫廷文人再创作的民间文学，以诗歌和戏剧（泰国的戏剧也是诗剧）为主体。印度文学从内容到形式对泰国的古代文学影响极大；高棉文学、爪哇文学和中国文学在不同的历史时期也对泰国的古代文学产生了影响（栾文华，1998：4）。由于这一时期的时间跨度非常大，曾两度出现文学的鼎盛期[①]，出现了大量优秀的文学作品，故大陆学者对泰国古代文学的研究占了很大比重，呈现出按年代进行系统引介分析、研究对象较为集中的特点。

（一）论著方面

较为系统的有栾文华的《泰国文学史》，对文学史的分期、文学内容和形式的演变发展进行分析，而且对重要作家及其作品进行评价（1998）。金勇的《泰国民间文学》，通过泰国历史文化、神话传说、民间故事、民间歌谣、戏剧、熟语与谜语等介绍泰国民间文学的主要内容和民族特色（2011）。裴晓睿、熊燃的《〈帕罗赋〉翻译与研究》，对长篇叙事诗《帕罗赋》进行了全面梳理，从诗学解读、美学欣赏、翻译研究和语言学等方面进行多角度、多层面的分析，体现了东西方学者对这一经典作品的共同关注和不同研究视域（2013）。此外，尹湘玲主编的《东南亚文学史概论》、庞希云主编的《东南亚文学简史》和覃德清主编的《东盟文学》等系列丛书也对泰国文学进行了系统的介绍。

（二）论文方面

研究对象集中在《三国演义》等中国古典小说的翻译及其对泰国文学的影响、《拉玛坚》（改编自印度史诗《罗摩衍那》）、《昆昌昆平》等文学作品上。如刘莉、李学仙（泰）的《泰国“三国热”成因及其现代表征》，分析了由文明盛望形成的中泰心理相容、由政商移民造就的血脉相融以及由政治、审美需要促成的价值相容是促使《三国演义》能够在泰国文化领域、社会领域和民众意识领域扩散的主要原因（2014：75-78）。金勇的《泰文〈三国演义〉经典译本产生的原因分析》，指出曼谷王朝一世王基于战争实用性、政治训谕价值、当时中国文化在泰国影响力与日俱增等考虑将昭帕耶帕康（洪）版《三国》提升至“国家文

---

① 泰国古代文学的第一次鼎盛期在曼谷王朝二世王时期（公元1809—1824），第二次在曼谷王朝三世王时期（公元1824—1851）。

学”的高度，大大加速了其在泰国的本土化进程（2011：84-88）。裴晓睿的《汉文学的介入与泰国古小说的生成》，从小说文类生成的视角提出《三国演义》、《西汉通俗演义》等古典小说的移植开创了泰国文学史上小说文类的先河的观点（2007：114-118）。陈俊豪的《〈罗摩衍那〉中哈奴曼形象在泰国的发展》，认为神猴哈奴曼形象从母本《罗摩衍那》到泰国的《拉玛坚》，变化不明显，基本保留了母本的形象（2013：131）。傅光宇的《〈罗摩衍那〉在泰北和云南》，通过比较两者间的异同，得出两者均为印度罗摩故事长诗不同译文在新的自然环境与社会生活中的新发展与创新，是印度文化因子与各地文化传统结合后的新产物的结论（1997：45）。廖宇夫的《泰国〈昆昌昆平唱本〉女性形象对现实社会的影响》，指出《昆昌昆平》中女性形象对泰国现实社会起到教化的作用，并且对后世文学作品女性形象的作用产生影响（2006：66）。曹凌静、熊来湘的《〈红楼梦〉与〈昆昌昆平〉思想艺术特色的比较研究》，从思想内容、艺术特色和艺术成就方面进行比较，得出两者在艺术手法上同中有异的结论（2014：20-21）。此外，还有学者整体分析了影响泰国古代文学的因素，如李小梅的《泰国古代文学初探》一文回顾了泰国古代文学发展史，并分析影响泰国古代文学的宗教因素、外来文化因素和稻作文化因素等（2012：35-39）。裴晓睿的《印度诗学对泰国诗学和文学的影响》一文论述了印度古代诗学理论在泰国被接受、改造并最终衍化为泰国诗学的过程（2007：73-78）。雷华的《〈佛本生故事〉与泰国古代文学》，通过对古印度佛教经文《佛本生故事》对泰国古代文学在文学形式与思想方面的影响进行论述，指出在思想继承的同时，也存在批判（2005:69）。赖伯疆的《泰国戏剧古今谈》，追溯了泰国戏剧与印度和中国文化的渊源，介绍了绚丽多姿的泰国古典和现代剧，还分析了泰国当代剧坛的风貌和态势（1998：91-99）。以及范桂忠的硕士论文——《汉泰诗歌音乐性的对比》，通过汉泰语言音乐性的对比和“八Glaun”与近体诗音乐性的地对比，找到两种语言相同的与不同的文化特点（2010）。

三、大陆学者对泰国近代文学的研究

泰国的近代文学自曼谷王朝五世王时期起至曼谷王朝七世王时期止（公元1868—1928），处在古代文学向现代文学过渡、西方文学形式泰国民族化的时期，因此，文学形态的过渡性、思想内容的复杂多样性成了处于新旧交替时期的泰国近代文学的基本特征（栾文华，1998：131）。大陆学者对泰国近代文学的研究相对较少，究其原因，笔者认为主要因为过渡时期的泰国近代文学在思想和表现手法上尚未成熟，加之受到政治上的压迫和禁锢，以及二十世纪七十年代以来文学受到电视、录像带和声色犬马的娱乐活动的挤压和争夺而出现商业化的消遣文学，使得这一时期的文学作品的社会评价普遍不高。系统研究的论著有上文提及的文学史类书籍，如《泰国文学史》、《泰国文学沉思录》、《东南亚文学史概论》、《东南亚文学简史》和《东盟文学》等。此外，李健在《泰国近代文学的起因与发展》一文分析了泰国近代文学的起因及其经历的翻译编译、模仿改写、融合吸收和独立创作四个由幼稚逐步走向成熟阶段，从而引出亚洲各国近代文学发展规律的思考（2005：106-110）。而她的另一篇题为《论翻译在泰国文学史上的地位和作用——以近代文学为中心》的论文，论述了泰国近代文学翻译兴起的原因，包括泰国传统文学形式日渐式微，西方文学形式的冲击以及国王积极倡导文学翻译等，还指出泰国近代文学初期翻译的特点并提出几点思考（2008:71-75）。

四、大陆学者对泰国现代文学的研究

泰国现代文学自曼谷王朝七世王时期（二十世纪二十年代末）至今（公元1928— ）（如果加以细分，可以将第二次世界大战以来的五十年的文学称为当代文学），这时期的泰国文学完成了过渡的历史使命，在思想意识和艺术形式上都发生了重大变革（栾文华，1998：195）。泰国现当代文学作品，无论就其数量还是质量来说，在泰国文学史上都是空前的，其中成就最大的是小说。大陆学者对泰国现代文学的研究数量颇丰，主要体现在对单一经典文学作品的研究上，小说俨然成为研究热点。如吴圣杨的《泰国庇护制礼教文化背景与〈四朝代〉主题剖析》一文从庇护制礼教文化背景切入解读《四朝代》，分析了泰民族式被庇护者与庇护者形象（2010:40-49）。周婉华的《泰国历史小说〈四朝代〉中珀怡性格的文化意蕴》，指出珀怡顺从、宽容的性格特征折射出暹罗民族的审美情趣，寄托了作家的政治理想，其中“顺从”体现了封建文化中的“道德规范”，“宽容”则蕴含着佛教文化的“精神力量”（1996：40）。王素琴的硕士论文——《张爱玲〈倾城之恋〉与西巫拉帕〈画中情思〉比较研究》，从创作背景、人物形象与内容和艺术手法三方面进行对比分析（2010）。黄进炎、唐旭阳的《泰国小说〈画中情思〉的艺术风格》，分析了《画中情思》在人物塑造、语言运用、情节安排和心理刻画方面的独特风格（2013：74）。静怡的《20世纪初泰中文学中的女性悲剧根源分析——以西巫拉帕〈以罪斗争〉与张爱玲〈半生缘〉为例》，文章分析了泰中文学的女性悲剧根源有三个方面：一是社会现实和家庭制约的压迫，二是自身的软弱与变态的性格，三是命运的无法抉择（2015：105-107）。李欧、傅其林的《〈甘医生〉的叙事技巧评述》，展示了作家在小说中所运用的全知聚焦、回溯法、叙述时速等叙述策略，并对其接受效果做了阐发性评述（2000：53）。李健的《义素分析法与泰国小说〈风尘少女〉》，通过义素对比直观地显示出人物形象的异同，以及洞悉情节发展的必然性（1998：33）。李玉良的硕士论文——《〈骆驼祥子〉与〈判决〉之比较研究》，通过讨论这两部作品的创作比较、人物比较、其他人物之比较及社会学意义的比较，展示了这两部小说所揭示的社会、人性等问题（2010）。此外，还有《关于〈舟渡彼岸〉的艺术分析》、《泰国作家社尼·绍瓦蓬及其代表作〈魔鬼〉》、《高·素朗卡娘与〈悲惨生涯〉》、《女性主义视角下的中泰父权制批判者——丁玲与多迈索》和《泰国以国外为背景的长篇小说的创始者蒙昭·阿卡丹庚》，等等。

除了对作家和小说作品的研究外，也不乏对泰国现代文学的整体性研究，如邱苏伦、裴晓睿的《当代外国文学纪事：1980—2000：泰国卷》，以纪事的形式对这一时期的文学思潮和文学发展的状况进行客观的分析和总结概括，进行批判性的把握和吸收，展现了当代泰国文学的全景画面（2015）。李健的《泰国文学沉思录》以文集的形式，收录了作者对泰国现代重要作家及其作品的研究（2007）。李欧的《泰国小说发展历程及其特征》一文通过对泰国小说发展史的回顾，剖析了泰国小说“以文载道”的倾向、因模仿带来的创作技巧滞后和重叙事轻抒情的现实主义风格等特征及其原因（2003：156-161）。雷华的《论泰国现代文学小人物形象的特质》一文论述了泰国现代文学中的小人物虽身份卑微但不失人格尊严、不弃原则、不灭反抗之志与精神博大的个性以及产生这一文学现象的原因（2001:42-41）。

五、大陆学者对泰国影视文学和泰华文学的研究

（一）泰国影视文学方面

大陆学者对泰国影视文学的研究，有较强的时效性，大体可分为三大类，第一类是纯影片和电影事业介绍的影视资讯类文章，如《亚洲影坛新“龙头”泰国》和《泰国电影作品》等。第二类是对某部或某类影片进行解读，对其特点及成功经验进行解析（以恐怖片的研究居多），如《泰剧中的文化传播——以〈蜜色死神〉为例》、《影片〈想爱就爱〉对泰国社会的透视》、《佛与魔的艺术——解读泰国恐怖电影》、《对泰国动作电影崛起的反思》和《近年泰国影视热播的文化

艺术探析》等。第三类是从电影艺术和理论的角度对泰国电影作深层次的研究，如《用民俗与想象触摸历史——泰国史诗电影述评》、《新世纪泰国电影文化及其表演形态》、《中泰家庭伦理剧比较研究》。值得一提的是，不少学者独辟蹊径，或研究泰国电影中的华人形象（如《泰国电影中华人形象浅析及其转变历史原因分析》)，或研究泰国电影的商业化及本土文化危机（如《全球化进程中的本土文化危机——以泰国恐怖片〈鬼鼓〉为例》)，或研究泰国电影的“殖民化”现象及其反殖民意义（如《港台的“在地经验”、后殖民文化及其抵制策略——以中国台湾、香港及泰国电影文化为核心》)，不一而足。

（二）泰华文学方面

泰华文学在二十世纪八十年代以来出现繁荣，这得益于泰国政治气候渐趋宽松，特别是自1992年3月解除了限制华文教育的禁令以来，泰国渐渐出现了“中文热”（栾文华，1998：362）。泰华作家在创作的同时，也翻译和介绍泰国文学；而他们的作品也常被译载在著名的泰国杂志上，这表明了泰国国内对华文文学的接纳和承认，华人和泰人在精神上也加强了沟通和联系。大陆学者对泰华文学的研究主要集中在对知名泰华作家（司马攻、梦莉、曾心、牡丹和马凡等）的散文研究上，如《追求“尺水兴波”的艺术技巧——略谈司马攻三篇不同类型的微型小说佳作》、《冰心与梦莉散文创作比较研究》、《曾心散文研究》、《论华裔泰文女作家牡丹小说中的华人女性形象》和《谈马凡的微型小说》等。除个体研究外，也不乏整体研究，如张国培的《20世纪泰国华文文学史》一书中阐述了20世纪泰华文学的萌芽、勃兴沉寂、以及复苏等时期的文学概况（2007）。张训涛的《泰国华文文学的文化特质及与政治之关系》，从佛教、社会政治与泰华文学的关系，指出泰华文学是一门特色鲜明、有着独特文化内涵和文化取向的文学艺术（2004:41-46）。张长虹的硕士论文——《文化心理的观照——中国与泰华的新文学关系侧探》，通过价值观念、道德情操、民族性格、艺术审美等几个心理层面，探讨中国新文学在中华文化精神方面直接或间接地影响泰华新文学（2001）。

四、结语

大陆学者对泰国文学的研究特点可概括为研究热点突出、研究角度多样化、不乏创新之作等。从泰国文学史分期上看，研究热点为泰国现代文学研究；泰国古代文学研究次之，而泰国近代文学研究较少；从体裁上看，研究热点为泰国小说的研究，泰华文学的散文研究次之，诗歌的研究较少；从具体文学作品上看，研究热点为洪版《三国》、《四朝代》和《昆昌昆平》等；从学者身份上看，对泰国传统文学进行研究的学者多为泰语专业学者，而研究泰国影视文学以及泰华文学的学者多为影视传媒专业及汉语言文学专业学者。创新之作如李健的《义位变体与文学作品人物分析》，采用义素分析法对人物性格进行分析；方佳萃的《浅谈泰国小说〈甘医生〉现实型特征》，运用文学类型理论进行分析；曾心的《移民意识[①]在泰华文学的取向》，作者用敏锐的触角捕捉到新移民在与泰国本土文化磨合的过程中透过文学流露的移民意识。

参考文献：

[1]曹凌静，熊来湘.《红楼梦》与《昆昌昆平》思想艺术特色的比较研究[J].鸭绿江，2014,(11)：20-21.

[2]陈俊豪.《罗摩衍那》中哈奴曼形象在泰国的发展[J].中国校外教育，2013,(S2)：131.

[3]范桂忠.汉泰诗歌音乐性的对比[D].上海：复旦大学，2010.

[4]傅光宇.《罗摩衍那》在泰北和云南[J].民族文学研究，1997,(2)：39-45.

[5]侯营.中国古典文学对泰国文学的影响[J].泰华文学，2007,(4)：26-29.

[6]黄进炎，唐旭阳.泰国小说《画中情思》的艺术风格[J].广东外语外贸学学报，2013,(3)：71-74.

[7]金勇.泰文《三国演义》经典译本产生的原因分析[J].解放军外国语学院学报，2011,(2):84-88.

[8]金勇.泰国民间文学[M].银川：宁夏人民教育出版社，2011.

[9]静怡.20世纪初泰中文学中的女性悲剧根源分析——以西巫拉帕《以罪斗争》与张爱玲《半生缘》为例[J].无锡商业职业技术学院学报，2015，15(1)：104-107.

[10]赖伯疆.泰国戏剧古今谈[J].戏剧艺术，1998,(5)：91-99.

[11]雷华.论泰国现代文学小人物形象的特质[J].四川师范学院学报，2001,(7)：42-46.

[12]雷华.《佛本生故事》与泰国古代文学[J].西华师范大学学报，2005,(2)：69-72.

① 移民意识指客居异国他乡的知识分子，在陌生的环境遭受挫折，如浮萍漂泊，找不到属于自己的“家”而苦闷、惆怅、迷惘。在文学中表现为抒发寄人篱下与怀念家乡为主的“落叶归根”的思想。

[13]李健.义素分析法与泰国小说《风尘少女》[J].解放军外国语学院学报，1998，21(2)：29-33.

[14]李健.泰国文学沉思录[M].北京：世界图书出版公司北京公司，2007.

[15]李健.论翻译在泰国文学史上的地位和作用——以近代文学为中心[J].解放军外国语学院学报，2008，31(1)：71-75.

[16]李健.泰国近代文学的起因与发展[J].解放军外国语学院学报，2005，(1)：106-110.

[17]李欧，傅其林.《甘医生》的叙事技巧评述[J].四川师范学院学报，2000，(5)：53-55.

[18]李欧.泰国小说发展历程及其特征[J].当代外国文学，2003，(1)：156-161.

[19]李小梅.泰国古代文学初探[J].临沧师范专科学院学报，2012，22(2)：35-39.

[20]李玉良.《骆驼祥子》与《判决》之比较研究[D].泉州：华侨大学，2010.

[21]廖宇夫.泰国《昆昌昆平唱本》女性形象对现实社会的影响[J].东南亚纵横，2006，(7)：62-66.

[22]刘莉.泰国“三国热”成因及其现代表征[J].四川戏剧，2014，(1)：75-78.

[23]栾文华.泰国文学史[M].北京：社会科学文献出版社，1998.

[24]裴晓睿，熊燃.帕罗赋翻译与研究[M].北京：北京大学出版社，2013.

[25]裴晓睿.汉文学的介入与泰国古小说的生成[J].解放军外国语学院学报，2007，(4)：114-118.

[26]裴晓睿.印度诗学对泰国诗学和文学的影响[J].南亚研究，2007，(2)：73-78.

[27]邱苏伦，裴晓睿等.当代外国文学纪事(1980—2000)：泰国卷[M].北京：商务印书馆，2015.

[28]王素琴.张爱玲《倾城之恋》与西巫拉帕《画中情思》比较研究[D].泉州：华侨大学，2010.

[29]吴圣杨.泰国庇护制礼教文化背景与《四朝代》主题剖析[J].外国文学评论，2010，(3)：40-49.

[30]张国培2007.20世纪泰国华文文学史[M].广东：汕头大学出版社.

[31]张训涛.泰国华文文学的文化特质及与政治之关系[J].广东教育学院学报，2004，24(1)：41-46.

[32]张长虹.文化心理的观照——中国与泰华的新文学关系侧探[D].厦门：厦门

大学，2001.
[33]张振华，戈苑等.用民俗与想象触摸历史——泰国史诗电影述评[J].浙江传媒学报，2010，(4)：88-92.
[34]周婉华.泰国历史小说《四朝代》中珀怡性格的文化意蕴[J].思想战线，1996，(2)：39-43.

（作者简介：蒙昭晓，女，四川外国语大学东方语学院，助教，硕士，研究方向：泰国文化）

中国出境游市场的发展趋势及其原因

金福实

摘要：中国旅游研究院在北京发布了最新一部中国旅游经济蓝皮书《2015年中国旅游经济运行分析和2016年发展预测》，提到中国旅游行业的旅游总收入已突破4万亿。（中国旅游研究院.2015.8）在国内游、入境游、出境游三大市场中，出境游市场以12%的增长率继续保持高速增长。近年来，中国的出境游可谓是一匹“黑马”，在中国旅游市场，甚至是世界旅游市场上异军突起。2015年国内的出境游总人数超过1.2亿人次，出境游规模连续三年排名世界第一。而且，我国内地公民出境旅游消费总额连续5年居全球第一，成为世界第一大出境旅游客源市场，处于全球同类市场中居首的地位，带动了全球旅游行业的发展。面对如此旺盛的出境游需求和强劲的发展尽头，中国的出境游市场已成为全球关注的重点对象。大体上，中国的出境游特征有上亿人次、规模巨大，空间非均衡发展，购物为境外消费主体。因此，有必要对中国的出境游市场的发展趋势及其原因进行分析。

关键词：旅游业　中国出境游市场　发展趋势

一、中国出境游市场的现状

旅游业作为世界规模最大的产业之一，不论从它的总收入、就业、增值、投资和纳税等方面来看，都对世界和各国经济的发展有着重大的贡献。我们知道，一个国家的旅游市场是由国内游、入境游、出境游三大市场组成，这三大市场也共同组成了我国统一的旅游市场。中国旅游业虽然起步较晚，然而随着中国国民经济的高速发展也使我国的旅游市场发展迅速。旅游业作为精神文化消费的第三大产业说明国人已不仅仅是注重物质消费而开始关注精神消费。其中，自20世纪90年代以来，中国的出境游更是进入了一个快速增长的阶段，到目前成为亚太地区重要的客源输出国。

（一）中国出境游市场发展规模

中国作为全球人口数量最多的国家，其庞大的人口基数决定了巨大的旅游需求。在我国的经济社会稳定发展，特别是一直以来旅游主管部门对出境游没有采取任何限制性政策的宏观背景下，中国出境游市场规模得到突飞猛进的高速发展。2015年国内出境游总人数超过1.2亿人次，出境游规模连续三年排名世界第一。虽出境游人次已突破亿人次，但是在中国庞大的人口基数下所产生的旅游人次还是偏少。故中国的出境游在国际旅游业的潜力巨大，有相当巨大的发展空间，也是中国出境游蓬勃发展的基础动力。

（二）先富起来的部分人带动出境游

由于我国的特殊历史条件和特殊的国情下邓小平提出了“让一部分人先富起来”的政策，是让一部分人、一部分地区先富起来，以带动和帮助落后的地区。经过二十多年的经济发展和改革开放，让一部分人先富起来的目的基本达到，社会上已经形成了一部分的富人。就像当初提出的让先富起来的人带动其他人一起走向共同富裕一样，也可能是我国先富起来的一部分人，由于较高的经济收入，带动了中国出境游的发展，刺激着中国出境游的进一步发展。

（三）中国出境游市场增速高于入境游和国内游

在中国旅游业发展初期，中国出境游是较为不受重视的部分，发展较为缓慢。其不被重视的原因也是众所周知的历史原因导致的国民生活水平低下，人们思想相对保守，国家政策限制等。但随着改革开放的不断深化发展，社会经济水平进一步提高，中国出境游得到了突飞猛进的发展。起先中国出境游市场规模明显低于国内游和入境游市场的规模，但是经过多年的发展，在量上还是有很大的差距，却在增长率上出境游市场的增速明显快于其他两个市场。到目前为止，出境游市场的增速均居于三大旅游市场之首，而且仍保持高速增长。

（四）从旅游目的地分布来看出境游发展空间

从收集到的数据资料来看，目的地分布由国内 1.2亿的出境游游客中有 64%去往港澳台，其中香港 4635万人次，澳门 2636万人次，台湾 427万人次；20%去往亚洲其他国家，包括韩国（611万人次）、日本（490万人次）、泰国（349万人次）；7%去往欧洲、北美、澳洲，包括美国（256万人次）、俄罗斯（148万人次）、澳大利亚（98万人次）、德国（92万人次）。从出境游人次占总人口的比例来看，韩国接近 30%，日本为 13%-15%，美国接近 20%，俄罗斯超过 35%，南非在10%左右，巴西和印度则低于5%，而中国2015年出境游总人次1.2亿，总人口量为13.68亿人，出境旅游率达到8.8%，如果剔除7271万港澳台游的人次，真正的出国旅游率仅为3.5%，即使将分母换成7.5亿的城镇常住人口，出境旅游率和出国旅游率也仅为16%和6.3%。因此，从海外国家的出境旅游率看，中国的出境游市场至少还有2-3倍的空间。（中国产业信息网.2016.3）

二、中国出境游市场的发展趋势

中国的出境游是从20世纪80年代中期的港澳探亲游发展起来的，由于仅限于探亲旅游，出境游人数很少。中国真正的出境游市场的形成是从开放东南亚旅游市场开始的。1988年，除中国香港和澳门地区外，泰国成为中国出境旅游的第一个目的地国家，中国公民的出境游自此起步。1990年起，中国政府陆续允许公民赴新加坡、马来西亚、泰国、菲律宾为探亲旅游的目的地国家；1997年起，根据新的原则和程序，中国政府又陆续批准开放了一些中国公民可以自费出境旅游的目的地国家，使出境探亲旅游正式转变为中国公民自费出国旅游。（郑淑婧，2005:1）到2013年，与中国政府签订ADS协议的国家与地区超过140个，正式实施开放的旅游目的地达到116个，目的地范围覆盖涉及亚洲、大洋洲、欧洲、非洲与美洲。其中中国与这五大洲正式实施开放目的地的国家或地区分别有32个、10个、37个、19个和18个。因此，伴随着这种现实背景，中国出境游目的地的选择呈现多元化的特点。在这种多元化的趋势下，更好地掌握中国出境游目的地市场的信息对了解中国出境游市场的发展趋势有很大的帮助。下面是以我个人的观点提出来的几个中国出境游市场的发展趋势：

（一）中国出境游市场规模在原有基础上高速发展

改革开放之后，我国入境旅游的封闭红利得到集中释放，1978年至1986年8年间，入境旅游人数增幅超过11倍，至2000年的22年间，入境旅游复合增长率达到19.02%。相比之下，出境旅游无论在启动时间上还是在启动初期的发展速度上均不如入境旅游。从有统计数据的1993年开始至2000年7年间，出境旅游人次仅增长了1.8倍。随着封闭红利逐渐释放殆尽以及国民收入稳步增长，2001年成为我国出入境旅游市场增速反转的拐点。（荆艳峰.2006）2001年至2013年，入境游复合增长率下降为3.41%，同期出境游复合增长率达到18.77%，出入境市场轮动发展完成新一轮交替。收入增长、旅游偏好增强、人民币对主要货币的升值是促进中国居民出境旅游以及出境旅游支出增长的重要原因。据中国旅游研究院旅游经济重点实验室测算，人民币实际有效汇率升值1%，将导致中国出境旅游人数增长3.094%。假定其他因素不变，汇改以来人民币实际有效汇率升值拉动了中国出境旅游人数增长约110.61个百分点，是我国出境游持续高速增长的最主要原因。中国旅游研究院发布的消息指出，2016年中国将会继续蝉联全球出境游人次的世界冠军。2015年中国出境游的游客人次达到1.2亿人次，仅2016年上半年中国公民出境游的人数达到5903万人次，这一数据比上年同期增长4.3%。（中国旅游研究院网站）然而，这只是冰山一角，中国的出境游市场似汪洋大海，潜力无穷。目前拥有出境游证件的中国公民约为6500万人，相对于13亿的中国人口规模，中国的出境游市场比例还不到5%。随着国家经济的发展、国民总收入也不断提高，个人的收入水平也得到了提升，促使人们不断从物质商品需求转向精神商品的需求。而且依据经济发达水平政府制定的工作时间和度假制度也得到了很大的改善，使个人的休闲时间增多，也是出境游游客人数增加的重要因素之一。近年来，《国民休闲纲要》明确提出要完善带薪休假制度，进一步在法律层面上保证公民的休假权利，这也是得益于中国的经济发展状况，也相应地促进中国出境游市场发展。除此之外，还有很多比如国与国之间的关系、国家政策、货币汇率、旅游价格、游客的职业类型、教育水平等等都是影响出境游发展的因素。而这一切的一切都在不断地发展，给人们提供良好的出境游环境，这就意味着中国的出境游潜力依然巨大，未来将会有更多的中国公民涌入出境游的浪潮之中。然而随着时间的推移这都是属于正常的发展阶段，不是一时的发展变化，而是随着国家综合国力的增强必然会发生的趋势。

（二）中国出境游消费爆发式增长

中国出境游正在发生质的变化，进入消费升级的阶段。中国的游客已经不是单纯的买买买，而是希望安排奢华或者特色高端酒店、不再忙着赶行程、吃的必须是本地特色餐。中国游客出境购物已从买奢侈品为主，逐渐转向日用百货类，银联卡在百货公司和超市等场所的消费增长明显，中国游客出境旅游人均消费额居全球前列。已经出现了得中国游客者得天下的说法，从全球范围来看中国游客对目的地国的旅游业及经济发展，甚至对就业都有巨大的贡献。中国游客在海外消费的爆发得益于更加便捷的金融服务，虽然人民币在许多地区不是流通货币，但是兑换起来比前些年方便许多。再加上目前许多国家零售商为了抓住中国游客都在接收银联卡，还有很多商店及专卖店都在支持支付宝付款。此外，中国留学的花费不同程度地放大了国民出境消费的规模。据悉期限不满一年的中国留学生境外花费的亦被计入旅游外汇收入。据统计英国、美国、日本、澳大利亚、法国、加拿大、韩国和意大利的中国留学生占全国出国留学生的9%，我国留学生在这些国家的加权年均花费约为2.47万美元，如此算来在外停留时间不超过1年的出国留学生的花费总额每年为110亿美元，约占我国游客境外花费额的十分之一。（世界旅游城市联合会.2015.9）中国游客消费水平的提升和消费方式的多元化以及税收制度、国内产品质量、境外消费环境和促销策略等都对海外购物消费有着重要的影响。

（三）主要集中在亚洲的出境游将会向其他洲分布

根据中国旅行社协会给出的数据资料显示，中国出境游目的地大都集中在亚洲地区并且在中国出境游中占据着绝大部分的优势。就像上述所讲中国1.2亿人次的出境游游客中，有64%的游客前往港澳台地区。到目前为止，港澳台同胞来大陆地区的旅游访问活动一直被视为入境游，同样我国大陆地区的居民前往港澳台地区的旅游访问活动也视为出境游。那么，一直以来港澳台出境游受游客欢迎的原因大概是：第一，旅游活动的旅行距离相对较短，因而旅途所需的实践较少。第二，旅游费用相对远距离较少。第三，基本上不存在文化障碍，方便交流。第四，同时也是不要办理过多的繁杂手续。由于这些原因港澳台出境游一直保持着居高不下的地位，但是就目前的发展趋势来看，港澳台出境游明显降温，日韩及东南亚出境游继续火爆，欧洲出境游迎来火爆的场面，北美澳洲出境游增长也是相当平稳。其中赴韩国、日本以及东南亚出境游的人次继续保持高速增长，短途出境游倍受青睐。但是近年来因韩国出现中东呼吸综合征、部署萨德系统，与菲律宾等国的南海纷争以及泰国的政局动荡的影响，亚洲出境游出现了短暂的下滑现象。之后，随着居民收入水平的提高、欧元贬值、签证放宽、国内休假制度的完善，欧洲出境游开始出现火爆的现象。2015年前往德国、意大利、法国的游客人次分别比同期增长70%、41%、48%，出现了前所未有的高幅度增长。美国及澳大利亚的游客人次也继续保持较快的增长。

（四）主要集中在东部沿海地区的出境游产客向内陆地区发展

从互联网上和国家旅游组织发布的数据中得知，中国内地各省市及地区出境游客源市场主要集中在东部沿海地区。中西部地区的出境游产客能力还需要进一步开发，而其中的湖北、四川、山西和其他中西部城市在出境游中处于优势地位。那么出现东西部地区出境游客源差异的原因主要是中国区域社会经济发展的差异。东部沿海地区的经济水平明显高于中西部地区，因此相比于中西部城市来说东部地区的游客在出境游的花费上较为宽裕。另一原因就是东部沿海地区的人口密度明显高于中西部地区的城市，所以说在出境游人口数量在绝对量上明显要高于中西部城市。而且东部沿海地区的对外交通便利，签证的办理也更加方便，上述种种可以说是游客集中于东部沿海地区的原因。但是以目前中国经济的发展增速、世界各大企业进军中国中西部地区以及政府对中西部地区的大力开发，其中处于内陆中西部地区的重庆已经连续几年在全国的发展增速位列第一。可想而知，目前，中国的中西部地区的经济已经突破发展缓慢、得到了全面发展的契机。相应的东西部地区的出境游市场也会如鱼得水般爆发其潜力。

综上所述，我国社会经济高速增长、国民收入水平大幅提高的情况下，我国的出境游市场得到了很大的发展，也呈现出大规模发展趋势。前面已经对中国出境游发展的趋势及其原因进行了分析，但是就个人观点认为中国的出境游市场得到如此快速的发展虽然得益于中国经济的快速发展，也存在不容大家忽视的原因，那就是中国的国内游存在的一些潜在的问题。

我国的国内游主要存在以下几个问题：1.旅游成本高、体验差。由于受到我国旅游产业发展模式的制约，我国的国内游主要是观光旅游，每一种旅游类型都有其依赖的因素。观光旅游依赖于资源、度假旅游依赖于环境。以观光旅游为的核心的国内游，必须强化对景区的依赖性，形成了以景区为重心的门票经济。在旅游需求的推动下，我国的景区门票价格正不断提升。根据旅游行业市场调查分析报告数据显示，目前国内5A级景区中，门票价格大多过百元，部分甚至超过300元，虽说国家发改委的“禁涨令”已经实行7年，但是景区门票涨价的脚步从没有停止过。一项针对游客的调查显示，有高达89.2%的网友认为，中国景区门票“太贵了”，门票支出已严重影响对旅游的热情。我国景区门票价格的不断提升使旅游者的旅游成本提高抑制了我国国内游市场的扩张，阻碍了我国国内游市场的规模性发展。在服务质量和市场秩序方面，旅游者外出旅游就是花钱图个轻松买个愉快，获得良好的旅游体验，然而我国的旅游市场存在非法经营、欺客宰客、强迫消费等行为，大大满足不了消费者的需求。2.旅游产品需要转型，要解决国内游增长缓慢的问题，应考虑改变国内旅游产品的形态、提升国内旅游产品质量和降低国内旅游成本。我国的旅游发展初期，大家追求的是短暂式的观光旅游，随着旅游的日渐普及，游客已经不满足于简单一看，而是把旅游看成是一种繁杂工作后的调节，看成是一种轻松身心的有效手段，度假旅游就是放松的一种很有效的方式。观光旅游是以参观、欣赏自然景观和民俗风情为主要目的和游览内容的旅游消费活动。度假旅游是以度假和疗养为主要目的和内容的一种消费活动。由观光旅游向度假旅游为主体的转型，这不是说观光旅游就没有发展前途，而是观光旅游最为普遍的情况下对度假旅游的需要在不断上升成为其主流。观光型主要靠卖门票，休闲度假型则靠卖服务，所以旅游形态的转变更多地表现为服务能力的提升，服务提升了，旅游产品的质量就提高了游客的满意度也会相应地上升。3.相关政策的不足，在政府主导下的旅游产业发展促进旅游产品的有效转型是政策与制度的设计、政策与制度的供给是旅游产品转型的关键。(王晓丽.王学峰.2006）国家先前提出的旅游战略部署是围绕观光旅游提出的，但是随着度假形态和休闲形态的旅游发展，相关的政策与制度没有跟进，现有的许多制度和政策是难以跟得上旅游业的发展的。

我们要全面了解旅游业的发展趋势、分析其原因，找出阻碍旅游业无论是出境游还是国内游的问题，以促进我国旅游业的快速发展。不可否认的是，部分中国游客在出行秩序、礼仪、尊重当地风俗习惯等方面都还存在着需要改善的部分，作为游客、消费者应当考虑到国家和个人的形象，注重自己的行为举止，避免有损形象的事情发生。在全球化经济下长大的新一代旅游者，中国出境游游客在传播中国文化、提升中国国家形象的过程中，发挥积极的作用。而且中国公民出境游的发展在一定程度上展现我国大国形象、扩大国与国的经济交往、民与民之间的文化交流，特别是在我国贸易出口大量顺差的国际环境下，中国公民大规模的出境游也可以在一定程度上缓解国际贸易的摩擦，为我国社会经济的发展创造一个良好的国际社会环境。

参考文献：

[1] 郑淑婧.中国出境旅游市场潜力的空间分布及深入发展对策分析.干旱区资源与环境，2005，第19卷.
[2] 中国产业信息网.2016年中国出境旅游市场现状分析及行业发展趋势，2016.3.
[3] 中国旅游研究院.中国旅游蓝皮书，2015.8.
[4] 世界旅游城市联合会.中国公民出境（城市）旅游消费市场调查报告，2015.9.
[5] 荆艳峰.我国出境旅游发展趋势预测及建议.商业时代，2006.
[6] 王晓丽.王学峰.解读新形势下中国出境旅游政策变更.商场现代化，2006.

（作者简介：金福实，女，四川外国语大学东方语学院，硕士研究生）

国内智慧旅游研究的回顾和展望
——基于CNKI相关文献的统计分析

王文健

摘要：智慧旅游作为信息业与旅游业相结合的产物，在我国的快速崛起顺应了时代的发展和要求，同时也受到了大量国内学者的关注和研究。本文通过文献整理法，从国内智慧旅游文献的现状、文献的内容总结及智慧旅游应用对象三个大方面对我国的智慧旅游文献进行了统计分析，对以后学者对于“智慧旅游”的研究提供参考，从而为国内外学者更好地为我国智慧旅游的发展提供文献指导具有深远的意义。

关键词：智慧旅游；CNKI；统计分析

一、引言

自从2008年IBM公司首席执行官彭明盛提出“智慧的地球”概念以来，“智慧”一词已经被越来越多的人们所关注和应用。智慧，旨在以物联网、泛在网为基础，通过信息的查询、交流以及应用，方便人民的生活。随后，作为“智慧地球”的落脚点，“智慧城市”、“智慧旅游”等名词也相继提出。智慧旅游，顾名思义，是以游客为中心，借助信息科学技术，通过大数据的整理分析实现了旅游前、旅游中、旅游后的信息需求进而提高了旅游质量。

“智慧旅游”是时代的产物，也是时代发展的要求。这些年来，我国“智慧旅游”的建设发展程度不断地向前推进。2010年，江苏省镇江市在我国率先提出“智慧旅游”的概念并实施；2012年国家旅游局确定18个“国家智慧旅游试点城市”；随后，国务院又将2014年确定为了智慧旅游年。作为信息产业与旅游业的结合，“智慧旅游”在我国的快速崛起顺应了时代的发展和要求，同时也受到了大量国内学者的关注和研究，并成为研究的热点。本文通过文献整理法，在CNKI上搜索了主题为“智慧旅游”的所有文章，共计1528篇，时间范围是2010年1月1日—2015年12月31日。通过对其文献的整理分析，可在总结我国“智慧旅游”所有文献的现状和问题基础之上，为学者对于“智慧旅游”的研究提供参考，从而在日后更好地为我国智慧旅游的发展提供文献指导。

二、文献综述

通过搜索发现，基于CNKI有关“智慧旅游”文献整理的文章共有3篇。李加军，黄丽英（2015）对CNKI《中国学术期刊网络出版总库》中以"智慧旅游"为主题的研究文献的处理来源及方法、发文时间、出版源、下载与被引用情况、项目基金资助情况、涉及会议、核心作者进行了定量分析，以求找出国内智慧旅游的研究特点及研究趋势，为相关学者的后续研究提供一定的参考；韩雅博（2015）从年份发文情况、作者活跃程度、所发期刊状况以及论文主题四个方面进行分析；王蕴瑞（2015）从文献的处理来源及方法、发文时间、出版源、下载与被引用情况、项目基金资助情况、涉及会议、核心作者进行了分析。这三篇文献虽具有一定的参考价值，但只是对基于2014年及以前的数据进行了客观的现状描述并且是对“智慧旅游”文献的现有情况进行客观的反应，但不能反应“智慧旅游”文献的一些内容研究。

基于现有3篇文献，本文的创新点在于：1、分析发现，现有文献时间范围2010—2014年，针对样本较少的问题，本文搜集了2016年以前所有的主题为“智慧旅游”的1528篇文献进行分析，时间跨度更长，样本数据更大、更新，能准确地把握“智慧旅游”文献的最新发展现状和趋势；2、全文有针对性地从文献数量及构成、作者单位分布、研究内容分析、研究方法来分析，来说明现有“智慧旅游”相关文献的不足。3、首次对智慧旅游应用对象四个要素：游客、目的地居民、政府、企业这四个方面的文献进行了统计，亦可发现“智慧旅游”的一些研究内容。

（一）“智慧旅游”文献的现状

1. 文献发表数量

在CNKI上通过对主题为“智慧旅游”的搜索，共计文献1528篇。2010年，共计文献3篇；2011年，共计文献52篇；2012年，共计文献131篇；2013年，共计文献229篇；2014年，共计文献507篇；2015年，共计文献606篇。(如图1-1所示)。

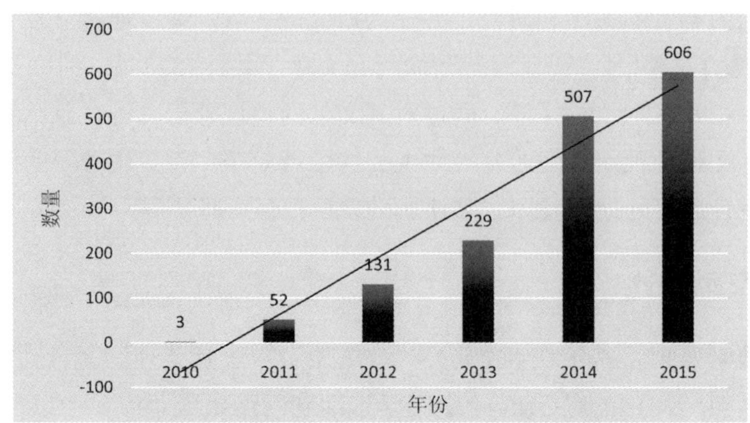

图1-1 CNKI主题为“智慧旅游”文献发表数量

数据来源：中国知网CNKI

通过图1-1可以看出，从2010年“智慧旅游”在我国的提出以及不断地发展，关于“智慧旅游”的文献也在不断地增加，足以说明“智慧旅游”引起了越来越多国内学者的研究和关注。2010年仅有三篇报纸有所报道，此后文献数量在不断地增加。2014年，国务院将此年确定为了“智慧旅游年”，此年研究“智慧旅游”的文献大幅度增加，从2013年的229篇上升到2014年的507篇文献。2015年是发表文献最多的一年，共计文献606篇。但是，“智慧旅游”作为一个新生的产物，还在不断发展和成熟当中，对其研究还有一定的过程，因此相对于其他的课题，研究数量相对较少，仍有巨大的研究空间。

2. 文献类型的组成

通过对其文献类型进行整理统计，发表期刊共计913篇，报纸报道共计461篇，会议报道共计19篇，硕博论文共计135篇。（如图1-2所示）

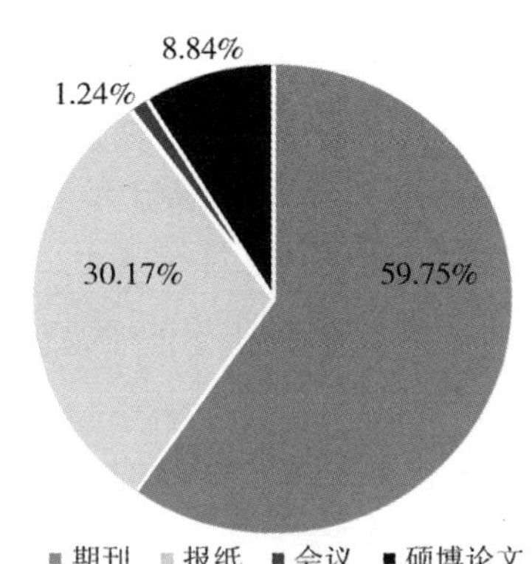

图1-2 CNKI主题为“智慧旅游”文献类型的组成

数据来源：中国知网CNKI

通过图1-2可以看出，“智慧旅游”的文献主要发表在期刊上（约占60%），而且每年发表的数量也是在呈递增上升的趋势（如表1-1所示）。期刊、报纸、会议、论文都在呈递增的趋势，同样表明了大家对于“智慧旅游”的关注程度在增加。

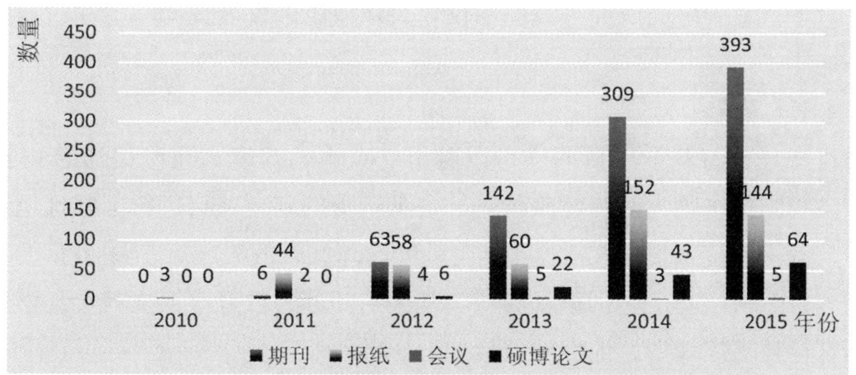

图1-3 CNKI主题为“智慧旅游”基于不同类型文献的数量统计

数据来源：中国知网CNKI

3. 文献的来源

通过图1-2不难发现，“智慧旅游”文献主要发表地点是期刊和报纸。统计表明，发表在期刊和报纸文献数量为1374篇（约占89.9%）。《中国旅游学报》（报纸）、《旅游纵览》（期刊）、《物联网技术》（期刊）、《商》（期刊）、《旅游学刊》（期刊）是发表“智慧旅游”最多的刊物，体现了这些刊物对于智慧旅游的重视。（如表1-2所示）

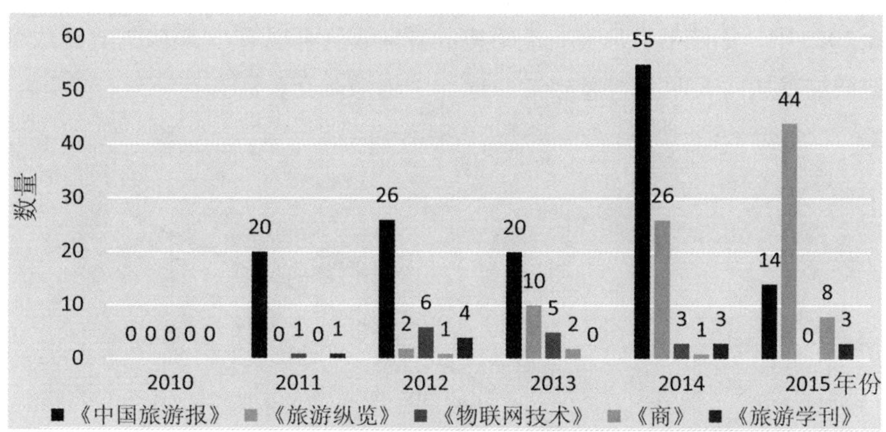

图1-4 CNKI主题为“智慧旅游”文献发表的出处统计

资料来源：中国知网CNKI

统计发现，旅游学科的文献共有1438篇，旅游软件及计算机应用学科的文献共有108篇，“智慧旅游”文献的发表不仅在旅游刊物上报道逐渐增多，同样也在在有关物联网、互联网的刊物（例如《物联网技术》）上发表数量也在不断增加，也充分说明了“智慧旅游”的发展是是借助于现在信息科学技术的进步所产生。对于智慧旅游的研究，我们不仅仅关注旅游的发展，同样关注“智慧”的进展。

4.文献的基金项目

通过智慧旅游基金项目同样可以看出受重视的程度。在搜集到的1528篇文章当中，我们把主题为“智慧旅游”的文献所受的基金项目进行了整理统计，统计发现，获得基金项目的文献共131篇，约占总文献的7.7%。其中最多的基金项目是国家自然科学基金、国家社会科学基金、江苏省教育厅人文社会科学研究基金、国家科技支撑计划，他们的数量如表1-1所示。

表1-1“智慧旅游”文献最多的基金项目

基金项目	数量
国家自然科学基金	35
国家社会科学基金	26
江苏省教育厅人文社会科学研究基金	15
国家科技支撑计划	7

资料来源：中国知网CNKI

同时，本文根据文献所受基金项目的年份进行了整理，其中最早的基金项目出现在2012年，如图1-4所示。通过基金项目数量可以看出，基金项目数量是在不断地增加，从而表明“智慧旅游”近几年越来越受关注。

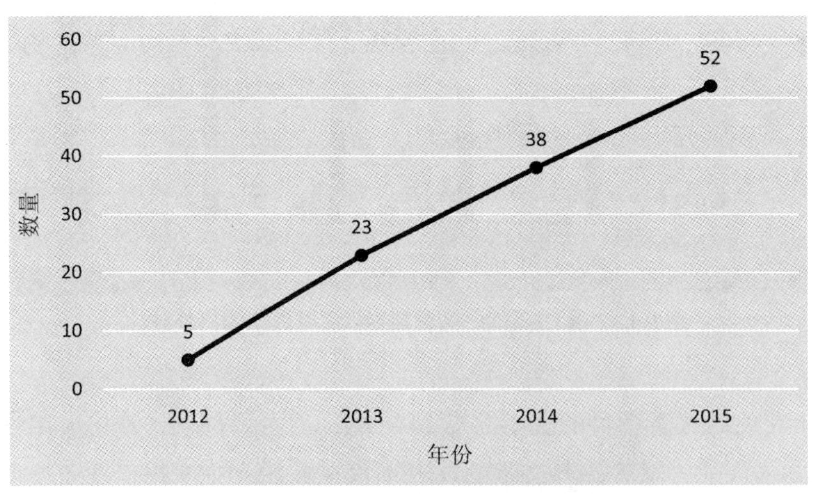

图1-5“智慧旅游”文献基金项目数量（按年份）

资料来源：中国知网CNKI

（二）文献内容的统计分析

对已有的文献按照内容进行分类，有关主题为“智慧旅游的概念、定义、理论”、“智慧旅游的发展 ”“智慧旅游的现状”“智慧旅游评价”的文献最多，如图2-1、2-2所示，本文也从这五个方面按照时间和主题进行了文献的整理统计。

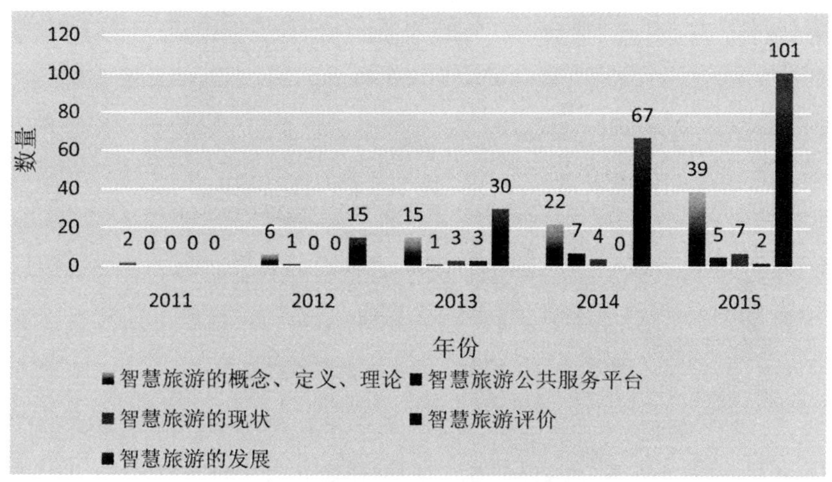

图2-1　“智慧旅游”按内容分类统计（总）

资料来源：中国知网CNKI

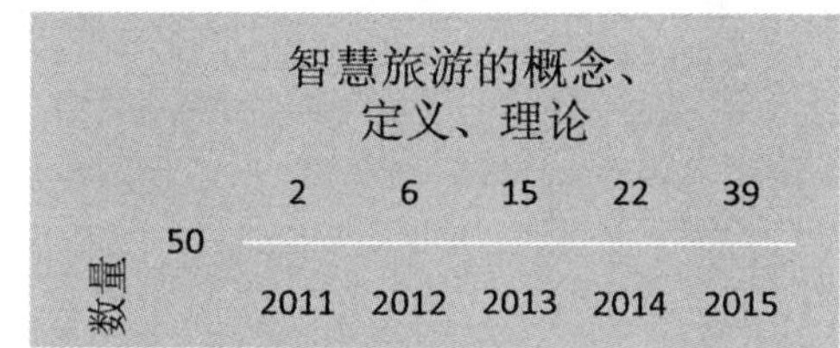

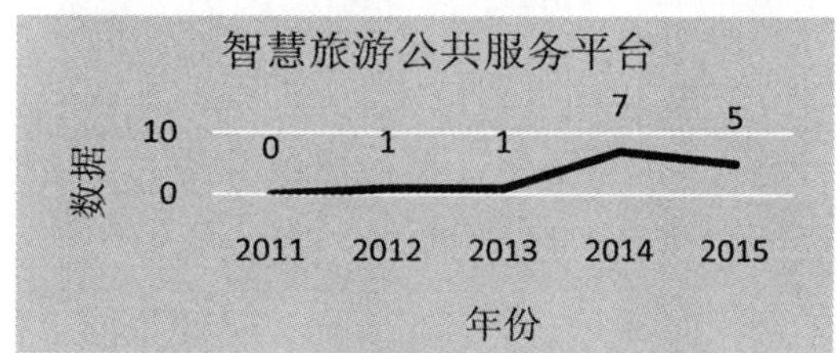

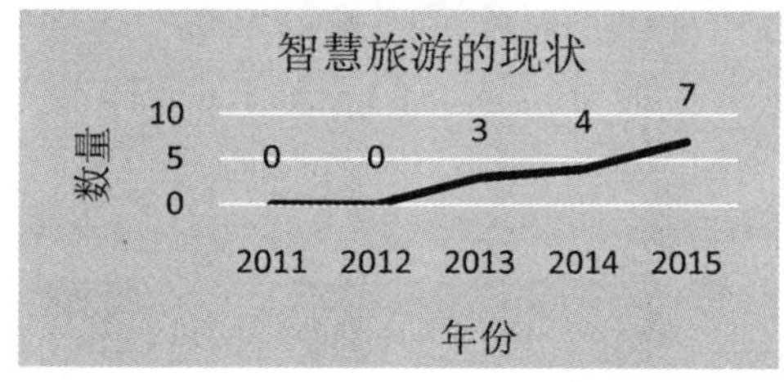

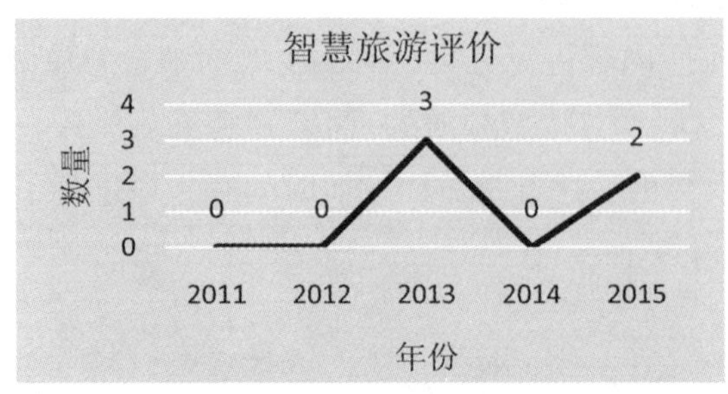

图2-2“智慧旅游”按内容分类统计（分）

资料来源：中国知网CNKI

基于现有文献，关于“概念、定义和理论”的文献共计94篇；“公共服务平台”共计15篇；“现状”共计15篇；“发展”共计242篇；“评价”共计5篇。由于“智慧旅游”刚刚在我国兴起，时间较短，对于已有的文献，基本都是定性分析的文献，学者们对于“智慧旅游”的研究主要集中在定义、现状、发展的探究等几个方面，相比之下，“智慧旅游理论体系”、“智慧旅游评价”等研究较少，为后来的研究提供了思路和方向。

1.智慧旅游概念、定义、理论

“智慧旅游”是旅游业与信息技术产业的结合而产生的结果，是社会不断变革发展的产物，也是科学技术发展到一定阶段的趋势。但是“智慧旅游”出现后，在定义方面一直没有统一的概念。本文整理得到的有关智慧旅游概念、定义和理论的文献共有94篇。虽没有统一定义，但在内容方面大同小异，其中以张凌云和李云鹏所提出的概念最具有代表性。

张凌云（2012）在已有的文献定义不足的基础之上，基于CAA框架体系提出了智慧旅游是基于新一代信息技术（也称信息通信技术，ICT），为满足游客个性化需求，提供高品质、高满意度服务，而实现旅游资源及社会资源的共享与有效利用的系统化、集约化的管理变革；李云鹏（2014）在梳理了国内外有关定义的情况下，从旅游信息服务视阈出发，强调智慧旅游以旅游者个体为核心、以信息服务为载体的支撑体系，以泛在化作为核心内涵，以旅游者行为方式、旅游业营销方式、管理方式和服务方式的根本性变化为主要外延。

大部分学者都赞同物联网、云计算、移动通讯技术、人工智能技术是“智慧旅游”的核心技术，以提高旅游品质、提高整体的效率为目的。在总结学者的观点后，本文认为，智慧旅游是以游客为中心，借助信息科学技术，通过大数据的整理分析实现了旅游前、旅游中、旅游后的信息需求进而提高了旅游质量。游客层面，借助于移动终端的基础之上实现旅游前查阅旅游当中的“食、住、行、游、购、娱”的相关信息和旅游中的互动体验以及旅游后的相关信息反馈和旅游后的评价；景区管理者层面，通过物联网的数据分析，及时地安排或者是组织相关的公共服务的调度；政府层面，掌握相关的数据信息，有效地实现了总体的把握和各个部门的信息交流，促进其集约化的发展。

2.智慧旅游的现状

2010年江苏省镇江市在我国率先提出“智慧旅游”的概念并实施，截止到今年已经是第七个年头了。7年内的时间里各地区的旅游智慧化程度推进得如何，同样受到了学者的关注。

张轫（2016）从智慧旅游的定义、现状、问题方面介绍了云南大理的智慧旅游发展状况，并给出了发展思路。同样的，在其他文献中提到的省份或者城市现状的还有河北省、吉林省、江苏省、山东省、辽宁省、山西省、甘肃省、安徽省，杭州市、黄冈市、秦皇岛市、温州市、洛阳市、大连市、南通市、襄阳市、松江市和佛山市等（排名不分先后），足以看出“智慧旅游”在我国的很多地方都得到了推行，但是大部分对于现状的分析文章都局限在了宏观的情况和问题的陈述，少量的文章提及到了“智慧旅游”的具体现状实施情况；蔡蓉蓉、顾婷婷、潘鸿雷（2013）则通过实地调查南京的酒店，介绍了南京的智慧酒店发展状况，进而对南京智慧酒店的发展趋势进行了分析；张龙（2015）介绍了我国智慧旅游软件的发展状况；龚诗雅（2015）则是基于移动终端的发展状况来对智慧旅游APP的发展提出了一些建议。

3.智慧旅游的发展研究

“智慧旅游”在不同的条件、背景下该如何发展也是国内学者关注的焦点。文献中除了一些城市发展模式外，彭丽、谭艳、周继霞（2014）以重庆合川区为例，探索了在智慧旅游背景下乡村旅游的发展模式；王虹、廖文喆（2014）针对我国国情和当前智慧旅游建设中的一些问题，从战略发展、科技发展、绿色发展、公共服务管理发展四个方面，论述了政府主导智慧旅游发展的必要性，明确了我国智慧旅游发展应走政府主导模式，提出了政府主导型智慧旅游发展建设模型，以及对我国智慧旅游的理论与实践提供科学依据；杨群（2016）在大数据背景下对智慧旅游的发展思路进行了探讨。

在不同的条件、背景下采取何种发展模式进行智慧旅游的建设确实是重中之重。如何在信息化的浪潮下冷静地分析自己的现状和能力，因地制宜地发展自己的比较优势。基于大数据的环境下，现有文献当中缺少数据的分析，是以后学者研究的重点方向。

（三）智慧旅游应用对象分类统计

张凌云（2016）阐述了智慧旅游针对旅游者、居民、政府、企业四大应用对象。基于这四个方面，本文对文献进行了统计整理，结果如图3-1所示。

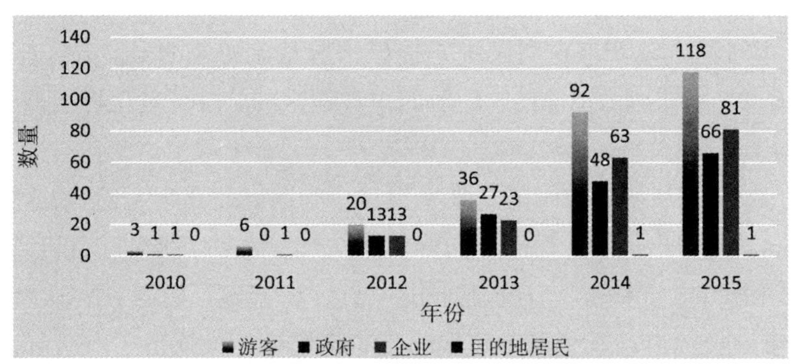

图1-1　智慧旅游应用对象文献统计（总）

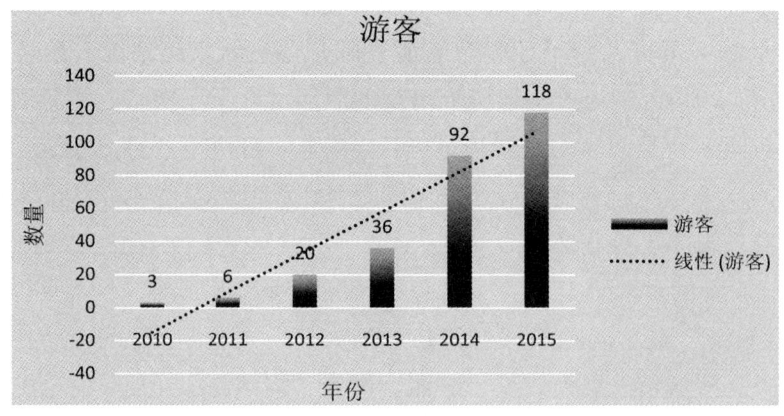

图1-1　智慧旅游应用对象文献统计——游客

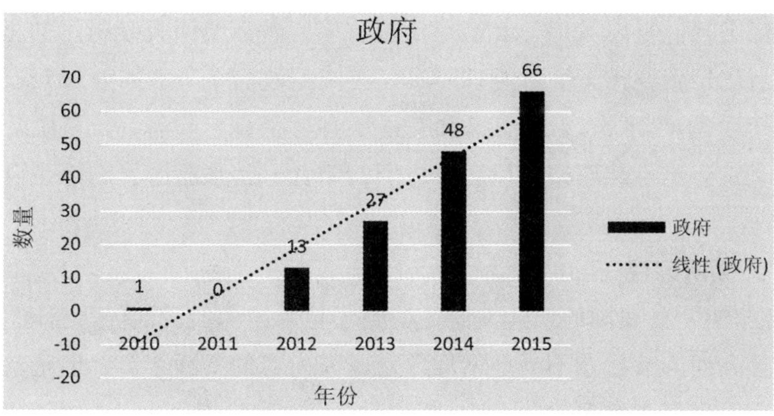

图1-1 智慧旅游应用对象文献统计——政府

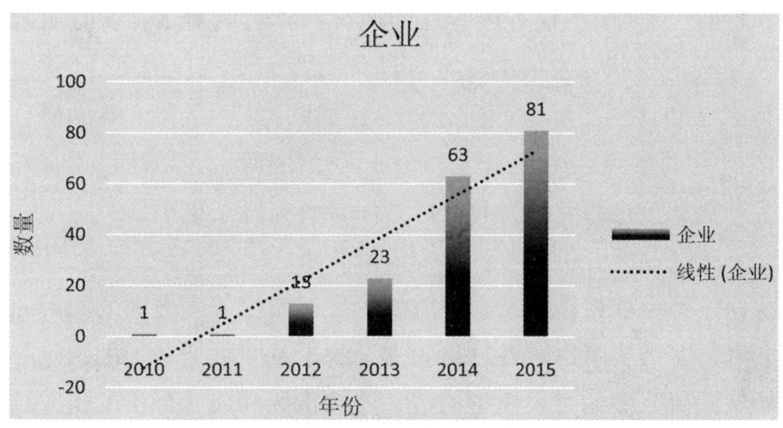

图1-1 智慧旅游应用对象文献统计——企业

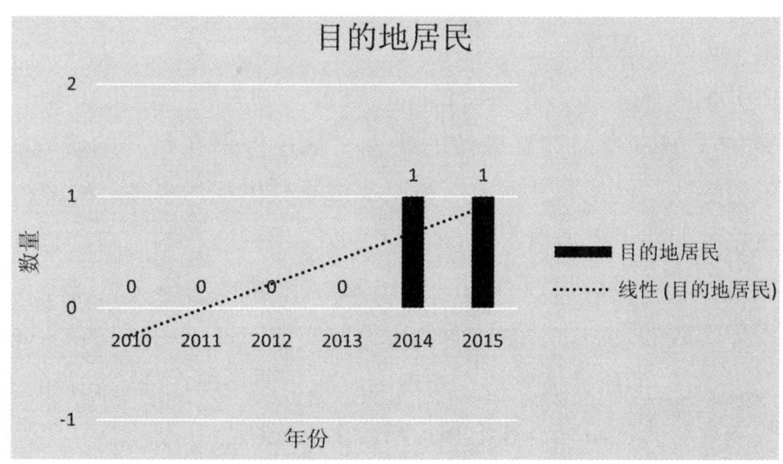

图1-1 智慧旅游应用对象文献统计——目的地居民

从表格中我们可以看出，文献对于智慧旅游游客的研究是最多的（文献数为325篇），其次是企业（文献数为199篇），再次是政府（文献数为167篇），目的地居民研究的最少（文献数为2篇）。相对于游客、企业和政府，智慧旅游目的地的研究少之又少。基于此表格可以启发我们的学者，智慧旅游目的地是以后的研究重点。

（四）文献研究存在的问题

“智慧旅游”在我国的快速发展，受到了越来越多的关注。尽管在文献数量、基金项目等方面的数量在不断地增加以及研究内容的不断丰富，但是基于当前文献，我们会发现存在很多问题。

1. 研究方面过于集中

如图2-1所示，文献的研究内容层面而言，学者们对于“智慧旅游”的研究主要集中在定义、现状、发展的探究等这几个方面。相比之下，“智慧旅游理论体系”、“智慧旅游评价”等方面研究较少；如图3-1所示，文献的研究目标层面而言，文献研究的重点集中在景区和企业两个方面，消费者和政府方面研究较少。纵观所有文献，在研究内容和目标方面，研究过于集中。

2. 研究方法以定性分析为主，缺少定量分析

由于数据的不可获得性以及智慧旅游的发展阶段等多方面的原因。智慧旅游的研究方法上，多数文献以定性分析为主，缺少基于数据之上的定量分析。这不符合国内外旅游研究中的主要模型构造、建造指标和回归分析的研究趋势。不同的城市、景区、酒店等该如何发展，我们需要数据的支持和分析，是学者们关于“智慧旅游”下一步研究时所关注的重点。

3. 理论与实践的脱离

生活中我们发现很多智慧旅游的项目已经“领先”于理论，理论不能很好地引导实践的发展。当前智慧旅游的研究文献还停留在最初的研究阶段，“概念”、“发展趋势”、“框架”、“研究对策”等都是其出现频率较高的词语。现实生活中，智慧旅游的建设已经取得了一定的成效，手机客户端“南京游客助手”已经成型，通过移动终端就可以查询南京15家4A级景区的事实状况等等。文献不能有效地指导实践的发展，智慧旅游的理论与实践已产生相脱节额的现象。不难发现，“智慧旅游”的研究还停留在宏观的层面，但是现在随着实践的不断进展，需要更多的微观层面的研究，理论和实践产生了偏离。

（五）宏观研究居多

当前智慧旅游的研究宏观层面居多，微观层面研究较少。在文献中涉及城市建设的文章不在少数，云南省、河北省、吉林省、江苏省、山东省、辽宁省、山西省、甘肃省、安徽省，杭州市、黄冈市、秦皇岛市、温州市、洛阳市、大连市、南通市、襄阳市、松江市和佛山市等（排名不分先后），足以看出“智慧旅游”在我国的很多地方都得到了推行，但是大部分对于现状的分析文章都局限在了宏观的情况和问题的陈述，少量的文章提及到了“智慧旅游”的具体现状实施情况。

（六）智慧旅游研究的展望

智慧旅游的快速发展，顺应了时代的潮流，是信息产业的不断发展的“结果”。本文对于智慧旅游文献的整理分析，对以后学者对于“智慧旅游”的研究提供参考，从而为国内外学者更好地为我国智慧旅游的发现提供文献指导具有深远的意义。

1. 研究方向的展望

智慧旅游信息产业和旅游产业的结合和产物，不仅仅是旅游产业单一的升级换代，涉及的是计算机、物联网、人工智能等多个方面的融合，是一个跨学科的、综合的命题，因此对于智慧旅游的研究有必要建立一个综合的体系和框架，全面地分析和综合地考虑智慧旅游的发展。未来的研究会涉及更多的微观层面的研究，同时对于消费者和政府层面的研究也会不断地增加；在涉及研究内容多样化的同时，真正的实现理论指导实践的发展。

2. 研究方法的展望

未来智慧旅游的研究方法在田野调查、问卷调查、信息查询、文献整理、文本挖掘方法基础，会出现越来越多的基于数理统计和计量分析的定量分析研究方法，基于数据基础上的文章会更好地指导智慧旅游的发展。基于本文所提到的文献的不足，望后来的学者在研究“智慧旅游”时，在现有的基础之上，不仅仅停留在“概念、理论”、“现状”等的研究，而是通过大数据的分析，在不同的背景下准确地探究发展的可行性，从而为我国智慧旅游更好地发展提供指导。

需要特别指出的是，本文的研究方法存在一定的局限性，难免会出现文章遗漏或者是重叠，会在以后的研究中不断地改进。

参考文献:

[1]蔡蓉蓉，顾婷婷，潘鸿雷.南京智慧酒店现状及发展趋势研究[J].对外经贸，2013，10:62-64.

[2]李加军，黄丽英.基于CNKI下智慧旅游研究文献统计分析[J].中国市场，2015，47:183-185.

[3]韩雅博.基于CNKI数据的智慧旅游研究文献统计分析及述评[J].商，2015，09:253-254.

[4]王蕴瑞.基于CNKI的国内智慧旅游研究论文计量分析[J].成都大学学报(社会科学版)，2015，02:30-34.

[5]龚诗雅，李鸣珂.智慧旅游下智能手机APP现状探析[J].美与时代(城市版)，2015，04:81-82.

[6]张凌云，黎巎，刘敏.智慧旅游的基本概念与理论体系[J].旅游学刊，2012，05:66-73.

[7]李云鹏，胡中州，黄超，段莉琼.旅游信息服务视阈下的智慧旅游概念探讨[J].旅游学刊，2014，05:106-115.

[8]张轫，杨运星.大理“智慧旅游”现状及发展问题研究[J].旅游纵览(下半月)，2016，03:145-146.

[9]彭丽，谭艳，周继霞.基于智慧旅游背景下的乡村旅游发展模式研究——以重庆合川区为例[J].农业经济，2014，12:49-50.

[10]王虹，廖文喆.政府主导型智慧旅游发展模式研究[J].社会科学论坛，2014，05:194-201.

[11]张龙.谈我国智慧旅游软件的发展现状[J].现代交际，2015，10:29.

[12]杨群.大数据下的智慧旅游发展思路探讨[J].特区经济，2016，03:139-140.

[13]张凌云.智慧旅游:个性化定制和智能化公共服务时代的来临[J].旅游学刊，2012，02:3-5.

[14]金卫东.智慧旅游与旅游公共服务体系建设[J].旅游学刊，2012，02:5-6.

[15]乔海燕.关于构建旅游公共信息服务系统的思考——基于智慧旅游视角[J].中南林业科技大学学报(社会科学版)，2012，02:27-29.

[16]姚国章.“智慧旅游”的建设框架探析[J].南京邮电大学学报(社会科学版)，2012，02:13-16，73.

[17]邓贤峰，张晓海.南京市“智慧旅游”总体架构研究[J].旅游论坛，2012，

05:72-76.
[18]刘军林，范云峰.智慧旅游的构成、价值与发展趋势[J].重庆社会科学，2011，10:121-124.
[19]朱珠，张欣.浅谈智慧旅游感知体系和管理平台的构建[J].江苏大学学报（社会科学版），2011，06:97-100.
[20]付业勤，郑向敏.我国智慧旅游的发展现状及对策研究[J].开发研究，2013，04:62-65.

（作者简介：王文健，男，四川外国语大学国别经济与国际商务研究中心，硕士研究生）

关于中越经济外交的一些思考
——从电商角度

任丹丹

摘要：近年来，电商作为一个新兴事物逐渐展露头角，尤其是11月后人们茶余饭后的热门话题便是双十一光棍节抢购。中国电商的热浪，已经席卷全球217个国家和地区。电商是经济的一部分，经济是外交的一个领域，如果在中越这两个邻邦之间的经济外交部分着重发展电商，则必然可以起到一些事半功倍的效果。本文拟对此问题进行探索，并在可行范围内提出建议。

关键词：中越；电商；经济外交；建议

一、一些基本概念

外交是一种充满活力的机制。作为国家之间进行和平交往的主渠道，以及通过既有联合又有斗争的方式，在国际关系原则指导下，在相互谅解与协调的基础上解决国家之间在各个领域的矛盾与冲突，促进国际社会的进步与稳定。随着社会的发展与需要，当代外交主要分为4种形式：多边外交、首脑外交、经济外交、公共外交。

经济外交在这些广义外交中有着特殊的地位和重要性，特别是在经济全球化趋势日益发展的今天尤其如此。从经济外交作为国家总体外交的组成部分的视角来看，经济外交具有两重涵义：一是国家以本国的经济力量为手段，为实现和维护特定的政治利益或对外战略意图制定和实施的对外政策与行为；二是国家维护本国的经济利益和拓展经济权益制定和实施的对外政策和行为。从国际经济关系的视角来看，国际经济是国际体制稳定与安全的要素。随着全球化的进展，经济外交的主体和领域发生变化，经济外交还应包括另一个重要涵义，即国家之间和国家间组织为建立稳定的国际经济秩序和有效公平的国际经济机制，促进全球经济繁荣与发展而进行的以政策协调和制度建设为基本内容的合作的外交行动。

经济外交涉及的范围很广，受篇幅限制，本文仅讨论属于经济范围内的新兴领域：电商。

狭义电商是指实现整个贸易过程中各阶段贸易活动的电子化，而广义电商是指利用网络实现所有商务活动业务流程的电子化。前者集中于基于互联网的电子交易，强调企业利用互联网与外部发生交易与合作；而后者则把涵盖范围扩大了很多，指企业使用各种电子工具从事商务活动。

电商区别于传统贸易，最大的特点是其依赖网络进行交易，而传统贸易更多的是面对面、人对人的交易。很明显，电商脱离了地域、时间、人力等各类传统贸易常受到的限制，可以更加高效率、低成本、透明化地进行交易。

二、现实意义

中国与越南山水相连、文化相通，中越两党、两国和两国人民是好邻居、好朋友、好同志、好伙伴。

但是这种唇齿相依的关系，却也不可避免地产生摩擦。2014年5月，越南爆发大规模反华运动，越共河静省委宣教部15日召开新闻发布会，称确认1名中国人在“摩擦中死亡”。越南外交部发言人黎海平15日称，根据越方统计，1.9万人参与了平阳省的暴动，上百家企业被砸，15家企业被烧毁，直接经济损失数十亿越南盾。6月9日，中国常驻联合国代表团临时代办、大使王民就越南非法强力干扰中建南项目事照会联合国秘书长潘基文，转去中国的立场文件《“981”钻井平台作业：越南的挑衅和中国的立场》，并要求秘书长将中国的立场文件作为联合国大会文件散发给联合国全体会员国。立场文件并附有中国企业在中国西沙群岛毗连区内的作业位置图以及长期以来越方承认中方对西沙群岛主权的相关材料。

然而，越南方面却并不认可。“越南新闻网”2014年8月1日登载旅美越裔太空科学家Thai Van Cau 的文章。作者妄称，越南对西沙群岛、南沙群岛拥有主权的历史证据比中国更清楚、更有力。同时，作者在文章中分析了未来10年南海争端的五种场景。

尽管两国领导人都在尽力维护“同志加兄弟”的友好情谊，但是我们也能很明显地感到一丝淡淡的不安。2013年10月13日，李克强总理访问越南，可是时隔7个月，越南就反华，由此可见，越南人并不买官方“首脑外交”的账。

我们注意到一个有趣的现象：二战时期曾经殖民过越南的法国和日本、发动越南战争的美国，其罪行自当罄竹难书，可是越南对他们却并没有太多的敌对情绪。日本的HONDA牌摩托车驰骋在越南的大街小巷，法式咖啡馆被视为贵族的象征，美国的电视剧、奢侈品更是深受年轻人的喜爱。

究其原因，很大程度上是三者是发达国家，能够给越南带去更多的经济利益。在经济全球化的今天，越南奉行“实用主义”，也不失为明智之举。但是，我们也应该注意到，老牌的发达国家正在渐入窘境。美国“次贷危机”是从2006年春季开始逐步显现的。2007年8月席卷美国、欧盟和日本等世界主要金融市场。至今也没有完全恢复。而彼时正值中国改革开放近30年，GDP已由1978年的3645.2亿元增长到249530亿元，排名世界第四。

时间又过去了七八年，这七八年来，世界继续聚焦中国。中国的GDP基本上每年都在增长，2013年GDP达568845 亿元，同比增7.7%。目前，中国已成为世界第二大经济体，仅次于美国。这其中最令人刮目相看的自然是中国的电商。2014年9月19日，马云的阿里巴巴正式在美国纽约登陆，立即吸引了世界的眼球。2014年双十一，阿里巴巴最终交易额突破571亿元，物流订单2.78亿，总共有217个国家和地区参与。

几番角逐，继2014年11月APEC会议之后，中国再次取得2016年G20峰会这一大型国际会议的举办权。世界都在看好中国，那么越南呢？作为中国的邻居，不论是地理还是历史，不论是民间还是官方，越南都有得天独厚的优势。我们期待，在中越两国领导人形成共识的十六字方针“长期稳定，面向未来，睦邻友好，全面合作”的指引下，中越两国的经贸往来不断加强。我们也有理由相信，中国电商刮起的飓风，也将引起越南经济翻天覆地的变化。

三、中越电商现状

中国方面，近几年电商呈蓬勃发展的趋势。到2014年上半年，各电商已经在市场上打拼出一片自己的天下。总的来说，天猫（阿里巴巴旗下网站）独占鳌头，拥有超过一半的市场，其次是京东、苏宁。(图1)

网购规模占社会消费品零售总额比例，也从2009年的2.1%增长到2014年的10%。(图2)交易规模也由2010年的4.5万亿元增长到预计2015年18.2万亿元。(图3)

网络零售市场交易规模也从2009年的2600亿元增长到2014年的27861亿元，5年增长了9倍。（图4）值得注意的是，我们熟悉的网络零售其实只占到了18.5%，只是冰山一角。B2B平台（即我们通俗意义上的线上批发）占76.9%，是零售的4倍多。由此推算，2014年，B2B交易规模将超过100000亿元。这是一个怎样的概念呢？2012年中越、韩越、日越双边贸易额分别是410亿美元、209亿美元、226亿美元，总计845亿美元，折合成人民币约5500亿，仅为上述中国2014年B2B交易规模的5%。

跨境电商中，金华一枝独秀。据有关统计数据显示，（2014年）前三季度金华跨境电子商务进出口额达12.5亿美元，预计全年跨境电子商务进出口额将达16亿美元。

越南方面，越南公布的2013年电子商务指数显示，越南电子商务持续发展，深刻融入到各个经营领域，与信息技术和传媒领域的发展密切关联，并成为经济与信息社会建设进程中的重要支柱之一。越南企业电子邮箱使用频率较高，83%的企业通过电子邮件接收订单。与此同时，43%的越南企业建有自己的独立网站，并约有35%的企业通过自己的网站接收订单。越南企业参与电子商务的比率为12%，接受调查的33%企业认为电子商务带来较高的经济效益。另一方面，大约有48%的企业使用在线公共服务平台。

上述电商，主要是指批发部分，而直接面对消费者的零售却面临尴尬。“据越南工贸部统计，2013年，越南在线支付比例仅占全国7200万张银行卡消费的19%，其余为现金支付。此外，由于网络销售出现欺诈行为，消费者对网购缺乏信心。”

越南几个主要的购物网站，如http://www.e24h.vn/buy/，http://www.vietnamesemade.com/，其主要面对的是高级顾客，即能看懂英语的人。而在越南，这部分顾客仅仅是金字塔上一角，并不多。至于像http://vatgia.com/home/这样比较“亲民”的网站，则常常没有客服。

笔者曾在越南看到一则类似于当当网的购物网站的广告，于是在该网站购买台灯，选择货到付款，结果却一直没能收到货。

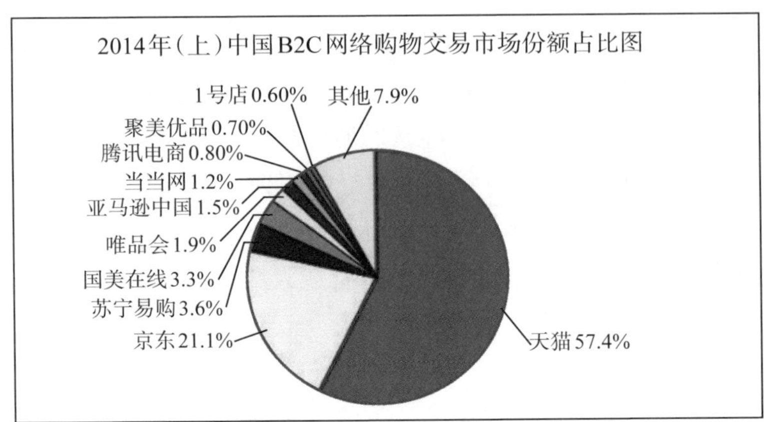

图1

数据来源：www.100EC.cn

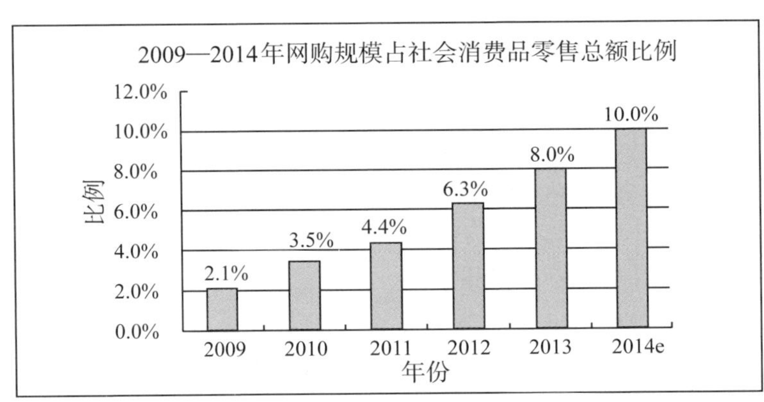

图2

数据来源：www.100EC.cn

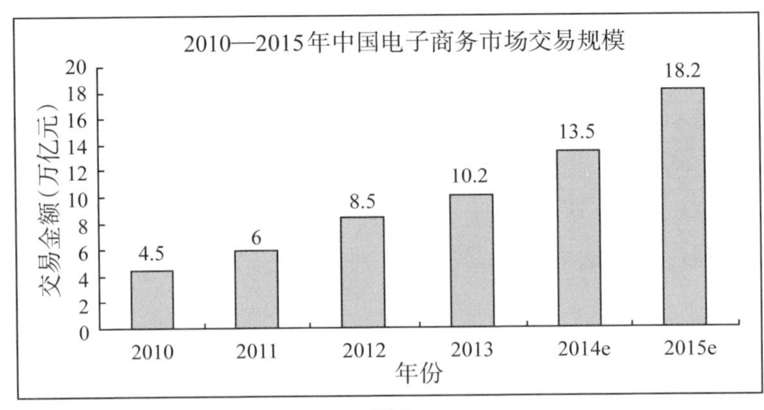

图3

数据来源：www.100EC.cn

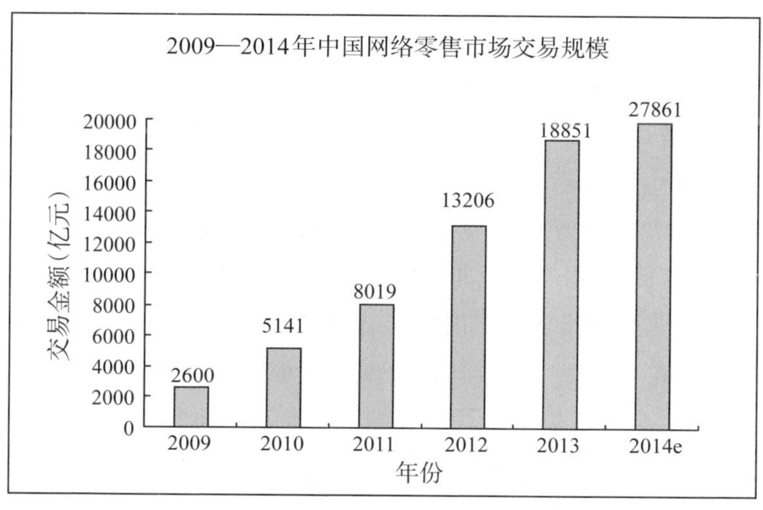

图4

数据来源：www.100EC.cn

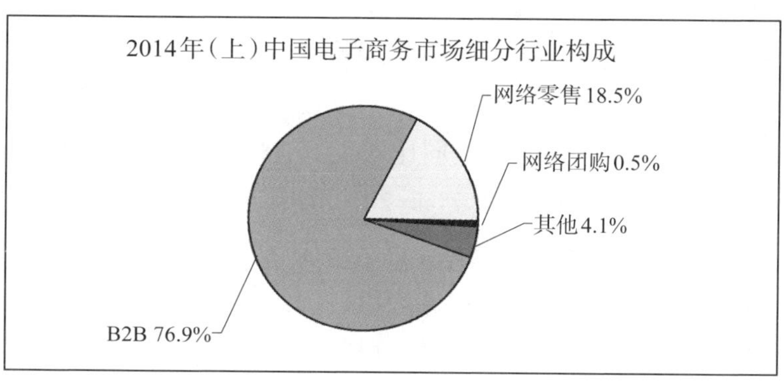

图5

数据来源：www.100EC.cn

四、中越电商外交可行性分析

随着APEC会议在中国举行，跨境电商又一次成为人们关注的热点。中央电视台在日前播出的新闻报道中称，跨境电商已成为APEC期间会内会外探讨的热词。一旦跨境电商走进人们的生活，那就意味着曾经只能在电视上、报纸上、杂志上看到的国外的一些商品，将可以供消费者自主选择，并且可以在短时间内送达。真正意义上的“足不出户，购遍天下”。

数据显示，从2011年以来，中国跨境电商交易额年平均增幅达30%，有研究机构预测，到2018年，中国将占全球跨境电商比例的50%，专家认为，随着跨境电子商务的兴起，中国在全球贸易链里的话语权也将获得提升。

跨境电商，既然可以把国外的买进来，自然也可以把国内的卖出去。对于中国人而言，其诱惑之大，可想而知。同样，我们认为，越南何不乘中国电商发展的风，快速发展本国经济呢？

河内超市协会会长武荣富表示，越南零售业要获得全面发展，必须发展电子商务，因此要加强信息和网络基础设施建设，提高电子商务经营水平和效率。就地理而言，越南拥有3000多公里的海岸线，其渔业非常发达，越南大型水产企业——明富水产品集团公司计划2014年实现净营业额达到11.715万亿越南盾和4217.4亿税后利润。这些数据比2013年增加了5.74%和5.74%。然而真正会亲自到越南谈生意的商家并不多。古代人们相信“酒香不怕巷子深”，近代发现琳琅满目的商品还真能盖住“酒香”，于是有了广告的概念。现代我们再来看看，发现广告也并不是就能百分之百地广而告之，就算让很多人听说了，可是要让买家和卖家能够实实在在地接触，也非易事。

2013年，越南对外贸易表现不俗，尤其在出口方面，其规模和增速超过了年初政府预定目标的10%，出口金额达1322亿美元，与2012年比增长 15.4%；与此同时，进口金额达1313亿美元，同比增长16.1%。2013年越南对外贸易额为8.63亿美元，相当于出口总额的0.7%。2013年中越贸易形势喜人，从贸易总量来看，中越贸易额达到了502亿美元，首次突破500亿元大关，与2012年比增长21.9%。中国是越南第一进口国，第四大出口国，仅次于欧盟、美国与日本，是越南最重要的贸易伙伴国之一。越南出口到中国的产品额达132.6亿美元，从中国进口的产品额为 369亿美元。如果电商发达，进口就可以不仅仅局限于以往的“关系”，而是可以透明地货比三家，然后在一个安全的平台付款，等待收货。如果美国的东西太贵，可以选择中国，如果中国的东西不好，可以考虑韩国。对于越南本国而言，增加了可以选择的机会。与此同时，出口方可以根据越南的需求，对已有的商品进行改进，从而更加符合越南人的使用习惯，帮助进口方能够更快更好地贴近消费者，从而获利。当越南民众可以更多更好买到物美价廉的“中国制造”之后，我们有理由相信，一些偏见会自动消除。

五、关于中越电商外交的建议及其可能带来的影响

从中国方面来看，要想支撑电商的发展，自然必须要有坚挺的金融系统、物流系统、网络系统。

中越实行电商外交，对于越南的金融系统而言，必当是一场脱胎换骨的升级。目前越南的银行卡手续还比较繁琐，ATM取款机不多，人们更多的是习惯现金交易。虽然电商可以货到付款，但是更多的则是要求用电子银行、信用卡、电子账户等形式交易。试想一下2014年双十一，阿里巴巴以571亿元破吉尼斯记录，那么越南要多久才能达到这样的宏伟目标？

双十一阿里巴巴物流订单2.78亿，京东1400万，总量突破5亿件，相当于37%的中国人或全世界8%的人每人1件包裹。如果这样的任务给越南，无疑是对越南物流系统的挑战，也就要求其员工合作、货运工具的升级。

11月6日，阿里巴巴宣布，其大数据团队自研的实时数据计算平台Galaxy，目前每秒可运算数据超过500万条，双十一当天每秒运算量将超过1000万条，日处理消息数将超过1万亿条。如果越南想要发展电商，其网络系统就不得不面临一场革命。

由此，笔者提出如下关于发展中越电商外交的建议：

1.要想富，先修路。当前中国的物流，一般不会超过5天，就可以将商品从卖家送达买家手里。商家发货——发货地小县城货运部——发货地主城货运部——收货地主城货运部——收货地小县城货运部——买家。每两个点之间的交接一般耗时一天，如果不是小县城，而是主城，则时间更短。笔者曾在成都某网店购物，次日就送达重庆，通知取货。当然，这也要求快递员吃苦耐劳，办事绝不拖拖拉拉。

2.创新安检流程。跨境电商毕竟不再像一般的电商那样，属于国内的“家务事”，一旦牵扯到两国，就会存在一些例如安全、关税等问题。如果按照一般的开箱验货，肯定会侵犯消费者的隐私，也会威胁货物的安全，遇上双十一这样的购物狂欢节，庞大的物流也无法实现逐一验货。所以对于电商物品的检查，我们期待可以有创新，比如统一包装，发货前安检；或者由卖家申请免检，交纳担保金。

3.大力培养人才。当越南顾客需要对商品进行了解的时候，顾客肯定是用越南语，而中国的电商对越南语了解的并不多，能够有效沟通的更是寥寥无几，所以首先应该培养销售客服。再者，目前中国的电商，如果产品出问题，一般是要求客户寄回维修。但是对于跨境电商而言，显然加大了其风险成本，自然应该培养其本地售后人员。跨境电商对交易平台的安全性要求更高，这就需要培养，甚至于中越联合培养网络工程师、程序员。

4.创新支付方式。中国电商催生了电子银行、支付宝等支付方式，那么对于中越跨境电商而言，涉及两种不同货币的转换，自然需要一种更加公平合理，能使双方满意的新型支付方式来满足。

5.稳定高层关系。众所周知，政治关系会直接影响经济交流。如果要想在中越两国间发展电商外交，自然离不开两国政府的支持。历史证明，国家高层关系越是稳定，贸易就会越活跃。

综上，如果中越发展电商，首先会促进越南的网络系统、金融系统革新，那么就需要大量的高级人才，如此一来就会间接刺激越南的教育。电商所需的物流、客服等方向的工作人员，又会大大地刺激越南的服务业，吸引更多的“农民”进城务工，从而加快越南城镇化的步伐。对运输的高要求，又会间接刺激越南的城市道路建设。电商的发展，又会牵动电子产品，尤其是电脑和手机的发展。如此一来，中越如果展开电商外交，对于中国的电子产品销往越南，也是一个极好的消息。此外中国人可以更方便地购买越南的手工艺品，而越南人也可以参加中国双十一的抢购。

不过我们也应该注意到一些可能存在的消极影响。毕竟中国的电商较之越南要发达很多，中国的制造业更是远胜越南。当大家可以在电商这一平台同台竞技的时候，越南的民族产业几乎不是中国的对手。该如何保护本国尚未成熟的工业，这是一个值得越南政府深思的问题。

展望未来，我们期待中越双边贸易在电商的带动下，在中越政府的合理扶持下，健康发展，欣欣向荣。同时，我们也相信，中越在经济外交中大力发展电商，会给两国人民带来实实在在的利益，反作用于政府层面，从而真正意义上实现“世世代代友好下去”。

参考文献：

[1]杨闯.外交学[M]，北京：世界知识出版社，2010,(1)：150.

[2]杨闯.外交学[M]，北京：世界知识出版社，2010,(1)：170；周永生.经济外交[M]，北京：中国青年出版社2004：1-28；何中顺.新时期中国经济外交理论与实践[M]，北京：时事出版社，2007：26-33.

[3]环球军事报道,《中国军方否认中越边境部队取消休假进入战备_军事_环球网》[EB]，http://mil.huanqiu.com/observation/2014-05/4996748.html，2014.5.16.

[4]常驻联合国代表团,《中国就越南非法干扰中建南项目照会联合国秘书长表明

立场》[EB], http://www.fmprc.gov.cn/mfa_chn/zwbd_602255/t1163702.shtml, 2014.6.9.

[5]环球军事报道,《越媒预测中越冲突5种场景 中国在2020前入侵南沙_军事_环球网》[EB]http://mil.huanqiu.com/observation/2014-08/5098303.html, 2014.8.7.

[6]刘铮,《马凯：改革开放以来中国经济年均增长9.67%_改革开放30年频道_红网》[EB], http://gaige.rednet.cn/c/2008/01/16/1420502.htm, 2008.1.6.

[7]中国经济网,《国家统计局公布2013年经济数据：GDP同比增7.7%_中国经济网——国家经济门户》[EB]http://www.ce.cn/xwzx/gnsz/gdxw/201401/20/t20140120_2161245.shtml, 2014.1.20.

[8]凤凰财经,《美媒称APEC期间 中国经济外交显成效|上证综指|贸易顺差_凤凰财经》, [EB], http://finance.ifeng.com/a/20141112/13268625_0.shtml, 2014.11.12.

[9]杨阳，李文博，李意安，马欢《移动端成双十一催化剂 电商明争销量暗斗支付》，经济观察报[N], 2014.11.17，第25版.

[10]本部分的图片与数据主要来源于2014年(上)中国电子商务市场数据监测报告http://www.100ec.cn/zt/2014bndbg/

[11]图中2014e表示2014年的数据是预测的。下图2014e、2015e也是预测的.

[12]古小松，越南报告：2012—2013[M]，北京：世界知识出版社，2013：137-139.

[13]本文美元兑换人民币，均按1：6.5的汇率计算.

[14]李婷婷,《跨境电商渐成外贸发展新业态 浙江金华成崛起新坐标—国际—人民网》[EB], http://world.people.com.cn/n/2014/1124/c157278-26081246.html, 2014.11.24.

[15]古小松，越南报告：2013—2014[M]，北京：世界知识出版社，2014年：140.

[16]驻胡志明市总领馆经商室,《越南电子商务发展面临阻力—中华人民共和国驻胡志明市总领事馆经济商务室》[EB], http://hochiminh.mofcom.gov.cn/article/jmxw/201410/20141000776990.shtml, 2014.10.29.

[17]李丽,《“跨境电商”成APEC热词_中国经济网—国家经济门户》[EB], http://nongye.ce.cn/hydt/201411/14/t20141114_2086353.shtml, 2014.11.14.

[18]驻胡志明市总领馆经商室,《越南电子商务发展面临阻力—中华人民共和

国驻胡志明市总领事馆经济商务室》[EB], http://hochiminh.mofcom.gov.cn/article/jmxw/201410/20141000776990.shtml, 2014.10.29.
[19] 北京福建水产农特产商会,《【国外渔业】越南扩大水产出口，土耳其改善捕捞养殖业，墨西哥颁布太平洋海域捕虾禁令，日本拟撤销水产品关税与捕黑金枪鱼减半》[EB] http://mp.weixin.qq.com/s?__biz=MzA3MzEyOTYwMw==&mid=200093427&idx=4&sn=f8b772753704bc2565723f9d7b6b0856&3rd=MzA3MDU4NTYzMw==&scene=6#rd, 2014.3.18.
[20] 杨阳，李文博，李意安，马欢.《移动端成双十一催化剂 电商明争销量暗斗支付》, 经济观察报[N], 2014.11.17，第25版.
[21] 张斌，周筱洲.《快递员改变中国》，经济观察报[N], 2014.11.17，第02版
[22] 杨阳，李文博，李意安，马欢.《移动端成双十一催化剂 电商明争销量暗斗支付》, 经济观察报[N], 2014.11.17，第25版.

（作者简介：任丹丹，女，四川外国语大学东方语学院，硕士研究生）

略论越南"船文化"

刘艳芬

摘要：船作为一种交通工具，已经渗透到越南民族物质和精神生活的方方面面，有着丰富的文化内涵。在越南众多独特文化中，船文化极具民族特色。它是越南地貌的一面镜子，同时也是越南人生活、思维、审美方式的反映。本文试图从越南船文化形成的原因、船与越南人的生产生活、船与信仰、船与艺术及成语俗语、歌谣五个方面来略论越南"船文化"，旨在更好地了解越南文化，进行跨文化交际。

关键词：越南；船；文化；

一、越南船文化形成的原因

客观事物的存在对文化的形成起决定作用，越南独特的自然地理环境是船文化形成的根本原因，丰富的海产资源是船文化形成的动力，交通的限制是船文化形成的外部因素。

（一）自然地理环境

越南位于中南半岛东部，濒临太平洋，属亚热带地区，海岸线长达3260公里，河流纵横交错、湖泊星罗棋布。（梁远，2008：4）红河和湄公河是越南的两大河流，其中湄公河支流众多，无数的河流和运河纵横交错。红河三角洲和湄公河三角洲地势低平，极易于船只的航行，于这两个三角洲之间，延伸着南北狭长的海岸线及平坦的沿海低地，这为船只的航行提供了便利的条件和保证。越南地处亚热带地区，雨季雨量充沛，充沛的降雨量为船只的航行提供了足够的水资源。

（二）海产资源丰富

因河流众多，海岸绵长，海域宽广，所以越南海产资源极为丰富。越南境内目前约有鱼类1000多种，包括海鱼和淡水鱼，主要有鲍鱼、墨鱼、红鱼、鳖鱼以及珊瑚、海参、海龟、玳瑁、珍珠蚌等珍贵海产，总计海鱼800多种，淡水鱼200多种。(古小松，2009：18）为了增加收入，提高生活水平，越南渔民不得不驶船捕捞丰富的海产资源。对渔民来说，船是他们致富的重要工具。

（三）交通的限制

陆路和水路是越南两大主要交通方式，与水路相比，越南陆路的发展受到了限制，如地形、技术、资金等，其仍处于发展阶段。特别在东部沿海，河网密布之地，水路成为人们出行的主要交通方式。水路，利用越南独特的地理环境即江、河、湖泊和海洋的“天然航道”来进行，通航能力几乎不受限制；加之投资少，建设和维护费用低；运量大，成本低；因运行持续性强还可以用于远距离的国际贸易。据以上优点，船已成为越南人出行或运输货物的首要选择。

二、船与生产生活

越南人依水而居，主要的交通工具是船只。船在他们的生产生活中占有重要的地位，很多捕鱼的渔民、运货的船夫都用船来安家，他们既可以用船来谋生又可以居住在船上，许多家庭聚集在一起，久而久之就形成了渔村。越南作家郑怀德在《嘉定城通志》中曾描写过19世纪越南南部的交通景观：家家户户都有船，船只随处可见，有的以船为家、有的乘船赶集、拜访亲朋好友、有的用船运货，狭窄的江河上船只络绎不绝。(Trần Ngọc Thêm，1999：213）比起在陆地上生活，他们更喜欢与船相伴，对他们来说，在船上生活反而更方便，他们同样可以在船上喂养家畜，并能保持清洁。

湄公河三角洲和越南西南部是水上市场的集聚地，这片领土带有浓浓的船文化气息。清晨，集市就已经开市。船上载满了居民要卖的东西，其中最常见的是水果和蔬菜。各家船上的一大亮点就是每只船上都会有几根竹竿，竹竿上挂着他们要卖的东西，这样顾客只需远远的看竹竿就知道可以在哪买到自己所需的商品。水上市场是当地居民进行商品交易的场所，虽然卖什么就在竹竿上挂什么，但是有三个特例：第一，不卖挂着的衣服，因为水上市场的居民通常生活在船上，而他们的衣服也需要在船上挂着晾；第二，没有挂着的小吃和饮品是可以卖的，因为这类东西不易于挂起来；第三，挂着甘蔗叶却卖船，有意卖船的船家只需在船上挂甘蔗叶即可。

越南较著名的水上市场有：Cái Răng 水上市场、Cái Bè 水上市场、Ngã Nam 水上市场、Phụng Hiệp水上市场、Phong Điện水上市场等。其中，Cái Răng 水上市场有潜力成为该片区最大的自产自销的水上市场。它主要经营的是各种农产品和水果的销售，如果到了芹苴而没有去Cái Răng 水上市场，那将会感到遗憾。该集市开市很早，从天还没亮就开市，一直到早上8、9点就散市。（Nguyễn Văn Hợp，2013：483）

随着消费者需求的增加，水上市场不只局限于水果和农产品，各种小吃和饮品也逐渐走进了人们的生活，比如：粉（phở）、米线、咖啡等。水上市场不仅服务了当地居民，方便了他们的生活，同时其独特的场景给外国游客留下了深刻的印象。

三、船与信仰

（一）赛龙舟

从古至今，船只与越南人的生活、信仰紧密相连。越南有些地区一直保留着赛龙舟的传统习惯，这个习俗得以传承是因为他们对船只有着较深的信仰。龙船在越南民间的庙会里带有神圣、庄重的色彩。人们认为举办庙会期间他们的民族英雄、武将和有功德的人会回到船上，所以凡是参会和观会的人都会向船只祈祷、求福。说到赛龙舟，就不得不提到岘港，赛龙舟是岘港的传统风俗和文化特色，岘港赛龙舟庙会将于每年农历正月在韩河举行，届时人们将会祈祷来年的风调雨顺和沿海地区人民生活的富裕。

然而，有些地区的赛龙舟庙会又独具特色。据当地人的信仰，“阳性”的龙船和“阴性”的凤船比赛才合理。同样，根据古阴阳信仰，富寿省陶舍乡的人们在制造参加比赛的船只时，把“阳性”的船造成鸟形，“阴性”的船造成鱼形，“阴阳”两船将于晚上进行比赛，祭礼结束后是“游泳盛宴”，人们以游泳的方式来祭奠各方神灵。

（二）画船眼

船的种类各异，各式各样的船被称作是人的灵魂。越南有画船眼的风俗，画船眼深具人文特性，是一大民间文化现象。人们一般会选好的时辰给船画上眼睛，每个地区人们的审美、造船师的技术会决定船眼形状、颜色及线条的不同。（Nguyễn Thanh Lợi，2009：7）他们相信船的眼睛在他们出海时能帮助他们打倒海上的妖怪而不受伤害；同时，渔民希望通过船眼睛的观望，能帮助他们捕捞到更多的鱼；一些出海经商的商人也祈祷船眼睛能帮助他们寻找到商机众多，财源滚滚的码头。（Trần Ngọc Thêm，1999：213）

四、船与艺术

船在越南人的生活中扮演着重要的角色，满足了人们出行的需要。当物质生活得到了满足后，船逐渐出现于越南人的精神世界中，在艺术创造过程中，船的身影随处可见。

水上木偶戏是越南的一种传统文艺表演，源于红河三角洲，当地遍布水田、池塘，农闲的时候农民就在水中挥动木偶作为娱乐。因船与越南人的生活紧密相连，越南人对船倍感亲切，所以船只就走进了水上木偶戏的艺术世界，在表演的时候，船通常以赛龙舟、帝王游玩、渔民捕鱼的场景出现。此时，我们可以借助于船而加深对越南农民生活及当地风俗的了解。

对歌是越南北宁、北江一带文化艺术的代表。对歌的男女双方在船上进行对歌，而观众就站在河岸欣赏，船与歌声、演员融为一体，形成了当地独特的文化艺术特色。

在越南的影视、摄影作品中，越来越多的船走进了观众的视野，比如：Áo lụa Hà Đông; Con thuyền số phận; Hương phù sa; Đất phương Nam等。在导演或摄影师看来，只有船才能体现出越南的特色及独特的魅力。通过媒介的传播，船的形象已被国际友人熟知，很多游客到越南旅游就会穿上飘逸的奥黛坐在船上穿梭于盛开的荷花间，并以此作为照片来留念。

五、船与成语俗语、歌谣

船在越南人的生活中广泛使用，它不只是一种简单的交通工具，而且还是越南人精神的寄托。在民间，人们喜欢用船抒发自己的感情，这种抒情方式在成语俗语、歌谣中显而易见，船在越南成语俗语及歌谣中蕴含着丰富的文化内涵。

Thuyền dời，nhưng bến chẳng dời. 本意：船动，但码头不移。寓意：比喻感情和意志坚定不移。（祁广谋，2006：126）通过对船和码头的观察，人们利用船灵活，能随处飘动的特点来反衬始终坚持自我的码头。正如坚定的感情和意志，没有什么能使之动摇。

Thuyền đua thì lái cũng đua. 本意：船走桨跟随。寓意：用来讽刺只会模仿别人、附和随大流之人。（祁广谋，2006：126）船和桨构成一个完整的系统，二者缺一不可。船之所以能前行是因为桨对水的冲击，船继续前进，桨也只能跟着摆动。人们觉得桨、船与附和随大流之人、被模仿附和的对象有着极高的相似之处，所以才把该寓意应用于生活中。

Thuyền mạnh vì lái，gái mạnh vì chồng. 本意：船因桨而健行，女因夫而荣显。（祁广谋，2006：126）寓意：妇女要依赖于丈夫生活。船与桨关系之密切正如妻子离不开丈夫。在越南民间看来，女人作为弱势群体，生活不能自立，只有通过丈夫才能改变自己的命运。总的来说，女人的生存离不开丈夫，此观点来自于儒教中的“三从”学说。

Thuyền không lái như gái không chồng. 本意：船没有桨正如妇女没有丈夫。该寓意同上，妇女要依赖于丈夫生活。船缺了桨，无法到达终点；妇女缺了丈夫，生活难以继续。

Thuyền nan chở đá，thuyền lá chở sắt. 本意：竹船运石头，大帆船运铁。寓意：比喻每个人根据自己的能力各司其职。竹船和大帆船根据自己的属性，选择自己能运载的货物，充分利用自己的特点，让其发挥最大的功效，实现资源的优化配置。

Thuyền to sóng cả. 本意：船越大浪越大。寓意：比喻职位越高责任越大。（Nguyễn Lân，2010：562）船越大激起的浪花也就越大，正如一个人拥有越高的职位，同时他所肩负的责任与职位就会成正比。人们巧妙地运用船与浪的关系来证明职位与责任的关联。

Thuyền xuôi gió ngược. 本意：船顺着行，风逆着吹。寓意：比喻遇到困难，身处困境。船顺着行，风作为助力也顺着吹，那么划船的人将很轻松就能到达自己想去的地方。相反地，风作为阻力逆着吹，那么划船的人将会很吃力，艰难地前行，甚至到达不了终点。以此形容人身处逆境时的无助，真是恰当不过。

Thuyền ơi có nhớ bến chăng，bến thì một dạ khăng khăng đợi thuyền về. 本意：船儿啊，可思念码头，码头痴痴地等待你的归来。寓意：比喻感情的执着和坚定。因船能到处漂流，四处闯荡，而码头具有稳定，坚固的特点，所以从古至今，船象征着出门在外的男子（或远行的人），码头象征着对感情执着、痴痴等待着爱人归来的女子（或留守的人），此歌谣完美地诠释了码头（留守的女子）对船（远行的男子）坚定的守护及爱情。然而，现在越南人对此句的理解存在争议，他们认为如果以更客观和全面的视角来解读这句歌谣，那么船和码头的象征意义并非如此。越南歌谣创作的灵感来自于人们生产生活的经验及自然万物，而生活中的码头不可能只迎接唯一一艘船的归来，甚至一个码头在同一时间可以等待多只船的停泊。虽然船是动态的，灵活的，但在特定的时间内，它只能停到一个码头边，在此意境中船和码头的形象与上述大为不同。尽管存在争议，但在文学作品中该歌谣仍然比喻女子对男子感情的执着和坚定。

五、结语

“船”在越语中不只是一种交通工具，它深具文化内涵，已经渗透到越南民族精神的方方面面。走进船的世界，我们可以解读越南人的思维、审美以及了解他们的生活、文化。无论在物质还是精神上，船在越南人的心中占有重要的地位。越南独特的地理环境是船文化形成的根本原因，当船广泛地应用于人们的生产生活后，越南人开始了对船的信仰，之后船文化便广布于越南的艺术、俗语成语及歌谣中。船不仅满足了越南人生活的需求，也给予了他们智慧和想象力，创造出既独特又富有内涵的越南民族文化——船文化。

参考文献：

[1] Trần Ngọc Thêm. Cơ sở văn hóa Việt Nam[M]. Nxb Giáo Dục, 1999.

[2] Nguyễn Văn Hợp. Non nước Việt Nam 63 tỉnh thành[M]. Nxb Thời Đại, 2013.

[3] Nguyễn Thanh Lợi. Tục vẽ mắt thuyền[J]. Nxb ĐHQG TPHCM, 2009.

[4] Nguyễn Lân. Từ điển thành ngữ và tục ngữ Việt Nam[M]. Nxb Thời Đại, 2010.

[5] 古小松.越南国情与中越关系[M].第三版.北京：世界知识出版社，2009.

[6] 梁远.越南水文化研究[J].广西民族大学学报，2008：4.

[7] 祁广谋.越语文化语言学[M].洛阳：解放军外语音像出版社，2006.

（作者简介：刘艳芬，女，四川外国语大学东方语学院，硕士研究生。）

论中韩文化之争——以“端午节”为例

徐绿枝

摘要：韩国端午祭申报世界非物质文化遗产的成功，在中国引起很大反响。中国端午节和韩国端午祭之争的本质，是对传统文化保护与发扬。事实上，端午节是中国的传统节日，2006 年成为第一批国家级非物质文化遗产，2008 年端午节列为国家法定节日，放假一天。2009 年，端午节成为世界人类非物质文化遗产代表作。受到中国端午节文化的影响，韩国也过端午节，以祭礼的方式迎接这一日子，所以在韩国称为“端午祭”。本文拟从韩国江陵端午祭申遗一事解析韩国端午祭的地方民俗传统，探讨韩国非物质文化遗产申报和保护的工作经验，并从韩国非遗文化产业开发思考我国非物质文化遗产保护与开发工作中的一些做法，希望能为我们的非物质文化遗产保护与开发提供参考意见。

关键词：端午节；端午祭；非物质文化遗产；申报和保护制度

端午节是中国的传统节日，又称为端阳节。其起源，可以追溯到春秋战国时期。每年农历的五月初五全国各地都以吃粽子、赛龙舟等活动庆祝这一节日。然而韩国端午祭的申遗以及申遗后的保护工作却走在了我们的前边。受到中国端午节文化的影响，韩国也过端午节，以祭礼的方式迎接这一日子，所以在韩国称为“端午祭”。1967年江陵端午祭成为国家级非物质文化遗产，2005年又成功申报世界级名录。除此，还有庆山端午祭在1971年列入国家级非物质文化遗产，法圣浦端午祭又于2007年开始申报国家级名录。我国非物质文化遗产保护工作起步稍晚，端午节于2006年进入第一批国家级名录，2008年成为国家法定节日放假一天。2009年，中国端午节列入世界人类非物质文化遗产代表作名录。从我国端午节申遗的过程来看，韩国江陵端午祭的申报在客观上对国端午祭的地方民俗传统，探讨韩国非物质文化遗产申报和保护的工作经验，并从韩国非遗文化产业开发思考我国非物质文化遗产保护与开发工作中的一些做法，希望能为我们的非物质文化遗产保护与开发提供参考意见。

一、中韩“端午”的历史渊源

（一）端午节起源

农历五月初五，是中国的传统节日端午节，迄今为止已有2000多年的历史。由于端午节的起源与稻作农业的起源有关，与水有关，每年农历5月正是涨水的季节，为了祈求大水不将水稻淹掉，每年的这个时候都要祭神，这样这个节日才慢慢在我国形成。后来我国的农耕文化传向海外，韩国的端午节受中国文化的影响而自然形成。因此，邻国韩国，每逢农历的五月初五，也有过端午节的习俗。且韩国人对“端午”的解释和中国人的观念是一样的。[①]

在中国，端午节又被称为“端阳节”、“重午节”，此外，端午节还有许多别称，如“五月节”、“粽子节”、“天中节”、“天长节”、“女儿节”、“龙船节”、“浴兰节”、“诗人节”、“地腊节”、“艾节”、“灯节”等等。据统计，端午节的名称在我国传统节日中叫法最多，达二十多个，堪称节日别名之最。端午节是我国民间夏季最重要的传统节日，中国的56个民族中，过端午节的就有27个，各地区、各民族虽然对端午节的叫法不同，但总体上说，过节的习俗还是基本相同的[②]。

韩国人也称五月初五为“天中节”、“重五”、“重午”、“端阳”、“五月节”等，这些多样的别称也是从我们中国流传过去的。但韩国语特有的词汇也称“端午”为“戍衣日”、“水懒日”、“上日”等，其含义是“神的日子”。

1. 中国端午节起源

尽管端午节年年过，但是关于端午节的由来，迄却不甚清楚。现代人提起端午节可能首先想到屈原，这主要是历代知识分子文化传播的结果。其实，关于端午节的由来与传说，史籍资料中有许多不同的说法，如纪念介子推说，纪念伍子青、曹娥说等。本文主要介绍如下几种传说：第一种说法，也是在民间影响最大、范围最广的看法，认为端午节是为了纪念投汨罗江而死的爱国诗人屈原；二是认为端午节起源于古代吴越民族对龙图腾的崇拜；三是说端午节插艾草、悬菖蒲都是为了夏日驱病防病，与古俗视五月为“恶月”、视农历的5月5日为“恶日”相应，所以端午节是起源于古代的避“恶日”。

纪念诗人屈原。据《史记》“屈原贾生列传”记载，屈原，是春秋时期楚怀

① 장서연, 한·중 단오 비교연구［D］.韩国外国语大学校 国际地域大学院，2010.

② 고학우. 한·중 단오문화 비교연구［D］.江陵大学校，2008

王的大臣。他倡导举贤授能，富国强兵，力主联齐抗秦，但却遭到奸臣强烈反对被罢默，流放到沅、湘流域。秦军攻破楚国京都后，屈原眼看自己的祖国被侵略，心如刀割，但是始终不忍舍弃自己的祖国，于五月五日，写下绝笔作《怀沙》之后，抱石投汨罗江身死。据说，屈原投汨罗江后，当地百姓闻讯马上划船捞救，一直行至洞庭湖，始终不见屈原的尸体。那时，恰逢雨天，湖面上的小舟一起汇集在岸边的亭子旁。当人们得知是为了打捞贤臣屈大夫时，再次冒雨出动，争相划进茫茫的洞庭湖。百姓们怕江河里的鱼吃掉他的身体，就纷纷回家拿来米团、黄酒等食物投入江中，让鱼龙虾蟹吃饱，以免糟蹋屈原的尸体。至此以后，在每年的五月初五，就有了龙舟竞渡、吃粽子、喝雄黄酒的风俗，以此来纪念爱国诗人屈原。①

吴越民族图腾祭。著名学者闻一多先生在论文《端午考》中的观点以及大量考古研究证实吴越地区从春秋战国以前开始，就是一个崇拜龙的图腾的部族。他们生活在水乡，不断饱受各种自然灾害、疾病的痛苦煎熬，于是每年的五月初五，他们都会通过祭拜图腾龙神，来祈求一年的丰饶与繁荣，希望龙神能保佑百姓，抵御各种灾害的侵扰。

避“恶日”说。据民俗专家考证，在先秦时代，普遍认为五月是个“毒月”、“恶月”，五日是“毒日”、“恶日”，所以五月初五为恶月恶日，是人们最忌讳的日子。端午日与夏至日又临近，这一时期，阳气最盛，各种蚊虫出现，而且时逢“重五”，五是阳数，重五也有“极阳”之意。中国传统文化讲究阴阳和谐，对于这种阳气极盛的日子一般认为不吉利，恶病病疫多泛滥。这一天，人们插艾草、悬菖蒲以驱鬼，薰苍术、白芷和喝雄黄酒以避疫，于是形成“躲午（五）”习俗，后来以讹传讹，遂成端午。

2.韩国端午祭起源

端午”这个词来源于中国的端午节。端是“开端”、“初”的意思，初五可以称为端五。农历以地支纪月，正月建寅，二月为卯，顺次至五月为午，因此称五月为午月，“五”与“午”通，“五”又为阳数，故端午又名端五、重五、端阳等。从中国流传过来的“端午”一词，与韩国江陵地区原本存在的祭祀活动结合起来就演变成了“端午祭”。在韩国，端午祭的时间和我国的端午节一样，都是农历五月初五。端午祭在韩国相当普遍，据韩国学者考证，端午祭祀活动最早可以追溯到古朝鲜时代，人们拜祭山神以求行路安全；拜祭海神，以求渔业丰收；

① 김지영.韩·中名节文化比较研究：语源，由来，风俗，饮食 中心［D］. 경기대학교 교육대학원, 2007.

拜祭部族神，以求村落平安。朝鲜时代文人南孝温的《秋江集》就有记载祭祀活动的内容。在1967年被确认为“无形文化遗产”之后，江陵端午祭的盛大活动恢复并发展起来。[①]江陵端午祭期间的祭祀仪式主要来自神话传说，他们所祭祀的神灵是“大关岭山神”、洞（村落）城煌，被神化的人物有十二位之多，如金庚信、国师城煌“梵日国师”、大关岭国师女城煌郑家女等。有关端午节的传说，流传到韩国的大概有四个，分别是纪念楚国诗人屈原的传说、纪念介子推、伍子青、孝女曹娥的传说以及道教风俗——向地祭祀的传说。同中国一样，这几种传说中占主导地位的是纪念诗人屈原。[②]

（二）端午节习俗及庆典活动

1. 中国端午节习俗

在中国，各民族、地区虽然对端午节的叫法不同，但总体上说，过节的习俗还是基本相同的。内容主要有：女儿回娘家，挂钟馗像，悬挂菖蒲，插艾草，佩香囊，赛龙舟，比武，击球，荡秋千，给小孩涂雄黄，饮用雄黄酒、吃咸蛋、粽子和时令鲜果等。其中最主要的习俗是龙舟竞渡，代表性的饮食是粽子。

龙舟竞渡。相传爱国诗人屈原投入汨罗江后，人们为了寄托哀思，荡舟江河之上，借划龙舟驱散江中之鱼，以免鱼吃掉屈原的身体。后来就演变成端午节举行龙舟竞渡的风俗。其实，早在战国时期就有“龙舟竞渡”，到吴、越、楚时，竞渡之习更加盛行。做竞渡游戏时，鼓声震天动地，万人欢呼雀跃，情趣盎然。时至今日，很多地区在端午节仍进行赛龙舟活动。龙舟竞渡已成为我国端午节的一大特色。

食粽子。粽子，古称“角黍”，传说屈原投江自尽后，人们为了使江鱼不要吃掉屈原的身体，就包了粽子投入江中喂鱼。后演变为吃粽子。粽子是中国历史上迄今为止文化积淀最深厚的传统食品。不仅由来已久，而且花样繁多，吃粽子的风俗，千百年来，在中国盛行不衰，流传至今[③]。

2. 韩国端午节习俗

韩国人的端午保持了较好的传承性，端午节主要的民俗娱乐活动有悬艾、食艾糕，穿着传统服装参加祭祀，跳假面舞，举行摔跤、射箭、荡秋千、拔河比赛等等。其中，江陵地区的端午祭祀仪式，是韩国唯一完整保留端午习俗的地区。

① 기효량. 한·중 세시풍속 비교 연구[D]. 중부대학교 대학원, 2014.

② 范利芬. 中国端午节及与江陵端午祭之略比试探汉民族文化和民族心理[D]. 兰州大学，2012.

③ 최나. 한·중 단오 풍속의 비교 연구[D]. 부산외국어대학교, 2011.
진로. 한중 단오 풍속 비교 연구[D]. 세명대학교 대학원, 2012.

江陵端午祭。江陵端午祭已成为民众共同参与的传统大型民俗祝祭活动，端午祭有着繁琐的祭祀仪式，且仪式比较完整。通常于农历4月初开始，持续一个月。祭祀活动有一套完备的程序，迎神和送神都由专门的祭官主持。除了举办多种祭祀仪式外，当地还会组织很多丰富多彩的游戏活动，主要有摔跤、荡秋千、射箭、农乐比赛等。除了祭祀、演艺、游戏等活动外，江陵端午祭还有打年糕、做艾糕、画面具扇子、用菖蒲水洗头等民俗活动。①1967年，“江陵端午祭”被韩国政府批准为国家级第13号“重要无形文化遗产”予以保护，它每年吸引国内外大量游客参与和观光，同时也使人从中了解韩国的民俗风情。2005年11月25日，由韩国申报的“江陵端午祭”被联合国教科文组织正式确定为“人类口头和非物质遗产代表作”。

通过前面的阐述，不难发现中韩两国端午节的异同之处。即两国端午节的时间相同，都是农历五月五日，且都属民俗节日，但是中国“端午节”只有农历五月五日当天，而江陵端午祭前后持续1个月，从农历4月5日开始到5月7日结束，不是局限于端午节这一天。作为两国共同的传统节日，都有着数千年的历史，经过不断地整合与变迁，迄今为止，都保存了很多纪念活动。中国端午节是以赛龙舟，吃粽子，配香囊，插艾草、菖蒲为主要内容。但江陵端午祭是一项规模很大的民俗活动。现在的江陵端午祭有数种祭典和假面舞剧，还有农民乐舞比赛、投壶、摔跤、打秋千、长跪比赛、跆拳道比赛、高校足球赛、棋王比赛、庙会等文娱节目组成。②同时我们可以看出，中韩端午节祭祀的对象不同。中国的端午节是祭龙王，而江陵端午节是祭山神。③

韩国端午节虽然从中国流传过去，但后来与韩国传统的祭祀活动相结合，形成今天著名的江陵端午祭；而中国虽也举国上下共同庆祝这一传统节日，但却没有形成统一规模。中国端午节属于节日型庆典，且从2008年起，端午节被定位法定节假日，旨在弘扬中华文化；韩国的端午祭则属祭祀型庆典。屈原是中国端午节普遍祭拜的历史人物，而韩国却没有。另外，因两国文化差异，端午节进行的民俗活动及传统饮食也各不相同。

① 이명련. 한·중 세시풍속 비교 연구[D].부산외국어대학교 대학원, 2006.

② 정삥삥.한국과 중국의 단오행사 비교연구[D]. 상명대학교 일반대학원, 2012.

③ 이묘. 한·중 단오의 비교연구[D]. 목포대학교 일반대학원, 2010.

二、韩国无形文化遗产（非物质文化遗产）保护制度

2005年11月，韩国江陵端午祭，被联合国教科文组织正式确定为人类口头和非物质遗产代表作。端午祭“申遗”成功后，韩国还拟将“韩医”申报为世界文化遗产。并已向联合国教科文组织提出文本申报。这是继端午祭成功申遗之后，韩国在文化上走向世界的又一重大举措。

韩国端午祭“申遗”的成功在国内引起了的广泛关注。从江陵端午祭“申遗”成功的案例我们可以看出，韩国充分挖掘了端午祭文化传统的内涵，凸现出与中国端午节的差异，使本来源于中国的节日，成为其相对独立的文化节日，最终抢先一步走向世界，并得到认可。笔者认为，韩国成功的原因在于其文化保护制度的完善和对文化传播的敏锐性，十分值得我们学习和借鉴。

目前韩国、日本、蒙古、新加坡等许多儒家文化圈的国家，都在积极申报非物质文化遗产项目，许多项目的渊源都在中国。为了捍卫中国文化源头的本源地位，不仅需要研究文化本身，更需要建立完善的保护和申报制度。本文通过对韩国遗产保护制度的分析入手，希望这一典型案例给我们带来有益的启示。

（一）以“文化财委员会”为核心的管理体系

韩国对文化遗产的严格管理源于他们以法律的形式制定出了一套完善的管理体系。在韩国，管理机构关系如下：国家总统—文化观光部下属的文化财厅—各地政府。

需要特别注意的是，上面所述只是韩国文化遗产管理、执行机构，而真正的决策机构则是由韩国文化财厅负责组建的文化财委员会。韩国的文化财委员会也是文化遗产保护工作中唯一的一个专门负责提供咨询审议的顾问机构。按韩国《文化财委员会规定》，这个委员会的委员必须由德高望重、学识广博的专家学者组成，相关官员不得介入。委员会委员分文化财委员和文化财专门委员两种。前者可参与全面咨询，而后者只能参与小范围的专业咨询。文化财委员的人数不得超过60人。

（二）积极的保存记录和传授教育

《韩国文化财保护法》认为：重要无形文化遗产，指的是如果不及时保存，消失的可能性极大的其保持者所具有的技能和艺能。其实从制定重要无形文化遗产认定制度的背后看来，本身就说明单靠艺术自身的力量，在本时代不能够坚持传承下去。所以我们要把重要无形文化遗产作为活生生的文化遗产加以保存，同

时又将其原貌传承子孙后代的义务。

对于文化遗产的保护，通常的做法是消极地保存记录。采谱、录音、摄影等记录，这是保存无形文化遗产的普通的方法，可作为传授教育的教材而使用。①

韩国在传统保护方法的基础上，推动了十分积极的保护措施，主要体现在以下两个方面：

第一，团体项目优于个人项目。

韩国政府为了扩充传授教育的空间，与市、道共同负担，从1973年开始每年一度为计划建设为原则，与个人项目相比，更注重团体项目，并在传承多种项目的地区，优先建立起重要无形文化遗产教育馆。另外，在1997年，汉城建成了重要无形文化遗产综合传授会馆，现作为进行传授教育、演出、展览、广告等活动的多功能的文化空间而使用。

第二，个人项目的“活态”监测与传承。

除了传授教育以外，被认定为技艺能保持者的个人，只要没有特别的理由，每年应该至少向市民公开其保持的技艺能一次。其理由如下：1. 检查传承状态，阻止其技艺能的退步，同时对其保持者通过不断磨练而达到的相关技艺能的提高程度进行检验。2. 指出由于保持者的偏见和执拗而引发的相关技能被歪曲的可能性，为专家提出批判与改善提供机会。3. 向市民普及及宣扬民族的传统技艺能。这是为了达到对其技艺能状态进行检查和向市民普及两大目的，而要求其履行的公开义务。公开报告分为中央报告和在其传承地区实施的自行报告。

（三）无形文化遗传海外传播的制度保障

文化遗产不仅是一个民族的遗产，同时也是人类的共同财产，韩国政府为了使其文化遗产在世界各国扎根而不断地进行努力。在世界范围内，对无形文化遗产进行认定，并在制度上进行传承的国家，韩国、日本等国家走在了前列。

韩国政府针对世界各国对于无形文化遗产缺乏深入认识的状况，在1993年举行的第142届联合国教科文组织的理事会上提出了联合国教科文组织的关于“普及无形文化遗产制度”的提案，最终此提案被采纳，走在联合国教科文组织普及无形文化遗产制度的前列。

之前认定的“世界文化遗产”的制度，韩国率先将将无形文化遗产列入遗产保护当中，并积极推进了会员国之间的充分合作。韩国政府通过向全世界推动

① 贺学君. 韩国非物质文化遗产保护的启示——以江陵端午祭为例［J］. 民间文化论坛，2006年第1期

无形文化遗产制度，向无形文化遗产指定为世界文化遗产的联合国教科文组织援助。每年文化遗产管理局召开国际的无形文化遗产制度运营的现场会介绍该制度。①联合国教科文组织为了使会员国迅速地实施该无形文化遗产制度，在1988年设立了“世界口传无形文化遗产奖”，并在1999年4月将这个奖的名称确定为“阿里郎奖”。

联合国教科文组织每隔两年，对世界范围内的口传及无形遗产杰作，以及对此遗产的保存做出贡献的个人和团体，授予此奖。

（四）完善的认定制度

1. 标准化认证制度

国家把在历史上、学术上、艺术上值得保护而地方色彩浓厚的项目指定为重要无形文化遗产。由专门学者的研究报告书、民俗艺术演出比较大会展出作品，以及由市、道知事将地方文化遗产委员会决议后，通过的项目予以建议。此外，有关专家的建议等等，都是重要无形文化遗产的审议对象。

文化遗产委员会判断其有认定的价值后，则由有关文化遗产委员或专家委员与其他有关学者实地考察，确认其技能与艺能的传承由来、内容、传承状态以及具有相关技能及艺能者的经历等，将其调查结果进行审议，最终由文化遗产委员会决定是否将其指定为重要无形文化遗产和认定为具有相关技能者。

2. 竞争性的认定制度

为了保存日益消失的传统文化，韩国政府从1958年开始举办了“全国民俗艺术演出比赛大会”。从1964年起，“全国民俗艺术演出比赛大会”被改称为“全国民俗艺术欢庆”，直到现在每年都坚持举办。通过比赛发掘文化项目，只有在比赛中脱颖而出的项目才能被列为重要无形文化遗产。1964年，以扬州别山台为代表的13种民俗剧在比赛中获得嘉奖，被指定为重要的无形文化遗产。

3. 动态性的认定制度

对于地方文化节为代表的民俗剧的演出，是根据时代的变化而变化的。以假面具为例，根据时间及场所的变化，他的台词内容发生变化，演出时间也有所变动。文化的传承具有二元化的保存与继承发展两方面。将非物质文化遗产按照原有的面貌、原有的台词进行保存是有悖于非物质文化遗产本质的，也不符合以传统的继承发展为目的的思想。非物质文化遗产是某一时代的产物，可以进行再创造。

---

① 陈连山. 从端午节争端看中韩两国的文化冲突[J]. 民间文化论坛，2011年第3期

4. 针对性、优先性认定制度

被指定为重要无形文化遗产的项目，与没有被指定的项目之间在申报的先后次序上有差异。被指定为重要无形遗产的项目被当成标准，因此对其他种类的艺术行为的评价被降低。重要无形遗产的项目一般是指三类项目：

（1）与他国有共存文化的项目。此类项目以端午祭、韩医、汉字为代表。

（2）濒临灭绝的项目。此类项目以方言为代表。

（3）具有本国典型特征的项目。此类项目以宗庙祭礼和宗庙祭礼乐、假面剧为代表。

三、对中国非物质遗产申报的启示

目前，韩国已有三项世界非物质文化遗产（我国仅有两项：昆曲和古琴），并且还在积极地申报。联合国也肯定了韩国在保护文化遗产方面的努力。韩国的文化保护制度给我们许多启示。

（一）申报的技术处理

1. 申报项目的筛选问题

在不断发生被别人抢申危机的情况下，为保护我国利益，中国申报世界文化遗产应优先考虑边疆和共存文化。中国应该列出一份源在中国、流在别国及跨国分布的文化遗产清单，按照这个名录，采取优先申报原则。同时采取扩容战略，争取通过和联合国教科文组织的交涉，改变每两年才能申报一个项目的局面，加大中国申遗的速度和力度。

中国申报世界文化遗产应有明确国际战略和国内战略。国际战略包括共存文化优先、边疆优先、分层级多渠道申报以及扩容战略；国内战略则包括联合申报、濒危优先、特色优先、农耕文化优先和少数民族文化优先战略。

2. 话语主动权的取得

从韩国官方对于端午祭的描述中可以得出，韩国在对端午祭进行申报时，回避端午祭的本源问题，突出其独立性，强调端午祭活动的历史悠久、影响范围大，重点突出端午祭的娱乐活动和纪念方式。打造好端午祭以后，再把其推向世界，使其优先取得话语主动权。中国在申遗时，应该注意强调文化文源性的问题，抓住世界遗产唯一性的特点，从而抢先获得话语主动权。[①]

① 钱爽. 民族文化的保护与传承——浅谈中韩端午祭之争[J]. 青年文学家，2009年第3期

（二）世界遗产保护方法的问题

1. 源头与源流——加强以中国文化为渊源的世界遗产的研究

中华文明在相当程度上影响了日本、韩国、朝鲜和越南等东南亚国家，所以这些国家在中医、时令、姓氏、宗教等方面与中国有相应的共存文化。同时，中国许多民族与周边国家垮境分布，许多文化跨国共有，对这些边疆共存的文化遗产，不管是单独还是合作申报，中国政府都应采取优先申报原则。应该深入研究这些边疆共存文化的中华渊源性，充分挖掘中国文化渊源的特征与证据，从而在申报时优先取得话语主动权。

2. 区域文化的"中国化"凸现——地区与地区的竞争与合作

文化的传播性是非物质文化遗产的重要特点。因此在整个国家甚至在整个文化圈都有同一遗产项目的不同表现形式。在申报时应该加强地区之间的合作。以端午节为例，其发源地虽是湖南，但其活动不只是在湖南举行。这一活动不是地区性的，而是全国性的。因此在申报时，各地区不能各自为政，应加强联系与合作，促进端午文化的发扬。

3. 一体化的多元共存——加强民族地区的保护

中国是一个拥有多元一体化文化的国家。在文化继承与保护工作中，应该创造文化的多元共存。多元共存不是容忍和漠不关心，也不是实质上同化少数民族文化或把少数民族文化掩入主流文化的托词。创造性的多元共存包括多种文化群体积极的和动态的共存。创造性的多元共存把当地社会环境和公共活动领域相结合，允许创造性地接触和转变。文化是多元化的，并没有优劣的关系。若只是重视汉族文化，将该文化当成标准，而过低评价其他民族文化，会产生错误。[①]这样的政策虽然会在遗产申报上暂时获得一定的成功，却对少数民族文化传承造成消极影响。

四、结论

韩国端午祭源于中国端午节，然而由于端午祭是"端午"的概念与韩国传统祭祀活动的结合，形成了独特的端午祭民俗活动。从节日的起源、节日类型、举行时间、举行目的、活动内容等方面看，这两个节日都有明显的差异，属于不同的节日民俗，因此韩国端午祭申请世界文化遗产与中国的端午节并无冲突。

① 张国强. 韩国江陵端午祭研究［J］. 湖北民族学院学报（哲学社会科学版），2009年第5期

同时，“他山之石，可以攻玉”，韩国的非物质文化遗产保护工作走在我们前面，有很多经验值得我们借鉴，从江陵端午祭申遗的事情来看，最为突出的是：建立了完整、完善的非物质遗产保护制度。①非物质文化遗产的利用和开发必须在真实、完整地保存传统的文化形态的基础上进行，这需要建立长效的监督系统、完善的资金运营机制和有力的行政管理体系，避免一些急功近利的做法。

参考文献：

[1]고학우. 한·중 단오문화 비교연구[D].江陵大学校，2008.

[2]기효량. 한·중 세시풍속 비교 연구[D]. 중부대학교 대학원，2014.

[3]김지영.韩·中名节文化比较研究：语源，由来，风俗，饮食中心[D].경기대학교 교육대학원，2007.

[4]이명련. 한·중 세시풍속 비교 연구[D].부산외국어대학교 대학원，2006.

[5]이묘. 한·중 단오의 비교연구[D]. 목포대학교 일반대학원，2010.

[6]장서연，한·중 단오 비교연구[D].韩国外国语大学校 国际地域大学院，2010.

[7]정빵빵.한국과 중국의 단오행사 비교연구[D]. 상명대학교 일반대학원，2012.

[8]진로. 한중 단오 풍속 비교 연구[D].세명대학교 대학원，2012.

[9]최나. 한·중 단오 풍속의 비교 연구[D]. 부산외국어대학교，2011.

[10]陈连山.从端午节争端看中韩两国的文化冲突[J].民间文化论坛，2011年第3期.

[11]范利芬.中国端午节及与江陵端午祭之略比试探汉民族文化和民族心理[D].兰州大学，2012.

[12]贺学君.韩国非物质文化遗产保护的启示——以江陵端午祭为例[J].民间文化论坛，2006年第1期.

[13]钱爽.民族文化的保护与传承——浅谈中韩端午祭之争[J].青年文学家，2009年第3期.

[14]杨琳曦.韩国非物质文化遗产保护制度对我国的启示——以端午祭申遗成功为视点[J].广西民族研究，2007年第1期.

① 杨琳曦.韩国非物质文化遗产保护制度对我国的启示——以端午祭申遗成功为视点[J].广西民族研究，2007年第1期。

[15] 张国强. 韩国江陵端午祭研究[J]. 湖北民族学院学报(哲学社会科学版), 2009年第5期.

(作者简介：徐绿枝，男，四川外国语大学东方语学院，硕士研究生。)

浅析越南佛教中的女性崇拜

张　睿

摘要：佛教是越南信仰人数最多、影响最大的宗教。佛教并不是越南本土宗教，但随着佛教与越南本土宗教信仰相结合，其渐渐已经被越南化，形成了自己的特色，其最突出的特点就是佛教中的女性崇拜。越南佛教中的女性崇拜与越南的稻作文化密切相关，稻作文化所特有的阴性文化——重女性，孕育了越南独特的女性崇拜。越南的女性崇拜力量非常强大，以至于当佛教传入越南之时都只有与之相融合才能得以发展，佛教与越南存在已久的女性崇拜相融合形成了独具特色的越南佛教。

关键字：越南佛教、女性崇拜、稻作文化

一、越南佛教的来源与发展

越南是一个多民族多宗教的国家，主要宗教有佛教、儒教、道教、天主教等，以及两个本土宗教和好教、高台教。其中最主要的就是佛教和天主教。佛教是越南最普遍，信仰人数最多的宗教。佛教传入越南的途径是多样的，随着历史的变迁，佛教在越南产生、发展，并于公元11—14世纪发展到顶峰，对越南文化产生了深刻的影响。概括越南佛教的来源以及随着越南历史发展变迁的过程可以寻找到越南佛教中女性崇拜的源头及其发展。

（一）越南佛教的来源

越南的佛教是经过多种途径传入越南的。在越南传播佛教的既有中国僧侣，也有来自中亚和印度的佛教徒。越南佛教既受到中国佛教的影响，又受到来自印度佛教的影响。一是通过陆路，大约于公元2、3世纪从中国传入。东汉末年由于中原战乱，大批僧侣、人民到交州避难，将佛教带入了交州地区。据古书记载，195年，东汉苍梧（今广西梧州地区）修行者牟子（又称牟博）奉母流寓交州

（今越南北部）向交州地区的人民传播佛教，并于交州完成了《牟子理惑论》，在当时影响非常大。这是佛教从陆路传入越南北部的早期代表。二是通过海路，从印度直接经海路传入越南。由于越南地处中南半岛，紧靠中国南部，并濒临泰国湾、北部湾和南海，在古代也是重要的交通要道，因此有许多中亚和印度的僧侣乘商船从海上到达交州。公元3世纪，中亚僧侣康僧会和印度僧侣支疆梁等先后从海路到达交州，翻译佛学经典，传播佛教。这些人成为了佛教南传的早期代表。[①]

3世纪以后，许多中国佛教高僧到交趾地区传教，并同交趾地区僧侣到印度取经。

中国佛教和印度佛教都先后进入到越南，在与越南文化交流时，都极大地影响了越南。但是由于越南受中国一千多年的统治，受中国文化影响大，更易接受中国文化，因此中国佛教对越南的影响更大，越南佛教就是汉传佛教的一部分，是属于大乘佛教。但是两者之间最大的区别在于越南佛教中的女性因素更多。这一时期，越南本土的民间信仰开始与佛教相结合，形成了既有原本佛教特色又有越南本土特色的越南佛教，其中最具特色就是“四法崇拜”。

（二）佛教在越南的发展

兴盛时期：自968年，丁部领平定“十二使君之乱”，建立越南第一个封建国家开始，经过黎、李、陈朝（10—14世纪），佛教在越南都十分盛行，并在李朝和陈朝时被尊为国教，许多高僧甚至有特权可以直接参与政事。十一世纪初李朝时期，出现“百姓大半为僧，国内到处皆寺”[②]的极盛局面，这对越南社会的政治、经济、思想文化都产生了极大的影响。这一时期，越南出现了许多关于观音的文学作品，而在越南观音绝大部分都是女性。其中最为出名的就是倚栏元妃。李圣宗时期的倚栏元妃因为会管理国事，爱护人民，被尊称为观音。

衰退时期：15—19世纪末，为了中央集权和封建制度的要求，儒教开始代替佛教进入越南的上层社会，儒教越来越受到重视，后黎朝把儒教推崇为国教，对佛教进行镇压，要求佛教僧侣还俗，并且只有庶民可以信仰佛教。但是在这期间也曾经有复兴佛教的小高潮，但是最终都未能发展起来。由于社会动荡、战乱，观音信仰得以快速发展，出现了《氏敬观音》、《南海观音》等反应人民生活和愿望的民间佛教文学作品。

① 陈继章、兰强、徐方宇：越南概况［M］，解放军外语音像出版社，2010版，101页

② 转自梁志明：略论越南佛教的源流和李陈时期佛教的发展［J］，印支研究，1984.3.21

振兴时期：从20世纪初到现在都是越南佛教的振兴时期。20世纪初，越南开始振兴佛教，并促成了10个佛教协会的诞生。1981年于河内召开了越南佛教代表大会，将越南佛教协会作为越南最高的佛教机构。佛教还开始重视发展高等、高级佛学教育，先后建立了3所高等学校，每年都有数千名学生毕业，并且可以到台湾、印度等地进行佛学交流。

佛教传入越南也有两千多年的历史，在这历史的长河里，越南佛教经过传入、兴盛、衰退、到复兴的若干起起落落。但是即使是在衰弱时期，佛教在民间也有一定的影响力。佛教在越南的发展过程中不断被吸收、改编和发展，逐渐形成具有越南特色的佛教文化，而在这发展过程中最具特色的就是佛教与越南本土民间信仰相结合而形成的女性崇拜。

二、越南社会中的佛教女性

佛教已经传入越南两千多年，在越南也经过起起落落，但是即使在其最衰落时期也在影响着越南社会。在面对恶，面临各种艰难困苦时，佛教所追寻的“善”会始终相伴。“善”字在越南佛教中更加集中地体现在越南女性当中，在越南的传说《氏敬观音传》中，在被别人打骂、冤枉也不生气，表现了佛家经典“忍辱”的思想；《南海观音传》中妙善用自己的手和眼睛医治自己的父皇并劝解父皇皈依佛门，这体现了对父亲的孝道。

越南佛教中的女性崇拜不止出现在传说当中，在历史人物和越南人民生活当中都可以看到越南佛教对女性的崇拜。在越南历史上也有被尊称为观世音菩萨的历史人物——倚栏元妃，她是越南女性与佛教的结合。在越南人民的生活中也可以看到越南女性在佛教的积极影响。

（一）倚栏元妃

十一世纪李朝时期，佛教活动非常频繁，每村必建寺庙，人们会在寺庙面前学习经书，此时的寺庙已经成为了人们精神文化的中心，在李朝时期，佛教一度被尊为国教。倚栏元妃原名黎氏燕，出生于京北（Kinh Bắc，现包括北江、北宁、和部分河内、兴安、谅山等地）[①]，在京北则建有越南最古老的寺庙——桑寺（chùa Dâu），是越南古代的佛教中心，她从小就受佛教思想的影响，心存善念，帮助穷苦人民。在她为李圣宗生了两个儿子之后被封为元妃。1072年，在李圣宗

① 京北的出处：https://vi.wikipedia.org/wiki/Kinh_B%E1%BA%AFc

去世之后，李仁宗继位，她又被尊为玲仁皇太后。

倚栏元妃由于出身穷苦人家，能够了解穷苦人民的疾苦，所以经常帮助穷苦人民，得到广大越南人民的爱戴。在李圣宗出兵攻打占城时，倚栏元妃就在京城管理国事，管理得非常好，深受人民喜爱。再加上她本身信佛，修建了许多佛寺，经常到寺庙与僧人探讨佛学，对佛教的发展做出了巨大的贡献，而存在于越南佛教中的女性崇拜，让人们自然而然地把她与佛教中的女性神联系在一起，因此被尊称为观音菩萨。倚栏元妃是越南历史人物中唯一一个被尊为观世音菩萨的人。河内嘉林县阳社村修建的“玲仁慈福寺”是越南人民在倚栏元妃去世之后所修建，这里既是寺庙又是专门供奉倚栏元妃的地方。

（二）村庙和越南女性

越南文化的社会单位是村社。[①]在越南，村社被建立了之后，村名会尊对村社有开创、保卫之功的人或历史人物为城隍，城隍就是村社的保护神。并会修建村亭，村亭既是处理本村村务的地方，也是村民聚会活动的场所，如有上级官员下来，则在此居住，更为重要的是这里是供奉、祭祀城隍的地方。[②]同时也会修建村庙以保存和发扬佛教信仰。村亭和村庙是越南村社的两个代表。

村亭里面主要是祭祀对村社有功的人、对人民有功的历史人物或传说人物，村亭的祭祀活动或者是处理村务等都是村子里有名望的男人，女性不能参加。在庙会（hội làng）时，妇女只允许参加一些娱乐活动而已。但是村庙则完全相反，妇女在村庙中占主导地位。

在越南有“村村皆有庙，无庙不成村”的说法，村庙在越南十分普遍。相比于男性来说，女性总是更加追崇心灵上的寄托。而佛教的慈、善、关心弱者、博爱精神更深受越南女性的推崇，并且越南佛教中的佛大部分都是女性，更加有亲切感，同时越南妇女也希望佛祖能够保佑自己的家庭、事业一切顺利。去村庙祭祀的主要是越南女性，村庙里的活动、事务主要也主要是由女性组织、处理。在村社当中，男性在村亭里占主要位置，男性在生活中主要是追求事业、权力。女性则在村庙中占主导地位，女性主要是追求心灵寄托。

三、越南佛教中的女性形象

越南地处东南亚最东端，紧邻中国南部，濒临南海，越南北部的红河三角

---

① Trần Quốc Vượng, Cơ sở Văn hóa Việt Nam, NXB giáo dục Việt Nam, tr47

② 孙衍峰：越南人的城隍信仰［J］，解放军外国语学院学报，2013.9

洲，土地肥沃，气候闷热，雨量多，有利于农作物的生长，越南是典型的稻作文化。稻作文化非常重视繁衍生息，而繁衍生息的代表就是女性，女性可以生产，可以孕育出天地万物和人类，因此在越南民间信仰中女性崇拜是极其重要的。在佛教还未传入越南时，越南就有了女性崇拜，在佛教传入之后，佛教与越南民间女性崇拜相融合，既保存着佛教的精髓，又添加了越南本土的女性崇拜，两者之间良性互动，从而形成了具有越南特色的越南佛教。

（一）越南佛教中的“女性化”现象

越南佛教中“女性化”现象并不少见。有部分原本在中国或者印度是男性的佛，越南人民根据自己的需要和信仰将其转变成女性；有部分是佛教传入越南之后，将越南本土的男性佛转变成女性。

观音菩萨女性化：印度佛教中的观音菩萨形象是男的，但是传入中国之后就变成了女性形象。越南佛教受中国影响，其观音信仰同样受中国观音信仰的影响。在中国观音菩萨是大慈大悲、救苦救难的代表，观音的慈可以给人们带来快乐，可以让人们从痛苦中解放，这就符合了越南人民的心理和愿望，让他们更能够接受观音信仰。古代越南妇女受到中国儒家思想的影响，需要遵守三从四德，生活得很辛苦，是最需要被解救的，因此女性的观音形象更容易被接受。中国观音在传入越南时思想、教义都是一样，连中国观音是女性形象传入越南之后也是女性形象都是一样的，只是女性形象观音在越南更为丰富和发展。当然在越南男性形象的观音也是存在的，但是女性形象的观音占主要位置。①越南人民还给观音加上符合越南本土特色的身世，有的借鉴中国的故事，改变时间地点等，例如：南海观音。有的则是完全由越南人自己创造，例如：氏敬观音。在越南寺庙中的佛像脸看上去都十分丰满、敦厚，更加偏向女性。

越南安江省州督市杉山地主婆（或主处婆Bà Chúa Xứ）女性化：根据法国考古学家1941年的实地考察判断，杉山地主婆原本是一个修建于公元6世纪的男性佛像，是著名的印度神话中三大主神之一的毗湿奴的坐姿。②这座佛像原本被遗弃在杉山山顶，后被越南人带回寺庙中，并根据自己的所愿重新装饰，成为了身穿丝绸衣服、颈带项链，该地区最有权势的神——地主婆。现在，在杉山每年阴历4月23—27日会举行杉山地主婆庙会，已经成为越南南部大型民间文化节之

① 乔氏云英：越南北方佛教女性神研究［D］，中央民族大学，2010.2

② 越南网站：杉山地主婆的出处http://tamlinhhuyenbi.net/threads/truy%E1%BB%81n-thuy%E1%BA%BFt-v%C3%A0-huy%E1%BB%81n-tho%E1%BA%A1i-v%E1%BB%81-b%C3%A0-ch%C3%BAa-x%E1%BB%A9-ch%C3%A2u-%C4%90%E1%BB%91c-an-giang.1429/

一，每年会有约200万人来此上香。

（二）佛母蛮娘和四法佛的形象

蛮娘在越南北宁省桑村里的寺庙里修行，一天蛮娘正在睡觉，一个印度和尚不小心从她身体上跨过，14个月后她生了一个女儿，和尚在返回印度时交给蛮娘一根锡杖，并告诉她在干旱时，将锡杖插在地里可以拯救人民，他念咒后把女儿放在天德河畔的桑树根洞里。和尚回去后，此地连续干旱三年，蛮娘用锡杖求得了雨，拯救了人民，桑树倒入河中，听到蛮娘的声音便靠岸。蛮娘叫人把桑树雕成四尊佛像，称为“四法”，佛名为法云、法雨、法雷和法电，象征着云雨雷电。后来蛮娘被尊为佛母，修行于祖寺（满舍），而四法佛则分别供奉在同一地区的四座寺。[①]

蛮娘可以被视为早期出现的母神形象，然后被佛教吸收与改造，产生了四法佛信仰。四法佛——法云、法雨、法雷和法电，都是与农耕文明密切相关的四种天象。在古代遇到自然灾害，朝廷都会派人去往四法佛供奉的寺庙祭祀，或者将佛像抬回京城，当自然灾害结束之时再将佛像抬回寺庙。

越南的女性崇拜力量非常强大，以至于当佛教传入交州之时都只有与之相融合。[②]而蛮娘生四法佛的传说正是证明这种融合。四法佛与越南自然、生殖崇拜相关，与稻作文化直接联系，在佛教传入之后，融入到女性崇拜之中，使外来的佛教有了越南特色。蛮娘和四法佛因此也进入了佛教系统，同时也形成了与佛教思想相符合的神话传说，蛮娘和四法佛也被搬入了寺庙里进行供奉。

四、小结

原印度佛教中女性佛极其少，但是传入越南之后却添加了许多女性色彩。这表现为从中国继承的观世音菩萨是女性，到创造出蛮娘、四法佛等越南特有的女性佛，这些都与越南是稻作文化的国家息息相关，也是佛教主动吸收越南本土信仰的表现，凸显了越南女性的非凡魅力。越南佛教中的女性崇拜与越南的稻作文化密切相关，稻作文化所特有的阴性文化——重女性，孕育了越南独特的女性崇拜。越南佛教中的女性崇拜是越南佛教中最具特色的闪光点。

---

① 蛮娘和四法佛的故事：http://www.cwhweb.com/news.php?id=5058

② Trần Quốc Vượng，Cơ sở Văn hóa Việt Nam，NXB giáo dục Việt Nam，tr100

参考文献：

[1][越]陈国旺.越南文化基础[M].越南河内：教育出版社，2014.
[2][越]陈玉添.越南文化基础[M].越南河内：教育出版社，2000.
[3][越]陶维英.越南文化史纲[M].越南胡志明市：胡志明市出版社，1992.
[4][越]陈国旺.文化学大纲和越南文化基础[M].越南河内：科学社会出版社，1996.
[5]陈继章，兰强，徐方宇.越南概况[M].河南：解放军外语音像出版社，2010.
[6]孙衍锋，黄健红，徐方宇.越南文化概论[M].河南：解放军外语音像出版社，2010.
[7]陈继章.越南研究[M].北京：军事谊文出版社，2003.
[8]孙衍锋.越南人的城隍信仰[J].解放军外国语学院学报，2013(9).
[9]梁志明.略论越南佛教的源流和李陈时期佛教的发展[J].印支研究，1984(3).
[10]徐方宇.越南熊王信仰研究[M].广东：世界图书图版社，2014.
[11]谭志词.中越语言文化关系[M].北京：军事谊文出版社，2003.
[12]乔氏云英.越南北方佛教女性神研究[D].北京：中央民族大学，2010.
[13]张秋贤.走向经济母神：越南女性母神信仰研究[D].上海：华东师范大学，2015.
[14]阮氏玉华.越南语佛教词语研究[D].湖北：华中科技大学，2011.
[15]阮曰陲.佛教在当代越南社会中的地位、功能与影响[D].湖北：华中师范大学，2014.
[16]潘氏冰心.越南观音菩萨[D].湖北：华中师范大学，2014.

（作者简介：张睿，女，四川外国语大学东方语学院，硕士研究生。）